Praise for *The Lexicographer's Dilemma*

"Lynch recognizes that grace, clarity, and precision of expression are paramount. His many well-chosen and entertaining examples support his conclusion that prescriptions and pedantry will always give way to change, and that we should stop fretting, relax, and embrace it." —*Boston Globe*

"Memo to grammar cops: Back off! A new book on the history of 'proper' English says you're just stuck up."

—**Laura Miller, Salon.com**

"Lynch's highly readable book will appeal to all users of the English language, from word buffs to scholars alike."

—*Library Journal*

"Lynch's book pleasingly delineates the conflict between those who have attempted to embalm English and those who have documented, and in some cases reveled in, its plasticity and mutability."

—*Financial Times*

"Lynch weaves the familiar with the obscure, to the delight of the reader." —*Post and Courier*

"A jolly and therefore readable account . . . From 17th-century Englishmen Jonathan Swift and Samuel Johnson to English's Americanizer Noah Webster, Lynch draws the battle lines between the prescriptivists, who prescribe a correct approach, and descriptivists, who analyze how language works. Lynch enlivens the narrative on a subject otherwise unglamorous to many readers."

—*Morning News*

BY THE SAME AUTHOR

Samuel Johnson's Dictionary (editor)
Samuel Johnson's Insults (editor)
Becoming Shakespeare

THE
LEXICOGRAPHER'S
DILEMMA

The Evolution of "Proper" English,
from Shakespeare to *South Park*

JACK LYNCH

Walker & Company
New York

Published by Walker Publishing Company, Inc., New York

All papers used by Walker & Company are natural, recyclable products made from wood grown in well-managed forests. The manufacturing processes conform to the environmental regulations of the country of origin.

LIBRARY OF CONGRESS CATALOGING-IN-PUBLICATION DATA

Lynch, Jack (John T.)
The lexicographer's dilemma : the evolution of proper English, from Shakespeare to South Park / Jack Lynch.
p.   cm.
Includes bibliographical references.
ISBN 978-0-8027-1700-9 (hardcover)
1. English language—Lexicography.   2. English language—History.   3. English language—Style.   4. English language—Usage.   I. Title.
PE1611.L96 2009
423'.028—dc22
2009019195

Visit Walker & Company's Web site at www.walkerbooks.com

First published by Walker & Company in 2009
This paperback edition published in 2010

Paperback ISBN: 978-0-8027-7769-0

3 5 7 9 10 8 6 4 2

Designed by Rachel Reiss
Typeset by Westchester Book Group
Printed in the United States of America by Quad/Graphics Fairfield

For three great teachers:
Bill Reinhart, Steve Dessants, David Jepson

Contents

Introduction

Everybody complains about the language, but nobody does anything about it—well, almost nobody. This book is an account of some of the people who did try to do something about it. It's about the rise of "standard English."

"There is no need to define standard English," wrote educator George Sampson in 1921. "We know what it is, and there's an end on't. We know standard English when we hear it just as we know a dog when we see it, without the aid of definition."[1] But do we really know what it is?—and if so, do we know how it got here? Even professional students of the history of the language are unclear on exactly what "standard English" means and how it came to be, and most of them only allude vaguely to the "eighteenth-century grammarians" who are supposed to have given us our modern notions of correctness and proper English.

This book poses a pair of questions: what does *proper* English mean, and who gets to say what's right? Our ideas of *correct* or *proper* English have a history, and we can learn about our language by reviewing that history. Today's debates over the state of the language—whether about Ebonics in the schools or split infinitives in the *Times*—make sense only in a historical context. This book looks back over the history of Modern English and traces the notion that some versions of the language are correct and others wrong. This is the story of the people who tried to "fix" or "improve" this messy language of ours.

A TYPICAL AMERICAN is expected to take a course in English for forty-five minutes a day, five days a week, thirty-four weeks a year, from the age of five to eighteen: that amounts to a lifetime of nearly 1,700 hours in the classroom, with many more hours outside it, learning the language that the overwhelming majority of American schoolchildren already spoke before they arrived at school. A college degree usually requires another three or four classroom hours a week for twenty-eight weeks in English composition, plus perhaps as much again in English literature—and that's for everyone, not just the English majors, who are expected to put in another four hundred or five hundred hours of class time on major English and American authors.

Since we spend so many hours being told what's right and wrong, we find it almost unthinkable that there was ever a time when proper English didn't exist. But when we look back about four hundred years, the linguistic world appears very different. The first impression that strikes a modern observer is chaos. We notice the capricious spellings right away. Here, for example, is a passage from Shakespeare's *Love's Labour's Lost*, as it appeared in the First Folio of 1623:

> He draweth out the thred of his verbositie, finer then the staple of his argument. I abhor such phanaticall phantasims, such insociable and poynt deuise companions, such rackers of ortagriphie. . . . this is abhominable.

By modern standards, Shakespeare's spelling is a mess: *thred* for *thread*, *then* for *than*, *poynt* for *point*, *ortagriphie* for *orthography*, and so on. And this little selection only hints at the anarchy of early modern spelling. The same word can be spelled several ways in a single poem. Shakespeare wasn't even consistent in spelling his own name.

Erratic spelling is just the beginning. By the standards of a modern ninth-grade grammar book, Shakespeare would be lucky to earn a C minus. His works are filled with gaffes no conscientious English teacher would permit in a student essay: double negatives ("thou expectedst not, nor I looked not for"—*Romeo and Juliet*), mixed metaphors ("take arms against a sea of troubles"—*Hamlet*), split infinitives ("thy pity may deserve to pitied be"—Sonnet 142), sentence-ending prepositions ("such stuff as dreams are made on"—*Hamlet*), singular *they* ("There's not a man I meet but doth salute me, / As if I were their well-acquainted friend"—*Comedy of Errors*), and *who* instead of *whom* as the object of a preposition ("To who?"—*King Lear*). If his collected works were submitted in English 101, the instructor would feel obliged to cover his pages in red ink, scolding him for hundreds of blunders.

Does this mean Shakespeare was a subpar writer, undeserving of the place he occupies in the literary firmament? Not at all. Shakespeare did nothing wrong—and not because he was some kind of rule-breaking rebel. It's not even because a genius like Shakespeare didn't need to follow rules, or because only those who know the rules can break them. Shakespeare *didn't* know the rules, but neither did anyone else in his day. The fact is that no one in 1600 ever imagined that the things we find troublesome in his writing might be problems. And even if Shakespeare wanted to get it right, there was no one around to tell him that, say, "the most unkindest cut of all" was a double comparative and therefore ungrammatical. There were no English dictionaries—at least none we would recognize as dictionaries—no grammar books, no guides to usage. Latin grammar and style were well documented, but English was mostly ignored by the scholars. There was no sixteenth-century equivalent of Fowler's *Modern English Usage* or Strunk and White's *Elements of Style*. Writers had to make it up as they went along, with no one to tell them whether they were right or wrong.

THE RESULT OF all this improvisation, as everyone knows, is a language that isn't the least bit ordered, tidy, or rational. If some Intelligent Designer were to sit down to plan a language, surely He—She? It?—wouldn't have created this tangled mess we call English. If the language were logical, the verb *to dust* wouldn't mean both "remove dust from" (as in "dust the bookcase") and "add dust to" (as in "dust the cookies with powdered sugar"). The noun *oversight* wouldn't mean both "careful scrutiny" (as in "they agreed to submit to the oversight of the committee") and "neglectful inattention" (as in "they lost everything because of an oversight"). *Cleave* shouldn't mean both "stick together" and "cut apart"; *bimonthly* shouldn't mean both "twice a month" and "every other month." But they do. The verbs *loose* and *unloose* shouldn't mean the same thing, nor should *flammable* and *inflammable*. And yet they do. The same illogic shows up in our phrasal verbs for the act of eating: *eat up*, *chow down*, *tuck in*, *pig out*. Which particle is the logical one for eating, *up*, *down*, *in*, or *out*? Reason tells us the same act can't warrant all four. But it does.

For centuries, English speakers lived comfortably with this state of affairs. Starting a little before 1700, though, some people decided to sort through the mess in the hopes of improving it. English writers and speakers began to develop a notion that some widely used forms of the language were *wrong* and should be avoided, even eliminated from the language altogether. Convinced that the only way to speak properly was to study the language, even native speakers of English began looking for English grammar textbooks, and the writers of those textbooks obliged by providing lists of thou-shalt-nots. In the eighteenth century, English grammarians sent the English-speaking world to school.

Linguists—professional students of how languages work—call this approach to language *prescription*, since it *prescribes* what's right and wrong. That's the sort of language instruction we usually receive in school, when we're told how we should speak and write. It's the force behind the textbook publishing industry, and it pays the bills for many popular writers on language like Lynne Truss, John Humphrys, and William Safire. Contrast this *prescriptive* approach to language with the *descriptive* approach taken by most academic linguists. A linguist working in a university rarely presumes to tell the world what's right and what's wrong, but simply analyzes how language works, without any regard for whether it's good or bad. Do many people split infinitives? Then it's enough to note that English infinitives are often split. Do many people say *infer* when they mean *imply*? Academic linguists note the fact and move on, without chastising the benighted multitudes for their ignorance. They care only about *describing* the way things are.

These two groups, the prescriptivists and the descriptivists, haven't gotten on together very well, and the struggle between them is at the heart of this book. And yet that struggle between the purists and the linguists is fairly new: in Chaucer's day, or Shakespeare's, most people wouldn't have understood what the debate was about. That's not to say people didn't recognize good or bad writers. Some authors have always been praised for their elegance or wit or beauty, or blamed for their clumsiness or dullness or ugliness. The difference is that very few were blamed for not knowing their own language. There was no widespread notion that native English speakers didn't speak proper English. That came into being only a few hundred years ago. And in historical terms, this is a remarkably short span.

THIS BOOK IS neither an old-fashioned call to arms to revive some linguistic golden age nor a self-righteous dismissal of those who worked to change the language. Instead it's an attempt to understand where these so-called rules came from and why. They were all the product of specific social movements, specific historical moments. More to the point, they were the product of real people: every rule has a human history. *The Lexicographer's Dilemma* is the story of some of the people who have surveyed the state of the English language, didn't like what they saw, and resolved to do something about it—and a few who, while disavowing any intention of improving the language, were expected to do so. In producing their dictionaries, grammars, spelling books, pronunciation guides, and even moral codes, they've been placed in an uncomfortable position, expected to declare what's right but aware that any proclamations will be ineffective. The characters who've taken up the charge are as interesting for their obsessions as for their erudition: the witty poet John Dryden, who apparently single-handedly invented a "grammar rule" observed for the next three hundred years; the sharp-tongued satirist Jonathan Swift, who called for a government-sponsored academy to issue rulings on the language; the polymath Samuel Johnson, who put dictionaries on a new footing; the learned Hebraist Robert Lowth, the first modern to understand the workings of biblical poetry; the crackpot linguist John Horne Tooke, whose bizarre theories continue to baffle scholars; the chemist and theologian Joseph Priestley, whose political radicalism prompted violent riots; the ever-crotchety Noah Webster, who worked to Americanize the English language; the overachieving physician Peter Mark Roget, who wrote, scribbled, scrawled, composed, indited, printed, put to press, and published the treasure-house of the language; the long-bearded lexicographer James A. H. Murray, who devoted his life to a survey of the entire language in *The Oxford English Dictionary*; the playwright George Bernard Shaw, who worked without success to make English spelling rational; and the foulmouthed stand-up comic George Carlin, the champion of unrestrained free speech who inadvertently wrote the law on censorship. In a sense, they've all been failures: despite their combined efforts, the language is every bit as messy and irrational as it was three hundred years ago. But all have shaped and influenced the language we speak today. To understand our language, we have to understand them.

A NOTE ON THE QUOTATIONS

Whenever possible, I've used the earliest printed version of each work I quote here. All my sources are cited in the notes, which give the shortened title and page numbers; a bibliography at the end provides full publication details on all the works cited. Since this is a book about the history of the language, I've preserved the spelling and punctuation of early sources. The only alterations I've made to quotations are eliminating obsolete typography—the long *s*, the *ct* ligatures, the running quotation marks—and regularizing the usage of quotation marks and closing punctuation. I supply a few explanations in [brackets]; when a passage is very difficult—as with some of the Middle English—I provide a complete paraphrase or translation afterwards.

Linguists use a number of conventions to reproduce different aspects of the language, with angle brackets, square brackets, slashes, and asterisks indicating different styles of transcription. I considered following these conventions, but in the end feared that the strange symbols would be too off-putting. I have, however, left the original spelling of my quotations untouched. We might see *greater then* (where we'd have *greater than*) or a possessive *it's* (where we'd have *its*). Spellings like this were stigmatized as wrong only after 1750 or 1800. Double letters and silent *e*'s were more common in the early modern era than they are now, but some words that are now spelled with double letters or silent *e*'s appeared without them. Thus we might see *alle* or *al* for *all*, and *booke* or *boke* for *book*. It's not unusual to see *i* and *y* interchanged and, perhaps most confusing to modern eyes, *u* and *v* were often reversed on the page. Thus, in a work of the sixteenth century, we might see a word like *vnwauerynge*, which would today be spelled *unwavering*. (It was always pronounced *unwavering*; the change affected only the form of the letters on the page, not the sounds they represented.)

Finally, I often give the dates when words and senses first entered the language. This information almost always comes from *The Oxford English Dictionary*, but it requires a few caveats. The first is that the *OED* records only the earliest *written* occurrence of a word. Many words were almost certainly circulating in speech for years, even decades, before someone got around to writing them down. Second, we can never be certain that we've found the very first occurrence, even in writing. "*OED* antedatings," discoveries of words and senses that precede those in the dictionary, turn up all the time. Still, despite its limitations, the *OED* is the best source of information we have on these questions. Rather than load every statement about the appearance of a new word with qualifiers—"probably," "apparently," "seems to have been first used," "the surviving evidence suggests"—I've chosen to give the dates from the *OED* and to trust readers to make the necessary qualifications themselves.

CHAPTER 1

Vulgarities of Speech

HOMO SAPIENS LEARNS TO SPEAK

HUMANS HAVE BEEN USING LANGUAGE for a long time, though no one knows how long exactly. Because sounds leave no fossils, clues about the early history of language are scarce. The subject has, nonetheless, prompted endless speculation. As one linguist put it in 1933, "How language originated nobody knows and everybody has told."[1] And, we might add, everybody has told with reckless abandon and precious little regard for fact. The speculation got so bad in the nineteenth century that on March 8, 1866, the newly founded Société Linguistique de Paris placed an official moratorium on papers discussing the subject: article 2 of its bylaws decreed, "The Society will accept no communication concerning either the origin of language or the creation of a universal language." More recent linguists have echoed the society's disgust with the subject. Writing in 1988, Noam Chomsky—the most influential linguist of the last half century—sided with the jaded nineteenth-century Frenchmen: "There is a long history of study of origin of language, asking how it arose from calls of apes and so forth. That investigation in my view is a complete waste of time."[2]

In the last two decades, though, evolutionary psychology has once again made language origins a hot topic, especially after Steven Pinker and Paul Bloom published a learned essay, "Natural

Language and Natural Selection," in *Behavioral and Brain Sciences*, a respected scientific journal, in 1990. What had once been forbidden is now becoming fashionable again, and several books and hundreds of articles on the subject appear every year. Oxford University Press has even started a series of scholarly books called Studies in the Evolution of Language. None of this means that our guesses are necessarily more accurate than they were two hundred years ago. We're still woefully ignorant about where language came from.

We can say with confidence that humans have been using language for more than five thousand years, because we have writing at least that old. We can also say that it has probably been less than five million years, because the fossil record tells us our earliest hominid ancestors had a larynx ill suited to speaking. But "somewhere between five thousand and five million years" is a frustratingly broad range. Virtually all linguists draw a line between animal communication and the tremendous richness and complexity of human language, but presumably our species had to move across that barrier. How we did it and when remain provocative mysteries. We can make a very conservative estimate, though, and say that human beings have been using language as we know it for about a hundred thousand years.[3] A language called "English" split off from the others around the year A.D. 500.

If language, then, is around a hundred thousand years old, and English is fifteen hundred years old, how old are "good" and "bad" English? When, in other words, did people begin singling out one variety and considering it correct, with all other widely used varieties deemed improper? Our notions of proper English are only around three hundred years old—a very recent innovation indeed. For just one third of 1 percent of the history of language in general, and for just 20 percent of the history of our own language, have we had to go to school to study the language we already speak.

AND YET, EVEN though attacks on bad English are fairly young in historical terms, they've become a big part of the modern world.

That's probably because they can be thoroughly enjoyable. It's fun to revel in well-phrased put-downs. Venom makes for good prose, at least as long as it's not directed at you. A favorite spectator sport in some corners of the journalistic world is watching an ill-mannered critic toss and gore a third-rate writer for his limp clichés and flaccid prose. It's the same kind of malicious glee we take in reading nasty reviews of bad novels or plays. Samuel Johnson raised a laugh when he looked at one poem and said that "though but fourteen lines long, there were six grammatical faults in it."[4] A twentieth-century inheritor of Johnson's mordant wit, Paul Fussell, offers a similarly biting critique of one of the most respected British novelists of the day in an essay called "Can Graham Greene Write English?" Fussell's answer is no. Greene's memoir, he writes, opens in its first sentence with "a freshman howler: 'An autobiography . . . may contain less errors of fact than a biography, but it is of necessity more selective. . . .' For *less*, read *fewer*." To the memoir publisher's touting of Greene as "the most distinguished living writer in the English language," Fussell responds that the claim is "impertinent and illiterate. . . . Actually Greene's writing is so patently improvable that it could serve pedagogic purposes, as follows." Then comes an amusingly vicious parody of an undergraduate final exam in an English composition class:

EXAMINATION

English 345: Expository Writing (Intermediate)
(One hour. Write in ink on one side of the paper only.)

The following passages have been written by Mr. Graham Greene in his book *Ways of Escape*. They have been passed by his editors and approved by his publishers, who assert that Graham Greene is "the most distinguished living writer in the English language." Rewrite each passage as indicated.

1. *Correct the grammar:*

    a. "I am not sure that I detect much promise in [*Orient Express*], except in the character of Colonel Hartep, the Chief of Police, whom I suspect survived into the world of Aunt August and *Travels with My Aunt*."

    b. "In my hotel, the Ofloffson . . . , there were . . . a gentle couple whom I cannot deny bore some resemblance to Mr. and Mrs. Smith. . . ."[5]

The long roster of Greene's grammatical and stylistic blunders keeps going—not only *whom* for *who*, but also misplaced modifiers, jargon, redundancy, and awkwardness. It's a bravado demonstration of curmudgeonly sarcasm that raises obnoxiousness to the level of performance art, and it has the potential to amuse everyone except Graham Greene himself.

As Fussell shows, bad writing often calls forth good writing. H. L. Mencken's description of President Warren G. Harding's linguistic proficiency is a minor masterpiece of the genre:

> He writes the worst English that I have ever encountered. It reminds me of a string of wet sponges; it reminds me of tattered washing on the line; it reminds me of stale bean soup, of college yells, of dogs barking idiotically through endless nights. It is so bad that a sort of grandeur creeps into it. It drags itself out of the dark abysm of pish, and crawls insanely up the topmost pinnacle of posh. It is rumble and bumble. It is flap and doodle. It is balder and dash.[6]

It almost seems worth it to suffer through the writing of a bungler like Harding in order to get sublime vituperation like this.

What's interesting about these attacks, though, is that they would have made no sense before about 1700. *Who* and *whom*, *less* and *fewer*—things like this may keep modern writers awake at night, but no one seems to have paid them any attention until the grammarians arrived on the scene. Under the old dispensation, people spoke and wrote English without self-consciousness. But we're products of the new dispensation; we live in the age of grammars and dictionaries, rules and prohibitions, and we're expected to know them all before we open our mouths or fire up our word processors.

THIS BOOK DISCUSSES the origins of many so-called rules of English, but we should be clear about what we mean by "rules." Grammatical rules or laws are not like the law of gravity, or even laws against murder and theft—they're more like rules of etiquette, made by fallible people, useful only in certain situations, and subject to change.

When linguists refer to rules, they mean the principles according to which "The boy sees the girl" counts as a legitimate English sentence while "See girl's boy the the" doesn't. While no one is sure how many such rules there are, one estimate places the count around 3,500. And though weary purists and frustrated schoolmarms complain that badly educated simpletons don't know the rules, almost every native speaker knows virtually all the real rules of English.

What's confusing is that most people don't *know* they know the rules of English. Two examples can take the place of many. Ask native speakers of English, "*My* and *mine* both mean 'belonging to me,' but when do you say *my* and when do you say *mine*?" Few will be able to give you a clear answer—at least, not without a long pause to run through various possibilities. They'll be able to produce examples, but few will be able to formulate a rule; only those with some training in linguistics will be able to explain the distinction between *attributive* and *predicate* positions. And yet it's very rare for fluent speakers to make a mistake in using these words—even though they've never heard of predicate position, they make use of the idea every day. They know the rule, but they don't know they know the rule. Or another: virtually every native speaker will say "the big red ball" rather than "the red big ball." We all know to put attributive adjectives that refer to size before attributive adjectives that refer to color, but no textbook bothers to spell it out. The real rules are the ones that native speakers don't need to be taught because they're absorbed unconsciously.

When most people talk about the rules, though, they mean something different. The real rules permit sentences like "I wonder where he got it from" and "It looks like he's done," but many people find them unacceptable: one ends with a preposition; the second uses the preposition *like* as a conjunction and has *is done* for *has finished*. A sentence like "I ain't got nobody," by these standards, is a train wreck: it uses the naughty word *ain't*, the past participle *got* for the present-tense *have*, and a double negative. Slang, obscenity, jargon—we've all learned in school that we're not allowed to use them, and for most people, these are the rules. And still virtually everyone gets them wrong.

And most people *know* they get them wrong. When I'm introduced at a party as an English professor, people immediately turn apologetic about their grammar and shuffle uncomfortably, fearful of offending me and embarrassing themselves. No one feels compelled to confess to engineers that they never got the knack of building bridges, or to doctors that they don't understand the lymphatic system—but nearly everyone feels a strange obligation to come clean to someone who is supposed to be an expert in "grammar." They know there's some difference between *lay* and *lie*; they know that *shall* and *will* are different somehow; they know that there's some rule about where to put *only* in a sentence—and yet they don't know what those rules are. They've been scolded for confusing *can* and *may*, but to no good effect. They know that there's a mark called the semicolon but haven't a clue what to do with it, and so they ignore it. They therefore have convinced themselves they're not using their language correctly. The only relief most people find is in the thought that at least some people speak worse than they do. It's a well-known fact that whole groups speak bad English, including school dropouts, some ethnic minorities, poor people, and the young—especially the young, who are believed to be incapable of forming coherent sentences. Most people speak improperly; only a talented and educated few get it right.

What, though, does it mean to say that *everyone*, or *almost everyone*, speaks incorrectly? There are some things on which everyone can be wrong—when Aristotle argued that heavy bodies fell faster than light ones, he was simply wrong: that's a fact that can be confirmed or denied according to objective standards. But language isn't gravity. To say everyone speaks the language badly is tantamount to saying an entire country drives on the wrong side of the road. Some maintain that *It's me* is wrong, and *It is I* is the only correct form, because the case of pronouns has to be the same on either side of a verb of being—but only comic book superheroes routinely say *It is I*. Doesn't that mean the old rule about pronoun case is no longer operative? The editors of *The American Heritage Dictionary* recently published a book called *100 Words Almost Everyone Mispronounces*—words like *acumen, banal, chimera, coup de grâce, debacle, desultory, forte, impious, lingerie, marquis, mores, niche, quay, respite, ribald*, and *viscount*. But if "almost everyone" pronounces *forte* as *for-tay* (instead of the traditional *fort*) or *niche* as *neesh* (instead of the traditional *nitch*), doesn't it mean that *for-tay* and *neesh* are now standard pronunciations? The first time an English-speaker pronounced the French word *forte* as *for-tay*, it was an unambiguous mistake. Ditto the second time. But what about the thousandth time, or the millionth? At some point the wrong version became right. How long can the tiny band of purists hold out against the rest of the world?

What infinitive-splitters, preposition-enders, double-negativizers, and *forte*-mispronouncers are violating are not grammatical rules but what linguists call the "prestige forms," the ones given special social status. Often they hold this special status for the most tenuous of reasons, but hold it they do. The alternative is "stigmatized" words or usages. And words, word endings, and word combinations move on and off the naughty list and the nice list as the years pass.

We can see how these forms work by looking at the most

stigmatized word in the language, *ain't*—the word that every five-year-old is taught is not a word. But why not? Just because. It originally entered the language as a contracted form of *am not* (passing through a phase as *an't* before the *a* sound was lengthened) and first appeared in print in 1778, in Frances Burney's novel *Evelina*. We have uncontroversial contractions for *is not* (*isn't*) and *are not* (*aren't*), so what's wrong with reducing *am not* to *ain't*? The problem is that it was marked as a substandard word in the nineteenth century, people have been repeating the injunction ever since, and no amount of logic can undo it. It's forbidden simply because it's been forbidden.

An anonymous work of 1826, *The Vulgarities of Speech Corrected*, is typical of the nineteenth-century excoriation of the word *ain't*. After surveying the various contractions with *not*—*don't*, *haven't*, *won't*—the author admitted that they're all offensive, though "some of these are much less vulgar than others." One in particular, though, was beyond the pale: "I mean the expression '*a'n't it*,'" which he labeled "the most vulgar and incorrect expression in common use." He advised readers to avoid it, reminding them that "you will never hear it employed by any well educated person, much less by correct or elegant speakers." Then comes a handy table of "vulgar" and "correct" ways of saying the same thing:

In order to make you more perfect in avoiding this vulgarity, I shall give you a few corrected examples of it.

VULGAR.	CORRECT.
I *a'n't a* going.	I am not going.
You *a'n't* able to do it.	You are not able to do it.
A'n't she come yet?	Is she not come yet?
A'n't I very lucky?	Am I not very lucky?
He *a'n't* ready.	He is not ready.
They *a'n't* gone.	They are not gone.
Those *a'n't* pretty.	Those are not pretty.
A'n't they going?	Are they not going?
It *a'n't* fine.	It is not fine.

He is very clever—*a'n't*   Is not Mr. Wilson very
   Mr. Wilson?   clever?
This flower is pretty—   Is not this flower pretty?
   a'n't it?

He concluded, "When you have mastered this easy lesson, you may then proceed to the other forms of contraction, which are by no means so bad as this vulgar *a'n't*."[7] Nearly two centuries later, that "vulgar" word continues to produce shudders among traditionalists.

THE BAN ON *ain't* is the classic example of a *shibboleth*. A passage from the Book of Judges sets the scene. The Gileadites and the Ephraimites were at war, and the Gileadites developed a clever way to spot Ephraimite spies:

> And the Gileadites took the passages of Jordan before the Ephraimites: and it was so, that when those Ephraimites which were escaped said, Let me go over; that the men of Gilead said unto him, Art thou an Ephraimite? If he said, Nay; Then said they unto him, Say now Shibboleth: and he said Sibboleth: for he could not frame to pronounce it right. Then they took him, and slew him at the passages of Jordan.[8]

The original *shibboleth* was an arbitrary word that Jephthah used to spot his enemies (it means either "ear of grain" or "stream"): the Ephraimites had trouble with the *sh* sound and, when asked to pronounce a word with *sh* in it, their failure revealed they were enemy spies. In its modern sense, a shibboleth is some mannerism, usually linguistic, that reveals someone's origins. Sometimes it relates to pronunciation, as with the original shibboleth, but it can also involve anything about the use of language that gives away the origins of the speaker or writer. Standard English, for example, uses the same form for the second-person singular and plural—*you* singular, *you* plural—but many other varieties use different forms, with terms like *y'all*, *youse*, and *y'uns* standing in for the plural form of *you*. Someone with a good ear for dialect can tell where a speaker grew up by tuning in to such clues. Shibboleths can also reveal other things about your background: If you use *whom* in conversation, you tell your listeners something about your level of education. Using *ain't*, on the other hand, serves as a shibboleth that you haven't learned the secret handshake of the hypereducated.

People have probably always depended on shibboleths of various sorts. We all do it unconsciously: when someone speaks with a regional accent, we make certain assumptions about the speaker; and when a writer uses words like *thusly* in an essay, we make other assumptions. Our concern, though, is with the way those shibboleths were codified and systematized in handbooks, grammars, and dictionaries. Only in the eighteenth century did people begin arguing that one had to *study* grammar in order to speak correctly. Here, for instance, is the opinion of one grammarian, John Brightland, writing in 1711: "To Speak and Write without Absurdity the Language of one's Country," he asserted, "requires a Grammatical Knowledge of it; for without That 'tis impossible so much as to Read, Sensibly, the Books written in our Own Language: Nor indeed, can an Author write Intelligibly (that is, with a Clear and Determinate Sense) without Conformity to Grammar-Rules."[9] In one sense, this is perfectly true: it *is* impossible to speak, write, or read "without Conformity to Grammar-Rules." Where he misses the mark is in assuming that these rules have to be *studied*.

Brightland was not alone. Another eighteenth-century grammarian, Thomas Wilson, author of *The Many Advantages of a Good Language*, wrote in 1718, "For want of *Grammars* . . . the generality of Speakers and Writers abound with . . . false Grammar," and he insisted that "without *Latin* a Man cannot learn *English*." Even the Greeks and Romans, he said, didn't speak or write well until the grammarians showed them the light. He concluded that "without an *Ars loquendi*, that is, without something of a regular

Grammatical Way of joining Words together, there can be no such thing as an intelligible Language."[10] Others agreed. The Abbé Gedoyn, writing in 1728, insisted that we can't hope to achieve "Correctness and Purity of Language" until we've been taught "both the Knowledge of Rules and Practice. Rules are requisite to shew and guard us against the principal Vices of Speech. We must therefore study them."[11]

The argument about the need for study is still made today. We need the rules of English, say the prescriptivists, in order to communicate clearly. And they're right—at least about the actual rules of grammar. But it's too easy to use "clear communication" to justify any linguistic prejudice, and this is why it's so important to distinguish the different kinds of rules. As one arch-prescriptivist, Dwight Macdonald, put it in 1962, the wanton disregard for traditional English "is debasing our language by rendering it less precise and thus less effective as literature and less efficient as communication."[12] But do these traditional rules of grammar and style really preserve clear communication? Many defenders of correctness like to invent confusion where none actually exists. A Victorian purist, for instance, told a story about a supposed mispronunciation: a teacher once corrected a student's misspelling of *Venice* as *Vennice*. The teacher, given to pronouncing an *h* where speakers of standard English wouldn't, "put his pen through the superfluous letter, observing, 'Don't you know, sir, there is but one *hen* in Venice?'" The student then marveled "*how uncommonly scarce eggs must be there*."[13] But was there ever such a ninny? If the elimination of a dangling participle or a split infinitive has ever saved a human life, the fact is not recorded in the history books. That's because most of the prescriptivists' rules, despite the passion with which they're proclaimed and enforced, don't really improve clarity. Even many of the most flagrant violations of the traditional rules are perfectly clear. "I ain't got nobody" is, *pace* Macdonald, perfectly "efficient as communication."

We can go further: following these traditional rules doesn't always make for good writing or good thinking. In 1957 Noam

Chomsky gave a now-famous example of a sentence that is perfectly grammatical without meaning anything: "Colorless green ideas sleep furiously."[14] Even though it's nonsensical, it doesn't violate a single rule of grammar. Neither is grammar the same as elegance or gracefulness. Sentences can be both meaningful and grammatical and still be bad. Business writers are notorious for turning out grammatical but ugly bureaucratese, but no one is better at grammatical obfuscation than academics. For a while the *Journal of Philosophy and Literature* ran an annual "Bad Writing Contest," seeking to find the worst bit of English published in the previous year. One of the winners was the British philosopher Roy Bhaskar, who in *Plato, Etc.: The Problems of Philosophy and Their Resolution* blessed the world with this marvel of mystification:

> Indeed dialectical critical realism may be seen under the aspect of Foucauldian strategic reversal—of the unholy trinity of Parmenidean/Platonic/Aristotelean provenance; of the Cartesian–Lockean–Humean–Kantian paradigm, of foundationalisms (in practice, fideistic foundationalisms) and irrationalisms (in practice, capricious exercises of the will-to-power or some other ideologically and/or psychosomatically buried source) new and old alike; of the primordial failing of western philosophy, ontological monovalence, and its close ally, the epistemic fallacy with its ontic dual; of the analytic problematic laid down by Plato, which Hegel served only to replicate in his actualist monovalent analytic reinstatement in transfigurative reconciling dialectical connection, while in his hubristic claims for absolute idealism he inaugurated the Comtean, Kierkegaardian and Nietzschean eclipses of reason, replicating the fundaments of positivism through its transmutation route to the superidealism of a Baudrillard.[15]

The sentence—yes, it's a single sentence—is utterly unintelligible, and not only to lay readers; even most professional philosophers stare at it in mute incomprehension. But there's not a single "grammar error" anywhere in its 136 words.

Conversely, writing can also be in-your-face ungrammatical but still be effective, even beautiful. A sentence like "You ain't seen nothin' yet," though only five words long, manages to transgress half the rules in a first-year composition handbook—the stigmatized word *ain't*, the past participle *seen* in place of the past-tense *saw*, the double negative, the truncated ending of *nothing*—and yet it's as plain as can be, and a hundred times more effective in context than "You have not yet seen anything." It's good English, even if it's "bad grammar." Even more forceful is the statement by Bartolomeo Vanzetti on April 9, 1927, as he answered the court clerk's question, "Have you anything to say why sentence of death should not be passed upon you?"

> Yes. What I say is that I am innocent. . . . The defense have had a tremendous work to do in order to collect some evidence, to collect some testimony to offset and to learn what the testimony of the State had been. And in this consideration it must be said that even if the defense take double time of the State about delays, double time than they (the State) delayed the case, it would have been reasonable just the same, whereas it took less than the State. . . . I would not wish to a dog or to a snake, to the most low and misfortunate creature of the earth—I would not wish to any of them what I have had to suffer for things that I am not guilty of. I am suffering because I am a radical and indeed I am a radical. . . . I am so convinced to be right that you can only kill me once but if you could execute me two times, and if I could be reborn two other times, I would live again to do what I have done already.[16]

The writing is often unidiomatic ("I would not wish to a dog," "I am so convinced to be right") and sometimes downright ungrammatical ("even if the defense take double time . . . than they (the

State) delayed"), and yet there is a dignity—a tragic dignity—to the broken English. Bad writing isn't the same as bad grammar any more than good writing is the same as good grammar.

EVEN DISCUSSING THESE questions can cause tempers to flare. Passions run hot when the discussion turns to language. Defending Vanzetti's radical politics is one thing, but defending his end-of-clause preposition ("things that I am not guilty of")—that's going too far. People of very different opinions—friends who can discuss politics, religion, and sex with perfect civility—are often reduced to red-faced rage when the topic of conversation is the serial comma or an expression like *more unique*. People who merely roll their eyes at hate crimes feel compelled to write jeremiads on declining standards when a newspaper uses the wrong form of *its*. Challenge my most cherished beliefs about the place of humankind in God's creation, and while I may not agree with you, I'll fight to the death for your right to say it. But dangle a participle in my presence, and I'll consider you a subliterate cretin no longer worth listening to, a menace to decent society who should be removed from the gene pool before you do any more damage.

And, even though most people are convinced their own use of the language is bad, they're still willing—even eager—to declare their pet peeves. Newspaper editors used to receive many such proclamations, but Internet message boards are now the preferred forum. "You know what I really hate?" comes the question, followed by a list of grievances, some of which can be downright eccentric. The phrase *went missing*, for instance, has been part of the language for a century and a half; while it's a little more common in Britain and the Commonwealth than in the United States, it's perfectly standard across the English-speaking world.[17] Still, it provokes bizarre and passionate reactions, usually because of its apparent illogicality (you don't *go* anywhere; you just *become* missing). The complainers rarely express trouble with *go hungry*, *go crazy*, or *go native*, all of which use the infinitely versatile verb *go* in similar ways. But there seems to be something uncommonly irritating about the phrase *went missing*. Here's a selection of actual comments about it on an Internet discussion board:

> I don't care where it came from or what it's [*sic*] English origins are. In my mind it will always remain a bastardization of the English language. To discover that it originated in England, of all places, horrifies me! Simply put, it is a stupid phrase!

> I find it very distressing that somehow this abomination has crept into our language from out of nowhere and is being accepted and promoted by the media. Stop the insantiy [*sic*]!

One writer finds it "silly and obnoxious"; another "illiterate and superfluous." Some, it seems, suffer mental and physical anguish when it appears:

> Everytime I hear it, it sounds like someone is scratching their fingernails on a blackboard!

The usage is even enough to prompt some people to contemplate violence:

> OMG I can't stand that phrase! It makes me mad, and I want to hurl something at the television when I hear it!!!

Others, perhaps more coolheaded than the television-destroyer with a fondness for exclamation points, still see it as an opportunity for action:

> It is a degradation of the English language. When I hear a reporter use the phrase, I note the time and the story. When I am on the computer, I e-mail the news program and

express my objection to this phrase. I would encourage
others to do the same and maybe we can keep this ignorant phrase off the TV news.[18]

IN TRYING TO tell the story of how these modern ideas about a "degraded" English came to pass, I'm bound to provoke more than my
share of annoyance, both from those on the permissive and the re-
strictive ends of the spectrum. Many will remain convinced that
bad English is bad English and always has been, and that defending
it is akin to allowing standards to decline. The same impulse has
led many ill-tempered grouches to send angry letters to magazines
and newspapers, lamentations for a lost age of proper English usage. But there has never been a linguistic golden age. As soon as
people stopped complaining about the illiteracies of the past, they
switched to complaining about the illiteracies of the present.

Treating cultural history as a story of decline is always ill-
advised. It's satisfying to indulge in nostalgia for the good old
days—almost invariably in one's youth—before society went to hell.
That was back when boys had respect for their elders, when girls
dressed decently, and when music still sounded like music. The
problem is that *every* aging population has had the same fears about
the rising generation. It's been going on forever: it's hard to find
any society that is not convinced that things have gotten much
worse since the good old days. We can look all the way back to the
very beginning of our literary tradition, to the first book of
Homer's *Iliad*. There the warriors Agamemnon and Achilles have
had a falling out, and the old man, Nestor, lectures the squabbling
princes, advising them to put aside their differences. In doing so he
recollects the days of his youth, back when men were real men.
Alexander Pope's translation of 1715 put it well:

> Young as you are, this youthful Heat restrain,
> Nor think your *Nestor*'s Years and Wisdom vain.
> A Godlike Race of Heroes once I knew,
> Such, as no more these aged Eyes shall view![19]

One of the founding works of Western literature shows us a council of the mightiest heroes, engaging in the most heroic acts—and yet, off to the side, an old man is convinced that things were better when he was young. The world, it seems, has been on a fast track to hell since time out of mind.

More than a century ago, when Harvard University was first beginning to offer courses in English composition, a prominent educator, L. B. R. Briggs, published a list of students' linguistic failures. "Spelling," he wrote, "is bad, and probably always will be." He was ready with examples: "*loose* for *lose* is so nearly universal that *lose* begins to look wrong; *sentance* prevails; *dissapointed* and *facinating* are not unusual." Moreover,

> Punctuation is frequently inaccurate—that is to say, unintelligent and misleading. The apostrophe is nearly as often a sign of the plural as of the possessive; the semicolon, if used at all, is a spasmodic ornament rather than a help to the understanding; and—worst of all—the comma does duty for the period, so that even interesting writers run sentence into sentence without the formality of full stop or of capital.[20]

All of these objections are heard today, often with the suggestion that things were better once upon a time. But we can see that even the best-educated Americans of the 1880s made the same sorts of blunders that people today regard as signs that things are getting worse.

Anyone who studies history knows there never was a golden age. English, it seems, has been in a state of crisis, besieged by barbarians, for as long as it has existed. People were grousing about misbehaving youngsters in 1700; they continue to grouse about them today; and today's youthful transgressors will someday bemoan the next generation's ignorance. It's a pity most of us won't be around to hear today's teenagers recalling, "Back in my day, we listened to death metal and gangsta rap, not that crazy music you kids like nowadays . . ."

But it's still useful to cast our attention back on the history of the language. For most of the last fifteen hundred years, virtually no one worried about getting the language right. Around four hundred years ago, though, there was a change, which provides a useful place to begin an inquiry into proper English.

CHAPTER 2

The Age in Which I Live
JOHN DRYDEN REVISES HIS WORKS

WRITERS ARE NOTORIOUS FOR SECOND-GUESSING themselves. Most of them don't like to let go of their manuscripts, and will keep tinkering with them—trying to make this sentence clearer, that paragraph punchier—until a publisher forcibly yanks them out of their hands. And once their works are on the press and it's too late to make further changes, those writers immediately feel a kind of literary buyer's remorse. That's one reason why authors appreciate the chance to revise their old works when it's time to prepare a new edition for the press: they get to correct their blunders and sharpen the language of the early draft.

But one particular act of revising—by the poet and critic John Dryden in 1684—is about more than the usual authorial vanity, and it deserves particular attention. The changes Dryden made to his works give us the opportunity to explore the state of the English language at the end of the seventeenth century, when ideas about the language were undergoing a seismic shift.

JOHN DRYDEN WAS born in London in 1631, fifteen years after Shakespeare died. The mid-seventeenth century was a difficult time in England—civil war broke out when Dryden was nine, and the king of England was beheaded by rebel forces nine years later—but, at least when he was young, Dryden remained reasonably well insulated from national strife. He attended the distinguished Westminster School, where he studied under the legendary Richard Busby. Among Busby's students were architect Sir Christopher Wren, scientist Robert Hooke, theologian Robert South, philosopher John Locke, poet Matthew Prior, and politician Francis Atterbury. Dryden received the best education seventeenth-century England had to offer.

Westminster School was famous for its attention to rhetoric, one of the seven ancient liberal arts, alongside grammar, logic, geometry, arithmetic, music, and astronomy. The word *rhetoric* has in recent years degenerated into a mere term of abuse—good-for-nothing politicians are said to resort to "rhetoric" when they mean to hoodwink us—but in the seventeenth century the word meant simply the effective use of language, a skill every writer hoped to master. And Dryden was one of the most distinguished rhetoricians to come out of a distinguished school: before he left, he had published his first poem, a royalist elegy to a recently deceased friend combined with a glance at the execution of Charles I.

Upon leaving Westminster, Dryden enrolled at Trinity College, Cambridge, in 1650, and received his B.A. four years later, finishing first in his class. Over the next few years he published a few poems, many of them praising the parliamentarian government that was set up by the rebel forces to run the country in the 1650s. He really came into his own, though, after the Restoration brought the exiled King Charles II to the throne in 1660. No longer a supporter of the parliamentary forces, Dryden had become a royalist once more, and his *Astræa Redux* celebrated the king's return from France to Dover in England with positively messianic excitement:

> And now times whiter Series is begun
> Which in soft Centuries shall smoothly run;
> Those Clouds that overcast your Morne shall fly
> Dispell'd to farthest corners of the sky.[1]

Whether the Restoration Charles II brought ever-dawning day to the nation is a question for historians to debate, but there's no doubt that Charles's ascent to the throne was good for Dryden. One of the king's first acts was to reopen the public theaters after eighteen years without any public drama in London,[2] and Dryden decided to try his hand at writing for the stage. By the 1670s he found his dramatic voice in a string of successful plays, both comedies and tragedies. And even as he was at work as a playwright, Dryden kept on writing nondramatic poetry, including the long *Annus Mirabilis* (1667), as well as critical prose. His *Of Dramatick Poesie, an Essay* (1668), with its famous praise for William Shakespeare, was one of the first great works of literary criticism in the language, prompting a later critic, Samuel Johnson, to declare him "the father of English criticism, . . . the writer who first taught us to determine upon principles the merit of composition."[3]

Not everyone was a fan. Dryden's conversion from Anglicanism to Roman Catholicism alienated many English Protestants, who also accused him of cynically switching his allegiance from the parliamentarians to the king for the sake of political advancement. He managed to make most of his enemies, though, by offending them with his writing, for Dryden was one of the most sharp-tongued satirists of his day. In works like *Absalom and Achitophel* and *The Medal*, he held up his political enemies to ridicule and turned them into public jokes. He entered a nasty war of words with several minor poets, most notably Thomas Shadwell, in his mock-epic poem *Mac Flecknoe* (1682). There Dryden imagined another bad poet, Richard Flecknoe, who "had govern'd long: / In Prose and Verse, was own'd, without dispute / Through all the Realms of Non-sense, absolute." This absolute monarch of non-sense was looking for a successor to the throne, and he settled on the third-rate versifier Shadwell (lightly disguised behind his initial and a dash):

> Sh—— alone my perfect image bears,
> Mature in dullness from his tender years.

Sh—— alone, of all my Sons, is he
Who stands confirm'd in full stupidity.
The rest to some faint meaning make pretence,
But Sh—— never deviates into sense.

The ghosts of Shadwell and Flecknoe now suffer the indignity of being known to history almost solely as the targets of Dryden's lampoons.

Dryden's willingness to satirize other writers prompted many of them to fire back. But even as he engaged in satirical fisticuffs, hardly anyone questioned John Dryden's skill as a writer: his poetry, plays, and criticism had earned him tremendous respect, enough to promote him to the position of England's poet laureate. By the time he published his career-topping translation of Virgil's *Aeneid*, he was the nation's preeminent writer. We still quote Dryden's magisterial translation when we think of the opening lines of the *Aeneid*: he gave us "Arms and the man I sing."

IT'S HARD TO imagine a more successful literary career than Dryden's. But when, at the height of his fame, it was time to republish some of his works in a new edition, Dryden wasn't happy with what he had written early in his career. He decided it was time to make some changes.

They weren't big changes; a full century passed before a critic, Edmond Malone, even noticed them. But they were interesting enough to deserve comment. Malone looked closely at *Of Dramatick Poesie*, carefully comparing the first edition of 1668 with the second of 1684. He noted that in that sixteen-year period, Dryden "appears to have revised and corrected it with great care." Malone promised to "subjoin the principal variations between the two copies."[4]

Some of those variations are straightforward—cleaning up ambiguities, striving for greater clarity in his word choices, that sort of thing. Dryden worked to make his prose less wordy and more direct. In those sixteen years he had apparently fallen out of love with the preposition *upon*, so he changed most occurrences of that word to *on*, as when "a funeral elegy *upon* the duke" became "a funeral elegy *on* the duke." He made other single-word changes: he revised the vulgar *wench* to the more pristine *mistress*; he tossed the obsolescent *garboils* for the more modern *disorders*. In the first edition he had stumbled into an Irish bull when he wrote "A good Poet never concludes upon the first line, till he has sought out such a rhime as may fit the sense," meaning *conclude* in the sense of "settle on"; he realized that "concluding" on a "first line" was absurd. When he revised the work, he nixed *concludes* for *establishes*.

Other changes were less stylistic and more grammatical. He made explicit the antecedents for some pronouns, for instance, to clear up some ambiguities—an *it* in the first edition might be replaced with a more specific noun. He caught a problem with subject-verb agreement, changing "there *appears* two actions in the play" to "there *appear* two actions." He also realized that when he wrote "especially him *who* you first described," he should have written *whom*, and made the change in the second edition.

None of these changes are especially noteworthy; they're the sorts of things any writer might do when given the chance to revise. The most curious class of corrections, though, arose from Dryden's habit of shuffling his prepositions. Whenever they appeared at the end of a sentence in his first edition, he felt obliged to move them in the second edition. He began relocating end-of-sentence prepositions to the beginning of a phrase, trading, say, "the age I live *in*" for "the age *in which* I live." Where the first edition had "*which* none boast *of*," Dryden substituted "*of which* none boast."[5] And so on, through dozens of changes.

WHY DID DRYDEN bother? It wasn't because ending sentences with prepositions was wrong—no one, it seems, had ever worried about it before, at least not in print. David Crystal, one of the most distinguished linguists writing today, examined the evidence and offered a number of possible answers: maybe Dryden liked ending sentences with more important and resonant words; maybe he was experimenting with different prose rhythms—"But above all, Dryden, a classical scholar, would [have] been influenced by Latin grammarians."[6]

Dryden knew his Latin, and Crystal is almost certainly right that his knowledge of Latin influenced his English. Dryden even admitted to trying to improve his English style by translating his own writings into Latin and then translating them back into English, convinced that the discipline of subjecting his works to the rigors of Latin grammar would make them better.[7] Others in his day did the same. One of the recurring accusations directed at seventeenth- and eighteenth-century grammarians is that they understood only Latin grammar, and expected English—a language built on a very different foundation—to conform to Latin plans. It's true that many early commentators on the English language were afflicted with a keen case of Latin envy. And it may be that Latin grammar motivated Dryden's movement of his prepositions. The Latin language allows much greater flexibility of word order than English: objects can come before subjects, verbs can come at the beginning or end of a clause, and so on. But Latin doesn't allow a preposition to appear after the noun or pronoun it governs: it must be in the *pre-position*, whence the name. Dryden decided the same policy should apply to English. He's the first writer on record to do so.

Dryden did explain this distaste for sentence-ending prepositions. His friend William Walsh, who in 1691 had published *A Dialogue concerning Women: Being a Defence of the Sex*, asked Dryden for suggestions on how he might improve his book. Dryden obliged by sending an advice-filled letter that began with some flattery: "There is not the least occasion of reflecting on your disposition of the piece," he said, "nor the thoughts. I see nothing to censure in either of them. Besides this the style is easy and naturall." After the compliments, though, came a few cavils. "In the correctness of the English there is not much for me to animadvert"—not much, but something. "Be pleasd therefore," he continued, "to avoid the words, don't, can't, shan't, and the like abbreviations of syllables." Why? Because they "seem to me to savour of a little rusticity." Contractions were used by rural bumpkins, not civilized gentlemen. (The English language preserves this prejudice of city life over country life in many words. The well-bred could aspire to *courtesy*—something learned in the *court*, near the centers of political power; they might also be praised for being *urbane*, which clearly shows its kinship with the word *urban*. At the other extreme, those who lived in the rural villages came to be known in the law as *villeins* or *villains*.)

Dryden's concerns about Walsh's writing went beyond contractions. "I find," Dryden wrote, "that you make not a due distinction betwixt that, and who; A man *that* is not proper; the relative *who* is proper. *That*, ought alwayes to signify a thing; *who*, a person." And where Walsh had written that "Conversing with fair Ladies . . . draws us into Inconveniencies, which we do not at first see the Consequences of," Dryden suggested the same revision he had used in his own work: "I hinted somewhat of concludding your Sentences with prepositions or conjunctions sometimes, which is not elegant, as in your first sentence—(See the consequences of.)" Walsh obliged, revising his opening sentence in the published version to read "draws us into Inconveniencies, of which we do not at first see the Consequence."8

Shuffling prepositions hardly seems epoch-making. But in some ways what Dryden was doing was genuinely new, and it marked a major shift in the way English speakers thought about their language. For many centuries people had worried about whether they got the language right. Dryden, on the other hand, was wondering whether the language was right. Dryden didn't think the problem was with Walsh or with himself. He thought the problem was with the English language itself. The *language* wasn't correct. It wasn't proper.

HOW DID DRYDEN know? He couldn't turn to grammar books or even dictionaries; though a few existed, not one was considered really authoritative. There was no one to tell him that sentence-ending prepositions, *that* for *who*, and contractions like *don't* were improper. He had to reach that conclusion on his own.

It raises an unavoidable question: who gets to say what the correct or proper version of the language is—what words mean and the order in which they should be arranged? There have been many answers to that question, but one of the most important comes from the Roman poet Quintus Horatius Flaccus—better known as Horace—in his poem *Ars Poetica*, "The Art of Poetry," written in 18 B.C. There he described the fate of many words in the Latin tongue:

> Multa renascentur quae iam cecidere, cadentque
> quae nunc sunt in honore uocabula, si uolet usus,
> quem penes arbitrium est et ius et norma loquendi.

A literal translation: "Many words will be born again that have now sunk into oblivion, and many will die that are now held in respect, if that's what usage chooses—usage, which has the power over the judgment, the law, and the rule of speech." The idea is that "usage" or "custom" dictates what's correct in the language—in other words, that propriety emerges from the collective wisdom of crowds. Questions in language are not resolved by a government committee or voted on by a board of distinguished academics. They're not settled by fiat. They change the same way the width of neckties and the length of skirts change: standards emerge more or less organically out of the collective practice of the multitude. No one is in charge, and correct language is simply what's dominant among the majority of competent speakers and writers. Horace's pithy phrase *norma loquendi*, "the rule of speaking," is often used to refer to this belief that correct English emerges out of the collective verdict of the entire English-speaking community.

Horace's answer seemed to satisfy most English speakers for centuries. With Dryden, though, we begin to see something different: usage or custom begins to be edged out in favor of other principles.

People had been blamed for their lapses and errors in language before, but they were blamed for *not* speaking or writing like everyone else—for violating traditional idioms, or using foreign words, or putting words together in ways that most people didn't. Dryden was among the first to level criticism at those who *did* speak or write like everyone else. And in this respect he was typical of his age: people were beginning to think the English language itself was in bad shape. English was corrupted or impure or improper. Dryden was eager to remold the language.

He wasn't alone in his worries about grammar. Many English speakers were paying unprecedented attention to the language late in the seventeenth century. Bemoaning the state of the language wasn't new; a complaint tradition stretches back many hundreds of years. But the earlier grievances about English looked very different from their seventeenth-century incarnations. Most worries about the language before the 1660s had to do with its adequacy to express everything that needed to be expressed: did it have all the words it needed, or was it necessary to introduce words and idioms from other languages?

Englishmen had long felt inferior next to their Continental brethren. The French, Italians, even the Spanish and Germans—all had produced impressive dictionaries and grammars to codify their languages. English seemed to lag behind. Some Englishmen fretted that the language itself wasn't capable of the full range of literary expression. In 1545, for instance, England's poet laureate, John Skelton, feared that English wasn't up to the task of expressing lasting literature. He worried about "frowardes" (difficulties) that would keep English speakers from expressing themselves fully:

> Our language is so rusty
> So cankered and so full
> Of frowardes and so dull
> That if I wolde apply

> To wryte ornatly
> I wot not where to fynd
> Termes to serue my mynde.[9]

"The speche of Englande," a fifteenth-century commentator noted, "is a base speche [compared] to other noble speches, as Italion Castylion and Frenche, howbeit the speche of Englande of late dayes is amended."[10]

Dryden's concerns were different. He wasn't bothered by the lack of vocabulary, but by the lack of *elegance*, to use one of Dryden's favorite words. It was a favorite of his contemporaries, too. John Evelyn called for translations "out of the best orators & poets, Greek and Latin, and even out of y[e] moderne languages," hopeful that writers would pick up some of the "elegancy of y[e] style."[11] Another favorite word for the ideal to which they aspired was *politeness*. One of Dryden's younger contemporaries, the journalist and novelist Daniel Defoe, called for an institution that would offer lectures "on the Nature, Original, Usage, Authorities and Differences of Words, on the Propriety, Purity, and *Cadence of Stile*, and of the Politeness and *Manner* in Writing." These lectures would chastise "Irregular Usages," correct "Erroneous Customs in Words," and aid in "bringing our *English* Tongue to a due Perfection."[12] The terms he uses are significant: Defoe, like Dryden and Evelyn, was haunted by the thought that the language lacked politeness, propriety, and purity, and that "Perfection" had to be imposed from without. *Norma loquendi* was being neglected: if even "Customs in Words" might be erroneous, then the usage of the masses can't be our guide to what's right.

COUNTLESS ENGLISH WRITERS of the time, both professional and amateur, were worrying, just like Dryden, Evelyn, and Defoe, about whether they were using the language properly, and whether the language itself was capable of being used properly. At least some of these concerns were probably the result of larger cultural shifts taking place in the late seventeenth century.

Dryden's early career shows him going back and forth between two political parties: the parliamentarians, who ruled the country at the time he took his degree at Cambridge, and the royalists, who were on the rise after the Restoration in 1660. The political turmoil was the result of a series of civil wars in the mid-seventeenth century. During those turbulent times, many distinguished old families lost their wealth, whether through extravagant expenditure or simply through picking the losing side in the wars. It was no easy thing to give up the estates on which their ancestors had lived for generations, and while many in the upper ranks were coming down, some in the lower ranks were on the way up. Big shifts in the economy restructured the entire society.

The Industrial Revolution would not get under way in earnest until the late eighteenth century, but many of the changes that became clear in that era were already beginning a hundred years earlier. Most important, this was the beginning of Britain's great age of empire, as exploring vessels were followed by merchant vessels, and North America, Africa, Asia, and eventually Australia started pouring money into British coffers. Much of it was dirty money—the British were deeply implicated in the slave trafficking of the seventeenth and eighteenth centuries—but it was money all the same, and it helped to transform English society. The very basis of the economy was shifting, as money assumed greater importance than land. Jonathan Swift put it forcefully in 1710: "power, which according to the old maxim was used to follow land, is now gone over to money."[13] Large estates inherited from ancestors had always been the only "real property"—we still use the term "real estate"—but for the first time, it was possible to work your way into the upper echelons of society, rather than being destined to remain in the socioeconomic class into which you were born. As a result, a few people born into the lower ranks found themselves with enough money to travel in circles previously reserved for the aristocracy. The numbers were still small—most of the population suffered under an appalling standard of living, some of them barely above subsistence level—but the changes were beginning.

The transformation didn't take place evenly throughout Britain.

The countryside was, at least for a while, largely untouched by the new prosperity, but the cities were becoming very different places. London in particular was growing rapidly, increasing from around half a million souls when Dryden was achieving fame in the 1670s to more than a million in 1800. And the metropolitan area was peopled not by longtime aristocrats who had owned land there for generations, but by go-getters from the countryside who arrived with dreams of making it rich. Most failed, as we can see in William Hogarth's illustrations of the dirty underside of eighteenth-century London life, with all the traps that awaited those who hoped to find a living in the city. But some actually managed to earn large amounts of money in trade or manufacturing, and increasingly they settled in London's newly fashionable neighborhoods— not the City, the square mile surrounded by the old Roman walls, but the more elegant West End. This class mobility plays a big part in the history of good English, which was tightly tied up with what it meant to be part of the middle class.

THERE'S NO SURER way to make historians roll their eyes than by using the phrase "rise of the middle class," a magical incantation that has been used to characterize every historical era from 1350 to 1950. Nearly every movement in Europe or North America in those six hundred years has been explained away with reference to a "newly emergent middle class." But the period from the late seventeenth century through the eighteenth really was marked by a newly self-conscious group of people who were no longer peasants but still were excluded from the traditional aristocracy. They thought of themselves as members of a newly important social rank, what Defoe's most famous creation, Robinson Crusoe, identified as "the middle State, or what might be called the upper Station of *Low Life*."[14]

Upward social mobility has plenty of obvious advantages, but there's at least one significant downside: it can produce crippling anxiety. Anyone who has had the experience of attending his or

her first formal dinner in distinguished company will recall the ter-
ror of using a fish fork during the salad course, eating a bread-roll
off a neighbor's plate, or holding out the water glass when wine is
being poured. This anxiety is itself the product of social mobility.
The traditional aristocracy doesn't suffer from the same fears:
people born into such families become accustomed to refined manners early in life. They know not to applaud between the movements in string quartets, they know not to rest their elbows on the
tables, and they know to address a duke as *Your Grace*—they learn
these things in their cradles, because their families have been immersed in that kind of culture all along. But newcomers to the
good life—they're a different story.

It was the self-conscious and insecure newcomers who wanted
guidance on how to behave in their new world. The late seventeenth
and early eighteenth centuries see the rise of a kind of publication
known as the conduct manual, the ancestor of modern etiquette
guides by the likes of Emily Post and Judith Martin (better known
as "Miss Manners").[15] The job of these manuals was to ease the
anxiety of social arrivistes as they made their way in an unfamiliar
culture. And advice on how to speak proper English—which is to
say, the kind of English the aristocrats learned in their cradles—
often appeared alongside advice on the proper fork.

ONE OF THE more important eighteenth-century conduct books
makes the connections between etiquette and language clear.
Samuel Richardson—whose *Pamela*, published in 1740 and 1741,
is called by some critics the first true English novel—wrote a book
called *Letters Written to and for Particular Friends, on the Most
Important Occasions: Directing Not Only the Requisite Style and
Forms to Be Observed in Writing Familiar Letters; but How to
Think and Act Justly and Prudently, in the Common Concerns of
Human Life*. It contains 173 letters, all offering templates for real-
life situations, just awaiting minor adjustments to make them suitable to any occasion. Are you an uncle, charged with chastising a

rowdy nephew for hanging out with a bad crowd? You might look to Richardson and begin your letter this way:

> *Dear Nephew,*
>   I am very much concerned to hear that you are of late fallen into bad Company; that you keep bad Hours, and give great Uneasiness to your Master, and break the Rules of his Family: That when he expostulates with you on this Occasion, you return pert and bold Answers.[16]

Or perhaps a neighboring family with a new child has asked you for a recommendation on the wet nurse you used. In that case, here's how you might reply:

> MADAM,
>   The Bearer is Mrs. *Newman*, whom I recommended to you as a Nurse for Master. You will be pleased with her neat Appearance and wholesome Countenance. She lives just above Want, in a pleasant airy Place, and has a very honest diligent Husband, with whom she lives very happily, and the Man is exceedingly fond of Children, very sober, and very good-humour'd; and they have every thing pretty about them.[17]

Or are you a father, concerned that your daughter's French lover is not right for her? Richardson suggests you might start with this letter, and adapt it to your needs:

> *Dear* Polly,
>   I cannot say I look upon Mr. *La Farriere* in the same favourable Light that you seem to do. His frothy Behaviour may divert well enough as an Acquaintance; but is very unanswerable, I think, to the Character of a Husband, especially an *English* Husband, which I take to be a graver Character than a *French* one. . . . If after Marriage his

present Temper should continue, when *you* are a careful
Mother, *he* will look more like a Son than a Husband.[18]

On he went, through nearly two hundred models that offer
examples of style and sentiment proper to the occasion. From
Richardson, insecure social climbers might learn not only the
proper manners for their new station in life, but also the proper
manner of expression. Richardson's audience, after all, was not
people who had been accustomed to writing for generations. His
book was instead for people whose grandparents couldn't read a
word, and whose parents were just barely literate—but who now
found they were expected to read, to write, to manage servants,
and to correspond with the rest of the world.

Richardson's generation was more literate than any that came
before. Reliable estimates of literacy rates are notoriously difficult
to come by, because the act of reading rarely leaves traces. Historians have generally used the ability to sign legal documents as a
proxy for literacy, assuming that someone who has signed a will or
a contract was probably able to read as well. It's a tenuous conclusion. Since reading and writing were usually taught as separate
skills, there were probably many people who knew how to read without being able to sign their names, and it's at least possible that a
few people learned to sign their names without really knowing
how to read. Still, the ability to sign a legal document is probably
correlated with literacy, and those numbers show sharp increases
in the decades after about 1660. The evidence suggests that more
people were reading and, at least as important, that more people
were writing. Those people new to writing were looking for guidance on how to do it well.

Not all the manuals were aimed at the same audience, though a
surprising number of them gave similar advice on language. Daniel
Defoe, famous today for *Robinson Crusoe* and *Moll Flanders*, offered his own guidance to the mercantile classes in *The Complete
English Tradesman*. People in business needed to learn to write, he
argued, and especially to write in a style appropriate to their station

in life: "a tradesman's letters," wrote Defoe, "should be plain, concise, and to the purpose; no quaint expressions, no book-phrases, no flourishes, and yet they must be full and sufficient to express what he means, so as not to be doubtful, much less unintelligible."[19] What does that mean? Defoe gave a series of examples of good and bad style. He also recommended that a master should give his apprentices exercises in writing so they can get the appropriate style down:

> the first thing is to let him write letters to his dealers, and correspond with his friends; and this he does in his master's name, subscribing his letters thus:
>
> *I am,*
> *for my master* A. B. *and company,*
> *your humble servant,*
> C. D.
>
> And beginning thus:
>
> Sir, I am order'd by my master *A. B.* to advise you that—
>
> Or thus:
>
> Sir, By my master's order, I am to signify to you that—
>
> Or thus:
>
> Sir, These are by my master's order to give you notice—[20]

"Nothing is so common," wrote another conduct-book author, "as to write Letters: But it is not a common Thing to indite them well." Still, in this new world of social mobility, "The Necessities of Life oblige almost all Manner of Persons to have Recourse to an Epistolary Correspondence," and yet "To succeed in this Kind of Composition is not so easy as generally thought." The author there gave advice for negotiating different social classes: "Three Things, in my Opinion, need only be observed in Letters. 1. To take care not to be haughty in writing to Superiors. 2. Not to demean yourself in addressing an Inferior. 3. To hold an equal Rank with Equals."[21] In keeping with these principles, he offered dozens more models: "Example for the Piety of a Lady"; "Of the Epistle Dedicatory"; "Letter to a Lady of Quality, on the Death of her Daughter"; "To a great Man, on his being re-instated in Favour at Court."

NOWHERE DID RICHARDSON, Defoe, or most of the other conduct-book writers give advice explicitly about grammar, but it's implicit throughout their books: they gave models of an accessible style appropriate for the occasion. A few of these guides, though, did mix explicit advice on language with more general advice on behavior in society. An anonymous book called *The Compleat Letter Writer* appeared in 1756; its title page promised not only "LETTERS On the most common *Occasions* in LIFE," but "ALSO, A Variety of more elegant LETTERS for *Examples* from the best modern Authors, on BUSINESS, DUTY, AMUSEMENT, AFFECTION, COURTSHIP, LOVE, MARRIAGE, FRIENDSHIP, *&c.*," and even "A PLAIN and COMPENDIOUS GRAMMAR of the ENGLISH TONGUE" and "a SPELLING DICTIONARY, Of such WORDS as *are alike in Sound*, but *different in Sense*. Very useful to the *English* Scholar." The author warned letter-writers against "the Shame of doing it ill," and therefore offered "a proper Collection of Letters . . . upon Subjects very various in their Nature. . . . *Business*, *Duty*, *Amusement*, *Affection*, *Courtship*, *Friendship*, and a Multiplicity of other Affairs that may require a *Letter*." With *The Compleat Letter Writer* by his side, the author claimed, "no Person can be at a Loss for a Pattern to direct him." He even boasted that his collection included a range wide enough "to answer the Purpose almost of every Individual, from the Boy at School to the Secretary of State."[22]

Another book on the same plan, *The British Letter-Writer; or, Letter-Writer's Complete Instructor* (probably around 1765), is accompanied by "a plain and easy English grammar"; George Seymour's *Instructive Letter-Writer, and Entertaining Companion* (1763), is accompanied by "a plain and concise GRAMMAR of the *ENGLISH* TONGUE; and some necessary Orthographical Directions"; James Wallace's *Every Man His Own Letter-Writer; or, The New and Complete Art of Letter-Writing Made Plain and Familiar to Every Capacity* (around 1782) includes "A PLAIN and FAMILIAR GRAMMAR, or an easy Guide to the Knowledge of the ENGLISH TONGUE." The number of subjects on which these guides presumed to offer advice kept growing as the century progressed. A work of 1770, for example, promised

> LETTERS On the most IMPORTANT, INSTRUCTIVE, and ENTERTAINING SUBJECTS, which may serve as Copies for *Inditing Letters* on the various Occurrences in Life,
>
> **PARTICULARLY**
>
> On Advice, Affection, Affluence, Benevolence, Business, Children to Parents, Compliments, Condoleance [*sic*], Courtship, Diligence, Education, Fidelity, Folly, Friendship, Generosity, Happiness, History, Humanity, Humour, Industry, Justice, Love, Marriage, Masters to Servants, Modesty, Morality, OEconomy, Parents to Children, Paternal Affection, Piety, Pleasure, Prodigality, Prudence, Religion, Retirement, Servants to Masters, Trade, Virtue, Wit, &c.[23]

IT'S SIGNIFICANT THAT these conduct manuals are among the very first works to explain English grammar to native English speakers. This is an important development, and a surprising one. There had been grammars of English for foreigners, things like George Mason's *Grammaire Angloise: Contenant reigles bien exactes* of 1622, offering advice on English grammar for native speakers of French. There were even books like Paul Greaves's *Grammatica Anglicana, præcipuè quatenus à Latina differt, ad unicam P. Rami methodum concinnata*, published at Cambridge University in 1594, an attempt to introduce an international community of scholars to the English language. The eighteenth-century etiquette books, though, were serving up advice on English grammar to people who were already native speakers of English.

Both the authors of these books and their audiences merit closer attention. These were not books by aristocrats for aristocrats; they were written by aspiring middle-class writers who hoped to pull other middle-class would-be writers up with them. That has important implications. Proper grammar wasn't imposed from on high, but aped from below. In fact, the upper classes have never liked conduct manuals and etiquette guides, because they threaten to blur the line between the to-the-manner-born aristocracy and the vulgar pretenders. It's therefore only natural that the earliest attempts to regulate the language were grassroots efforts. It wasn't a matter of aristocrats lecturing their social inferiors on how to speak; rather, the middle classes were imitating their social betters, hoping to pass among them unnoticed. Middle-class writers wanted to sound like their social superiors; outsiders wanted to sound like insiders.

There's no reason to assume that the speech of wealthy people living in Surrey or Buckinghamshire is automatically better than the speech of poor people in Lincolnshire or Yorkshire. But it was the wealthy people in Surrey and Buckinghamshire who had the political and economic power, and many not-quite-so-wealthy people from the rest of the country recognized the value of sounding like them. The people who benefited from class mobility feared that if they couldn't imitate the manners of the upper classes, they would be recognized as vulgar nouveaux riches, and so the hoi polloi scrambled to imitate the toffs. And what began as a mere preference or fashion—an attempt to sound like social superiors—eventually became codified as a law. Eventually it became axiomatic that correct English was the English of the upper classes, particularly those who lived in the "best" parts of the country, especially in and around London. To speak properly was to speak like the traditional aristocracy. To this day, good English usually means the English wealthy and powerful people spoke a generation or two ago.

———————

IF ANY EVIDENCE is needed that proper English came largely from those outside the traditional circles of power, we need only look at where the English language was first taught as a school subject. That began happening in the late seventeenth century in the "Dissenting academies," educational establishments for people excluded from the usual schools and universities. The Dissenters were British Protestants who did not belong to the Church of England, usually because they believed that it had not taken the Reformation seriously enough—that the Anglicans had retained too many Roman Catholic traditions.

Because Oxford and Cambridge were originally founded in the Middle Ages to educate the clergy—and because they held that function even into the nineteenth century—England's universities were officially closed to Dissenters in 1662. The Dissenters, recognizing the value of education while acknowledging that the Oxbridge universities were not for them, responded by founding their own academies. By many estimates, the best Dissenting academies far surpassed the universities. Without the weight of four hundred years of tradition, they were free to take new, experimental approaches to education. They were pioneers in what we now call the natural sciences, fitting out laboratories with chemical apparatus and air pumps long before the universities, and the cutting-edge philosophical theories of John Locke found a home among the Dissenters long before any Oxbridge academic paid attention to them. The ancient public schools and universities might prepare you for a position in the church or the government, but if you wanted to stay in touch with the latest scholarly trends, the Dissenting academies were the place to go. Another Dissenting experiment had to do with the language, for the academies trained their students in English— something that Oxford and Cambridge had never done. The old universities considered English and the other "vulgar languages" beneath them: lectures were in Latin, and the books studied were the classics of Greece and Rome. At some colleges, students could be fined for speaking anything other than Latin, even in the dining halls and dormitories. Most lectures at the Dissenting academies, though, were in English, and they often concerned English literature and the English language itself. Daniel Defoe was a Dissenter, and as a young man he attended Charles Morton's academy at Newington Green, one of the most reputable of the academies. He later recalled Morton's classes, in which "his pupils declaim'd weekly in the English tongue, made orations, and wrot epistles twice every week. . . . He taught his pupils to write a masculine and manly stile, to write the most polite English, and at the same time to kno' how to suit their manner as well to the subject they were to write upon as to the persons or degrees of persons they wer to write to."[24] The fact that his instructor lectured in English, not Latin, was still enough of a novelty that Defoe felt compelled to record it.

IT WAS IN these academies, filled with the quintessential outsiders, that we see some of the first systematic attempts to explain the English language for English speakers. But the Dissenters were just a part, although an important part, of the rethinking of English grammar and style. John Dryden, for instance, wasn't one of the outsiders; he was rich and powerful and lived at the center of power for most of his life. But he, too, shared many of the Dissenters' concerns. One of the remarkable things about these developments is just how uniform the concerns were across many strata of society. Nearly all these early discussions of English grammar were consistent in advocating a number of principles. David Crystal summarizes them in a series of bullet points:

- Left to themselves, polite people do not speak or write correctly.
- Grammars, dictionaries, and other manuals are therefore needed in order to instruct polite society in the correct ways of speaking and writing.
- No one is exempt. Even the best authors, such as Shakespeare, break the rules from time to time.
- And if even Shakespeare breaks the rules, this proves the need for guidance, because lesser mortals are even more likely to fall into the same trap.[25]

Learning to speak properly, therefore, meant avoiding *traps*— avoiding the two kinds of blunders known as *barbarisms* (errors in single words, usually a matter of spelling or pronunciation) and *solecisms* (errors in combinations of words, usually a matter of syntax or word forms). Speaking well was defined in negative terms: it meant not giving offense.

CHAPTER 3

Proper Words in Proper Places

JONATHAN SWIFT DEMANDS AN ACADEMY

WHY ALL THIS ANXIETY? WHY DID the newly literate middle classes feel so insecure about writing? Why did someone like John Dryden, one of the most revered literary figures in England and then at the top of his game, feel the need to revise his works to root out the "imperfections"?

Much of the concern arose from fear that the English language was changing. All languages evolve; no one—no writer, no committee, no government, no king—has ever been able to put an end to that. Languages have always been resistant to outside interference. At the end of the seventeenth century, the philosopher John Locke related a story about Augustus Caesar's inability to change the language of his subjects:

> Every Man has so inviolable a Liberty, to make Words stand for what *Ideas* he pleases, that no one hath the Power to make others have the same *Ideas* in their Minds, that he has, when they use the same Words, that he does. And therefore the great *Augustus* himself, in the Possession of that Power which ruled the World, acknowledged, he could not make a new Latin Word: which was as much as to say, that he could not arbitrarily appoint, what *Idea*

any Sound should be a Sign of, in the Mouths and common Language of his Subjects.[1]

There's something stirringly democratic about that freedom, but
there's also something worrisome. If the language is going to
change without regard for authority, it runs the risk of changing
helter-skelter without regard for order or logic—by shaking off
tyranny, it threatens to degenerate into mere anarchy.

Dryden's generation wasn't the first to realize that language
changes. Three centuries earlier, Geoffrey Chaucer, in *Troilus and
Criseyde*, made the point well:

> Ye knowe ek that in forme of speche is chaunge
> Withinne a thousand yeer, and wordes tho
> That hadden pris, now wonder nyce and straunge
> Us thinketh hem, and yet thei spake hem so.[2]

In modern English:

> You know, too, that there's change in the form of speech
> over a thousand years; words that once were valuable now
> seem to us wondrously odd and strange—and yet they
> spoke them that way.

Unlike Dryden and his contemporaries, though, Chaucer doesn't
seem particularly upset by this development. Speech changes—so
what?

But what had been for Chaucer merely a philosophical meditation became a serious practical concern a few decades later. The
author of *The Canterbury Tales* lived and died before the invention of printing; during his lifetime and for the next three-quarters
of a century, his works were copied by hand. But in the second
half of the fifteenth century a new technology arrived, bringing
with it profound consequences for the shape of the English language. And linguistic diversity was very much on the mind of people
in the dawning age of print.

One of the first expressions of real anxiety about language change appears in the works of William Caxton, the first printer to set up shop in England. Printers had good reason to be conscious of linguistic variation—they were, after all, working to create books that would last for generations, and a changing language would inevitably reduce the longevity of their wares. The rapidity of change in the fifteenth century was obvious even in one man's lifetime: "our langage now vsed," Caxton observed in 1490, "varyeth ferre from that. whiche was vsed and spoken whan I was borne." It seemed to be a time of rapid change: nowadays, he said, the language is "neuer stedfaste / but euer wauerynge / wexynge one season / and waneth & dyscreaseth another season." The "englysshe men," he worried, seem to have been "borne vnder the domynacyon of the mone"— like the moon, waxing and waning, always changing.

Worse still, "that comyn englysshe that is spoken in one shyre varyeth from a nother"—in other words, language varied within England, and things spoken in one part of the country could be unintelligible in another. Caxton told a famous story that made this problem clear. He described a merchant ship on the Thames, waiting for the wind to pick up before it could set sail. The sailors, growing impatient, went ashore for a snack. One, a cloth merchant from the north of England named Sheffelde, "cam in to an hows and axed for mete"—that is, came into a house and asked for food (*meat* then referred to any food, not just flesh)—and "specyally he axyd after eggys." But the woman of the house answered "that she coude speke no frenshe." French?—he had asked for *eggs*, not *œufs*. Sheffelde was angry, Caxton said, "for he also coude speke no frenshe. but wolde haue hadde egges." Still a blank stare from the woman. Finally, another sailor "sayd that he wolde haue eyren." *Eyren!* Then, wrote Caxton, "the good wyf sayd that she vnderstod hym wel." The problem? The word *eggs* was the form spoken in the north of England, but the southern form was *eyren*. When the northerner, Sheffelde, asked a woman from the south for *eggs*, she was baffled by his unfamiliar dialect and assumed he must be a foreigner. She had to wait for one of his colleagues from the south to explain that the hungry sailor wanted *eyren.* For Caxton this posed a real problem. "Loo," he wrote, "what sholde a man in thyse dayes now wryte. egges or eyren"? But English wasn't yet a single language, and all those varieties made for rough going. "Certaynly," Caxton lamented, "it is harde to playse euery man / bycause of dyuersite & chaunge of langage."[3]

Uneasiness about "dyuersite & chaunge of langage" had been a constant concern since the fifteenth century, but in the eighteenth that uneasiness turned into outright alarm. In 1711 the poet Alexander Pope put it memorably in his *Essay on Criticism*. When readers of Pope's day looked back on Geoffrey Chaucer, they had trouble making sense of him. Chaucer's Middle English can sometimes be remarkably direct and accessible, even across the ages, but there are also passages that hardly seem like English at all, such as this one from *The Canon's Yeoman's Tale*:

> Oure orpyment and sublymed mercurie,
> Oure grounden litarge eek on the porfurie,
> Of ech of thise of ounces a certeyn—
> Noght helpeth us; oure labour is in veyn.

Pope looked at such passages and worried that, after just a few hundred years, the language of England's greatest poet was inaccessible. And he feared that the same fate would eventually overtake John Dryden, who had then been dead for just over a decade:

> Our Sons their Fathers' *failing Language* see,
> And such as *Chaucer* is, shall *Dryden* be.[4]

With language change continuing unabated, Pope insisted, even the recent works of John Dryden would soon be as incomprehensible as the antique Chaucer. If their literature was to survive the ravages of time, someone would have to fix it, to hold it in place.

Pope wasn't the first to bewail Chaucer's fading away. As early as 1666, the great Continental scholar Franciscus Junius bemoaned the fact that he "knew not how to looke for a Commentator that should give anie light to Chaucers old language."[5] And Edmund

Waller, one of the most influential poets of the mid-seventeenth century, wrote a poem called "Of English Verse," in which he warned modern poets that their works were all too mortal:

> Poets may boast (as safely-Vain)
> Their work shall with the world remain.
> . . . .
> But who can hope his Lines should long
> Last in a daily-changing Tongue?
> While they are new, Envy prevails,
> And as that dies, our Language fails.

Even the greatest old poets in the language have succumbed to time's winged chariot:

> *Chaucer* his Sense can only boast,
> The glory of his Numbers lost.

"Numbers"—poetic meter—is now lost, and while we can still admire Chaucer for his "Sense," his poetry is closed to us. What, then, is a poet with thoughts of immortality to do?

> Poets that lasting Marble seek,
> Must carve in *Latine* or in *Greek*;
> We write in Sand, our Language grows,
> And like the Tide our work o'erflows.[6]

Writing in Latin or Greek, many poets agreed, was the key. Those languages were permanent, for the ages, not like this provincial Germanic dialect that couldn't be counted on to stay the same even month by month, let alone century by century.

THIS SENSE THAT English was changing only reinforced the opinion of many people—especially in the Renaissance—that English was a mongrel language, inferior to the dignity and permanence of the classical tongues, Latin and Greek. Most people took it for granted that Latin did not change at all during its golden age; only when the Roman Empire fell to the northern barbarians, the story went, did the language of the Romans begin its long decline into barbarism. We now recognize this as nonsense—Latin and Greek, like every language, changed substantially over the centuries—but the myth was widespread, and it contributed to the prejudice that linguistic change is always the same as linguistic decay.

At the end of the seventeenth century, Francis Atterbury repeated the conventional wisdom on the subject. When another author had the nerve to suggest that it was possible to date an ancient Greek book based on the forms of the language in it, Atterbury laughed scornfully: surely this rube must have known that the language of Homer and Plato wasn't subject to the fluctuations of a debased modern language like English. While "the *English* Tongue has undergone very considerable and surprizing Changes, especially in this Last Century" (before "we . . . in good earnest set about the Cultivating and Refining it"), the classical languages—Greek and Latin—were immune from degradation. "We have *Greek* Books," Atterbury insisted, "writ by Authors at almost Two thousand Years distance, who disagree less in their Phrase and Manner of Speech, than the Books of any Two *English* Writers do, who liv'd but Two hundred Years asunder."[7] Latin and Greek were the eternal languages, and therefore far superior to changeable English.

The task, then was to give a modern language like English the permanence of a classical language like Greek or Latin. Many seventeenth- and eighteenth-century thinkers were convinced the answer lay in an academy—a government-sponsored body that would be charged with arresting language change by writing dictionaries and grammars, establishing a standard of proper English, and using its power to force the English-speaking world to follow its guidance.

IT WAS AN age of learned academies. In 1582, one of the first scholarly societies, Italy's Accademia della Crusca, was founded in Florence, bringing together some of the most erudite thinkers and writers of the day. Among other tasks, they took it upon themselves to spell out the "official" form of the Italian language, publishing the *Vocabolario della Crusca*, a monumental dictionary, in 1612. A few decades later, the French followed the Italian model: in 1635, Cardinal Richelieu officially established the Académie Française, a group of forty distinguished French scholars who were authorized to rule on what was good French and what wasn't. Like the Accademia della Crusca, the Académie Française is still active today—apart from a ten-year hiatus during the French Revolution, it has been working on the language continuously—and its members have included luminaries like Voltaire, Montesquieu, Dumas fils, Victor Hugo, Louis Pasteur, Marcel Pagnol, Marguerite Yourcenar (the first woman member), Claude Lévi-Strauss, and Alain Robbe-Grillet. Even in the twenty-first century they continue to issue rulings on proper French.

Many seventeenth-century Englishmen thought the same model would work in their own country. Writing in 1660, one "R.H." imagined a utopian society that would show English readers the way to scientific, political, and linguistic enlightenment. In the world of the story, the New Atlantis, there is "in the Imperial City one Eminent *Academy* of selected wits," charged with reforming "all errors in books." Their job is "to purifie our Native Language from Barbarism or Solœcism," and they're to do this "by regulating the termes and phrases thereof into a constant use of the most significant words, proverbs, and phrases." The members of this learned academy have other responsibilities: they "translate the best Authors" and "make Dictionaries in all Languages."[8] But "purifying" English of its flaws was their most important charge.

R.H. had a grand project in mind. The academy of the New Atlantis was to be surrounded "on three sides with fair *Cloisters*, the Pillars and Arches being of *Mosaic*, of *Gold* and *azure*."[9] His scheme seems to be on something like the model of a modern university, though you'll look in vain for golden and azure pillars on the typical college campus. But although the fancy mosaics never materialized, a more realistic academy did open shortly after R.H.

published his vision of the future. In 1660, King Charles II—having spent years in exile on the Continent after his father's execution in 1649—returned to take the English throne, and he liked the kind of academy that the French and Italian rulers had sponsored. Just a few months after returning to England, Charles chartered the Royal Society of London for the Improvement of Natural Knowledge. In most respects, the Royal Society was a great success: the research it sponsored on the natural sciences contributed to the burgeoning scientific revolution of the seventeenth century, and much of the groundbreaking research on botany, zoology, chemistry, physics, astronomy, and a dozen other fields has appeared in the pages of its journal, the *Transactions*. Today, three and a half centuries after Charles II founded it, the Royal Society remains one of the most important scientific institutes in the world. Its fellows have included Christopher Wren, Isaac Newton, Humphry Davy, Michael Faraday, Charles Darwin, James Clerk Maxwell, and Ernest Rutherford, as well as foreign members like Sigmund Freud, Albert Einstein, and Richard Feynman. Current fellows include Stephen Hawking, Richard Dawkins, and Tim Berners-Lee, inventor of the World Wide Web.

If royally sanctioned institutes like the Royal Society could improve the state of natural knowledge so successfully, many reasoned, why couldn't the same be done for the language? In fact, some argued, it was impossible to improve one without improving the other. This was the age in which science as we know it was being born. At the beginning of the seventeenth century the systematic investigation of nature, supported by universities and government grants, didn't exist. No English university had scientific laboratories, and experiments were usually carried out by wealthy amateurs. What's more, even as late as the eighteenth century, there was no clear distinction between modern chemistry and old-fashioned alchemy: as enlightened a figure as Sir Isaac Newton devoted much of his time to alchemical experiments, searching for the philosopher's stone and the *elixir vitae*.

It's remarkable how much mysticism, spiritualism, and astrology were mixed in with the founding works of the seventeenth century's scientific revolution. The materialism of most modern scientific writing—the rejection of any supernatural causes—had not yet set in. Instead, seventeenth-century writers used a style that was rich in invocations of preternatural forces and ancient mysteries. And this fondness for the preternatural was evident in the prose style of the age. A typical example of scientific writing from the early seventeenth century is loaded with vivid metaphors and evocations of transcendent powers. Here is how Patrick Scot, writing for other chemists in 1623, described the element mercury:

> What then is the *Philosophers Mercury*, but *Wisdom the childe of heauen, and the glory of the earth? the pounding and mixing of the matter, is the beating downe and qualifying of our affections in the morter of a wise heart*; the feeding of it with more or lesse fire is, *the timely pressing and relaxing of our corrupt Will*, the fixation of *volatile*, is the *reduction of our inconstant running Wits, to the solidity of true Wisdome:* Lastly the *Redde colour* ioyned to the *White*, which crownes the worke, giues vs to vnderstand, that *perseuerance in vertue will gaine vs the garland of victorie ouer all foraigne incumbrances; and subdue our vnruly domesticke affections.*[10]

It's all very stirring—Scot's prose has a grandeur, even majesty, rarely found in modern chemistry textbooks—but does it teach us anything we need to know about mercury? It's very well to hear that mercury is wisdom, the child of heaven and the glory of the earth, but a working scientist in a laboratory might be more interested in its specific gravity or the way it reacts with other elements. By the 1660s, the metaphorical richness and grandiloquence that had been the hallmark of early seventeenth-century scientific writing was beginning to be viewed as an impediment to understanding.

This was the argument made by Thomas Sprat, who was charged with documenting the early days of the Royal Society shortly after its founding. In 1667 he gave "an Account of the *First Institution* of the *Royal Society*," hoping that his "Learned and Inquisitive

Age" would be inspired "to attempt some *greater Enterprise* . . . for the Benefit of humane life, by the Advancement of *Real Knowledge*."[11] But real knowledge couldn't be advanced until the language was reformed. Sprat was frustrated by the linguistic exuberance of his day and expressed his irritation with the "specious *Tropes* and *Figures*"—metaphorical and figurative language—that interfered with clear expression. He hoped, therefore, that "some sober and judicious Men, would take the whole Mass of our Language into their hands, . . . and would set a mark on the ill Words,"[12] thereby making English a suitable vehicle for proper scientific discourse.

It wouldn't happen on its own, though, and so Sprat called for a group that would enforce on the public "a constant Resolution, to reject all the amplifications, digressions, and swellings of style." He wanted English "to return back to the primitive purity, and shortness, when men deliver'd so many *things*, almost in an equal number of *words*."[13] Others had been thinking along the same lines around the same time. John Evelyn, famous today for the vivid accounts of seventeenth-century London in his diary, was a founding member of the Royal Society, and like Sprat, he hoped that the language might "be purg'd from things intollerable," and proposed "a Lexicon or collection of all the pure English words."[14] At the end of 1664 the Royal Society established a committee, which included both Evelyn and Dryden, "for improving the English language."[15]

MANY REMAINED CONVINCED that the Royal Society was the place to regulate the language, but as the seventeenth century turned into the eighteenth, and as the Royal Society made no progress on matters linguistic, critics began proposing new institutions to take care of the unfinished business. Science seemed to be in good hands, but the language needed its own academy. One of the Englishmen most passionate about planning a linguistic society was Daniel Defoe—but then Defoe, an inveterate schemer, was passionate about planning almost anything. One of his early major works, known as *An Essay upon Projects*, appeared in 1702, and it's filled with schemes for improving dozens of miscellaneous areas of life. The title page spells out just a few of the things he planned to accomplish:

> ESSAYS UPON Several Projects: OR, Effectual Ways for Advancing the Interest of the Nation. *Wherein are plainly laid down,* The Means by which the Subjects in general may be eased and enriched; the Poor relieved, and Trade encreased in the most material Branches of it, *viz.* in Constituting Seamen to theirs and the Nations Advantage, for Encouragement of Merchants and Merchandizing; for Relief of the Poor of Friendly Societies; for discouraging Vice, and encouraging Vertue; the Usefulness; of Banks and Assurances; to prevent Bankrupts; with the surest way to recover bad Debts; and many other considerable things, profitable and conducing to the great Advantage of the Nation in general.

One important way of advancing the interests of the nation in general, Defoe argued, was to establish an academy to regulate the language. France, Italy, and Spain had their national academies, but England had fallen behind. This was odd, wrote Defoe, because no one could deny that the Continental academies had been a great success: the French Academy had refined the French language so well "that we see it now spoken in all the Courts of *Christendom*, as the Language allow'd to be most universal."[16] He thought it was time to establish a similar academy in England.

Defoe's hopes for his own academy were similar to those of many other schemers: "The Work of this Society," he wrote, "shou'd be to encourage Polite Learning, to polish and refine the *English* Tongue." The academy would also assume some of the responsibilities of the censor, and purge the language of its "Irregular Additions." With the right people in positions of authority, the society would keep sloppy writers in line, "and no Author wou'd have the Impudence to Coin without their Authority." The *coining* metaphor is an old one—people had been "coining" words and phrases for a century and a half—but Defoe brought the dead metaphor back to life by equating unauthorized words with counterfeit currency. Under the new regime, he wrote, " 'twou'd be as Criminal then to *Coin Words, as Money*."[17]

DEFOE'S PROPOSAL OF 1702 attracted little attention, and he quickly busied himself with other schemes for the public benefit. But just a few years later another famous writer brought the idea for an academy to the attention of the entire nation. Jonathan Swift would someday be universally celebrated for *Gulliver's Travels*, but early in his career he was one of the most vocal partisans for the regulation of the language. Swift particularly disliked Defoe—the two were on opposing sides of most eighteenth-century political questions and mocked each other in their satirical works. But on this subject, the worth of a linguistic academy, Defoe and Swift were on the same side.

Swift had strong opinions on the state of the language—it was one of the very few subjects on which he was not a playful ironist. In *A Letter to a Young Gentleman, Lately Enter'd into Holy Orders*, he offered advice to a would-be priest, encouraging him to apply himself "a little more to the Study of the *English* Language." Neglecting good English, he explained, "is one of the most general Defects among the Scholars of this Kingdom." How, though, is one to get a good "Conception of a Style"? Swift was ready with an answer: "Proper Words in proper Places, makes the true Definition of a Style."[18]

A true definition, perhaps, but still rather cryptic. That's why he listed some specific faults to be avoided. "The first," he wrote, "is the frequent use of obscure Terms, which by the Women are called *Hard Words*, and by the better sort of Vulgar, *Fine Language*." This abuse makes most beginners' sermons incomprehensible. The best way to write well, Swift insisted, is to think clearly and to be direct, because "the Faults" in English expression "are nine in ten owing to Affectation, and not to the Want of Understanding." The speakers who made a mess of the language did so because they were too concerned to show off "their Learning, their Oratory, their Politeness, or their Knowledge of the World." The key is clarity: "When a Man's Thoughts are clear, the properest Words will generally offer themselves first, and his own Judgment will direct him in what Order to place them."[19]

We can find more of Swift's examples of bad style in one of the most popular periodicals in the country, a thrice-weekly paper called the *Tatler*. Though most of the essays were by Sir Richard Steele, Swift contributed number 230 to the series, which appeared in late September 1710. His article took the form of a letter to the editor complaining about "the deplorable Ignorance" of recent writers. Unless someone took action soon, Swift wrote, the "Corruption of our *English* Tongue" would eventually cause the language to "suffer more by the false Refinements of Twenty Years past, than it hath been improved in the foregoing Hundred."[20]

At the center of Swift's essay is a parody of a letter by a fashionable man-about-town, someone given to all the linguistic nonsense of his day. Swift highlighted the objectionable features with italics:

> *SIR,*
>
> I *Cou'd n't* get the Things you sent for all *about Town*----I *thôt* to *ha'* come down my self, and then *I'd h' bôt 'um*, but I *ha'n't don't*, and I believe I *can't d't*, that's *Pozz*---*Tom* begins to *gi'mself* Airs, because *he's* going with the *Plenipo's*-----'Tis said, the *French* King will *bamboozl' us agen*, which *causes many Speculations*. The *Jacks* and others of that *Kidney* are very *uppish*, and *alert upon't*, as you may see by their *Phizz's*-----*Will Hazzard* has got the *Hipps*, having lost *to the Tune of* Five Hundr'd Pound, *thô* he understands Play very well, *no body better*. He has promis't me upon *Rep*, to leave off Play; but you know 'tis a Weakness *he's* too apt to *give into*, *thô* he has as much Wit as any Man, *no body more*. He has lain *incog* ever since----The *Mob's* very quiet with us now----I believe you *thôt* I *banter'd* you in my

last like a *Country Put*----I *sha'n't* leave Town this
Month, *&c.*[21]

Swift objected to the dashes that separate sentences—the sloppy
writer's punctuation—sprinkled through the prose without much
thought for syntax. He also found some newly fashionable words
bothersome. We may not be distracted by words like *banter* and
bamboozle, but for Swift they were still recent coinages: the *OED*
has found no examples of *banter* before 1676 or of *bamboozle* before 1703. But Swift had a peculiar abhorrence for abbreviations,
especially those combining auxiliary verbs with the word *not*.

These contractions probably first appeared in the spoken language around 1600, and began appearing in writing after 1660:
shan't was first written down in 1664, *won't* in 1667, *don't* in 1670,
can't in 1706. Swift singles them out for particular scorn. He also
despises *he's*, a contraction of *he is*; *thôt* for *thought* (although it's
unclear how these two would have differed in pronunciation, since
the *gh* was silent in Swift's day as in ours); *upon't* for *upon it*; *h'*
for *have*; and *bôt* for *bought*. Another kind of contraction was
just as irritating, and that was formed by clipping away the end of
a word—not a function word like *can* or *is*, but a noun or a verb.
Some of Swift's examples strike us today as merely odd: since we
rarely speak of *plenipotentiaries*, we have little need to speak of
plenipo's; *hipps* hasn't survived as a short version of *hypochon-
dria*. A few others do survive, though, three centuries later, even if
they're not common: *pozz*, a short form of *positive*, and *rep* for
reputation.

The strangest of the lot is *mob*—strange because most English
speakers aren't aware that it's a contraction at all. But *mob* comes
from the Latin *mobile vulgus*, "fickle crowd," which was picked up
in English around 1599. By 1676, people were shortening it to *mobile* (pronounced with three syllables), and by 1688, it had become
common to shorten it even further, from *mobile* to *mob*. The word
has been in widespread use ever since. Swift's allergic reaction to it
is remarkable. One nineteenth-century editor described Swift's

quixotic quest to wipe the word from the language in a footnote to this passage: Swift, he wrote,

> carried on the war against the word *mob* to the very last. A lady, who . . . was well known to Swift, used to say, that the greatest scrape into which she got with him was by using the word *mob*. "Why do you say that?" said he, in a passion; "never let me hear you say that word again." "Why, sir," said she, "what am I to say?" "The rabble, to be sure," answered he.[22]

It's a good example of the kind of vehemence with which people follow their hatreds in language.

BUT THE *TATLER* essay and *A Letter to a Young Gentleman* are almost insignificant next to Swift's most important contribution to the language. While in those works he merely grumbled about what he disliked, in another work he offered what he saw as a practical solution to the problem of bad English. Fourteen years before *Gulliver's Travels* appeared, Swift stirred up public controversy with a forty-eight-page pamphlet called *A Proposal for Correcting, Improving and Ascertaining the English Tongue*. It took the form of a letter to Robert, Earl of Oxford and Mortimer, and Britain's lord high treasurer, and appeared on May 17, 1712.

The word *ascertaining* in Swift's title has a meaning it no longer carries: as the *OED* puts it, "To make (a thing) certain, definite, or precise, by determining exactly its limits, extent, amount, position, etc.; to decide, fix, settle, limit." (It's the same sense as in the U.S. Constitution, Article 1, Section 6: "The Senators and Representatives shall receive a Compensation for their Services, to be ascertained by Law.") Swift was proposing an academy that would correct, improve, and ascertain the English language—remove its faults, supplement its virtues, and then lock the whole thing down to stop its frustrating change.

He opened with a blunt statement of the problem: "our Language is extremely imperfect." Yes, there had been some recent improvements, but they were "by no means in proportion to its daily Corruptions," and most of those who think they're clarifying the language have only "multiplied Abuses and Absurdities," with the result that English now "offends against every Part of Grammar." He saw a trajectory in the history of languages: they began in rudeness, reached a point of perfection, and then tended toward decline. It had happened with Latin, which rose to perfection before begining to fall; it was also happening, he was convinced, with French, which in the last fifty years had received "polishing as much as it will bear," but now was becoming less expressive owing to "the natural Inconstancy of that People."[23] The fickle French were going to be the ruin of their own language.

The English language, though, had not yet reached the point at which decay was inevitable—it was, Swift was convinced, still on its way up. What's more, Swift imagined it might be possible to avoid the seemingly inevitable reversal of fortune, in which refinement is followed by decay. He saw "no absolute Necessity why any Language should be perpetually changing," and he speculated that if English "were once refined to a certain Standard, perhaps there might be Ways found out to fix it for ever." (If "for ever" was too ambitious, he suggested, we might hold out "at least till we are invaded and made a Conquest by some other State.") Authors in the English language, were they to receive the kind of guardianship he hoped to provide, might yet "have a Chance for Immortality."[24]

It was "perpetual change" that nettled him. But when he surveyed history, he thought he saw evidence that change could be withstood. "From *Homer* to *Plutarch*," he wrote, "are above a Thousand Years; so long at least the Purity of the *Greek* Tongue may be allowed to last." "The *Chinese*," he went on, "have Books in their Language above two Thousand Years old," and even "The *German*, *Spanish*, and *Italian*, have admitted few or no Changes for some Ages past."[25]

What was missing in England, he concluded, was an academy. Swift therefore proposed "that a free judicious Choice should be

made of such Persons, as are generally allowed to be best qualified
for such a Work, without any regard to Quality [i.e., social rank],
Party, or Profession." (He made no reference to sex—Swift's academy clubhouse would likely bear the motto NO GIRLS ALLOWED—
and it's probably safe to assume that, despite his disavowing
attention to "Quality," he'd have been horrified if anyone below
the rank of tradesman were admitted.) These men should get together and draw up a set of bylaws, though "What Methods they
will take, is not for me to prescribe."[26]

While the specific methods would be up to the academy members, Swift was clear about their guiding mission: to prevent a
number of chronic abuses of the language. One source of these
abuses was the "*Dunces* of Figure" throughout the town, fashionable boneheads "who had Credit enough to give Rise to some new
Word, and propagate it in most Conversations, though it had neither Humor, nor Significancy." And once a bad word had entered
the language, it spread like an infection, making its way through
plays and newspapers until it ultimately "became an Addition to
our Language." Another threat to good English came from the
poets, who, in order to get their lines to scan, had squeezed and
mangled good English words until they were barely recognizable.
English already had too many one-syllable words—a common
complaint among people who thought Latin superior to English—
but still, these poets, "to save Time and Pains, introduced that barbarous Custom of abbreviating Words, to fit them to the Measure
of their Verses," giving us even more monosyllables. The result has
been a medley of "such harsh unharmonious Sounds, that none but
a *Northern* Ear could endure"—that is, a barbarian from northern
Europe, not an inhabitant of cultured Italy. But these savage
northerners "have joined the most obdurate Consonants together
without one intervening Vowel, only to shorten a Syllable."[27] He
offered a catalog of offenders: "What does Your LORDSHIP think
of the Words, *Drudg'd*, *Disturb'd*, *Rebuk't*, *Fledg'd*, and a thousand others, every where to be met in Prose as well as Verse?" Their
"jarring" sound was so awful he was amazed that anyone could
stand for them.[28] (He didn't mention the fact that ancient Greek,

which he so admired, is actually riddled with consonant clusters that are hard to get the mouth around: Greek words like *sphinx*, *mnêmonikê*, and *pneuma*, in which all the letters were sounded, are at least as difficult as the English *disturbed*.)

Once the academicians roll up their sleeves, wrote Swift, "they will observe many gross Improprieties," and it's their job to "discard" them, however much these abuses may have been "authorised by Practice." *Norma loquendi* has no place: even widespread habits can still be illegitimate. The members of the academy might also find some obsolete words that "ought to be restored" to living English. The important thing, though, was to stop the perpetual change, even if it meant fixing the language before it had achieved perfection: better, he insisted, that "a Language should not be wholly perfect, than that it should be perpetually changing."[29]

Swift was confident that he was not an unreasonable man. "Where I say, that I would have our Language, after it is duly correct, always to last; I do not mean that it should never be enlarged." No, there are good reasons to add new words to the language— "Provided," of course, "that no Word which a Society shall give a Sanction to, be afterwards antiquated and exploded." The trick was to stop good words from falling out of use, so that old books would always remain readable. It would be a pity to see great English literature neglected "on account of unintelligible Words and Phrases, which appear harsh and uncouth, only because they are out of Fashion."[30]

So how did these proposals for an academy go? Some loved the idea, but not everyone was won over by Swift's recommendations. Within just a week of the appearance of the *Proposal*, a rival critic, John Oldmixon, rushed out *Reflections on Dr. Swift's Letter to the Earl of Oxford, about the English Tongue*. It's a surly ad hominem attack, lacking both the wit and the venom that make so much of Swift's writing worth reading. But Oldmixon draws attention to problems in Swift's scheme and is therefore worth reading carefully.

Swift, Oldmixon argued, "may as well set up a Society to find out the *Grand Elixir*, the *Perpetual Motion*, the *Longitude*, and other such Discoveries, as to fix our Language beyond their own Times." That kind of permanence is a dream, doomed never to become reality. Swift, Oldmixon insisted, meant "to Bully us into his Methods for pinning down our Language, and making it as Criminal to admit Foreign Words as Foreign Trades"—even though Oldmixon thought that admitting foreign words would enrich the language as much as free trade had enriched the nation's finances.[31] And in case anyone still believed Swift was a suitable regulator of the English language, Oldmixon trawled through Swift's published writings and found "such graces of Speech" there

> as, *Lord, what a Filthy Croud is here; Bless me! what a Devil has rak'd this Rabble together; Z---nds, what squeezing is this! A Plague confound you for an overgrown Sloven? Who in the Devil's Name, I wonder, helps to make up the Crowd half so much as your self? Don't you consider with a Pox, that you take up more room with that Carcass than any Five here? Bring your own Guts to a reasonable Compass, and be d—d.* I tremble while I repeat such Stuff, which I defy any Man to match in any Language, Dead or Living, *Pagan* or *Christian*; and yet this is the Eloquence, as is pretended, of a sound Orthodox Divine.[32]

Swift, in short, argued Oldmixon, was a bad writer, and no one who writes that badly can be trusted to serve as a guardian of the language. And while posterity holds firm in its belief that Swift was a far better writer than Oldmixon, in this case the inferior author carried the day. Swift never got to put his proposal into effect. Neither, for that matter, have any of his successors.

THE ROSTER OF names calling for an English academy is long and impressive, and yet, despite all their concerted effort, no

English-speaking country on the planet has an official government-sponsored academy. There is, in other words, no "official" standard of what's right or wrong in the English language. With all these important writers arguing for a linguistic academy, why was none ever established?

It's not for want of trying. Dozens of prominent Britons were clamoring for an academy, and in Colonial and Early Republican America, proposals were just as common: John Adams, who would go on to become the second president, wrote the Congress on September 5, 1780, about the French, Spanish, and Italian academies. Noting "their great success," he hoped their model would be imitated in the United States: "The honor of forming the first public institution for refining, correcting, improving, and ascertaining the English language, I hope is reserved for Congress."[33] Congress wasn't interested, though, and the proposal never got out of committee.

There are at least three reasons for the failure, the first of which is specific to English. The world's English-speaking countries, with their long tradition of favoring individual liberty, have never supported the kind of absolutist, top-down government that linguistic regulation seems to require. Britain, the United States, Ireland, Canada, Australia, New Zealand—all distrust centralized regulation. The thought that a government entity could tell people how to speak and write has been anathema to many rugged individualists, and it's hard to imagine any such scheme succeeding in a national legislature.[34]

The second reason for the failure to establish an academy has to do with deciding who would get to serve in it—who would get to regulate the proper words and their proper places. Thomas Wilson, writing in 1722, liked Swift's idea for an academy, and went even further, not only proposing such an institution but also signing on for the job himself. He and a few of his friends came together and began issuing edicts: "That which we propose to our selves," he wrote, "is, to examin the present State of the Language, to fix what is right by Grammars and Dictionaries, to fill up what is wanting, streighten what is crooked, and make it easy to be learnt and remembred by Youth and Strangers."[35]

Wilson's cheerful readiness to enlist is an example of one of the perennial problems with proposed academies: most of those who have called for regulation have taken it for granted that *their* version of the language would become the official one. But while two writers can unite in fellow-feeling when they're both railing against the barbarisms of the masses, they're almost certain to disagree on hundreds of the finer points of usage. And when it comes time to pick one set of rules as the official set, friendships evaporate all too easily.

But the third and biggest reason a linguistic academy wasn't formed in the English-speaking world is that, despite their august reputations, the academies in other countries have lousy records of stopping language change. The Continental academies with the highest profiles—the Académie Française and the Accademia della Crusca—have worked for centuries to ascertain their languages, but French and Italian continue to change. The Académie, for instance, spent much of the twentieth century fighting valiantly against the English interloper *le weekend*, advocating instead the native *fin de semaine*, but to no avail. Words like *le showbiz*, *les bluejeans*, *un parking*, and *e-mail* abound, despite the Académie's distaste for English imports. Its most recent round of recommendations includes these rulings: the verb *interpeller* "ne signifie pas 'attirer l'attention.' On ne doit pas dire, par exemple: *Cet évènement nous interpelle*, mais *s'impose à notre attention*"—it "doesn't mean 'get [someone's] attention.' You shouldn't say, for example, *That event interpels us*, but rather *catches our attention*." The properly French *fac-similé* "Doit être préféré à l'anglais *Reprint*"—"should be preferred to the English word *reprint*." And so on through dozens of examples.[36] But even though these proclamations come from *les Immortels*—the most distinguished literary figures in France, some of whom have served in the Académie for more than forty years—and they have the official backing of the French government, the odds are slim that they'll have any effect on the French language.

In a decade or two, even *les Immortels* will probably give up on *interpeller* and *reprint*. The situation is the same in Italy. The most recent supplement to the *Vocabolario della Crusca* grudgingly includes an entry for "Millennium bug," derived "Dall'inglese *millennium* 'millennio' e *bug* 'insetto.' "

Even today there are proposals for academies and societies— some to be sponsored by states, others to thrive as nongovernmental organizations like the Queen's English Society, founded in 1972. But history gives us little reason to expect much from them, and the smart money will be placed on *norma loquendi*—the unregulated habits of myriad speakers, working more or less in tandem but without any plan. English has been growing and changing haphazardly for fifteen hundred years and has never taken kindly to attempts at regulation. And yet the best writers have managed in spite of this—or perhaps because of it—to keep putting proper words in proper places.

CHAPTER 4

Enchaining Syllables, Lashing the Wind

SAMUEL JOHNSON LAYS DOWN THE LAW

ENGLISH SPEAKERS IN THE FIRST HALF of the eighteenth century were acutely pained by the lack of an authority in the language. Defoe and Swift were denied the academy they longed for, but still, some said, it might be possible for a true arbiter of proper English to issue authoritative edicts. If an academy couldn't do it, perhaps the author of a definitive reference book could. Maybe a dictionary could save the day.

And yet the English had fallen behind their rivals on the Continent when it came to dictionaries. The Italian *Vocabolario*, produced by the Accademia della Crusca, set the standard for that tongue for decades. A little closer to home, the Académie Française had produced the first edition of its four-volume *Dictionnaire* in 1694, and by 1740 it was already in its third edition. Even in Spain, the Academia Española published its six-volume *Diccionario de la lengua catellana* in parts between 1726 and 1739. In England? Nothing.

WELL, NOT *NOTHING*. Mythology holds that Samuel Johnson's *Dictionary of the English Language*, published in 1755, was the "first English dictionary." In 2005, on the book's 250th anniversary, the claim was widely repeated. Melbourne's *Herald Sun*, for example, called it "the very first dictionary of English"; the *Irish Times* made the same claim in the same words; the *Ottawa Citizen* noted, "It's been 250 years to the day since the appearance of Samuel Johnson's celebrated first dictionary of English." And it was not just the sestercentenary, to use a good dictionary word, that prompted these declarations. In 1998, both the *Independent* and the *Guardian* made the claim. Similar assertions appear in the *Boston Globe*, the *Observer*, the *Toronto Star*, the *Financial Times*, and the *New York Times*. In 2000, a helpful contributor to the Montreal *Gazette* clarified things for less enlightened readers: "I should explain that the Dr. Johnson mentioned above was neither pediatrician nor urologist, but the author, among other things, of the first Dictionary of the English Language."

But the legend is entirely without foundation. There were plenty of dictionaries before 1755. As early as 1582, for instance, a schoolmaster named Richard Mulcaster published a book called *The First Part of the Elementarie Which Entreateth Chefelie of the Right Writing of Our English Tung*. In a section titled "A perfit English dictionarie wished for," Mulcaster declared it "a thing verie praiseworthie in my opinion, . . . if som one well learned and as laborious a man, wold gather all the words which we vse in our English tung . . . into one dictionarie." It was a topsy-turvy world, he complained, in which people spoke foreign languages better than their own native language: "verie manie men, being excellentlie well learned in foren speche, can hardlie discern what theie haue at home."[1]

The first Englishman to answer Mulcaster's call with what we'd call an English dictionary was Robert Cawdrey, whose *Table Alphabeticall, Conteyning and Teaching the True Writing, and Vnderstanding of Hard Vsuall English Words, Borrowed from the Hebrew, Greeke, Latine, or French, &c. with the Interpretation thereof by Plaine English Words* appeared in 1604. With just 2,449 entries, it covered only a tiny fraction of the language, but it was a start, and other lexicographers soon took up the challenge. In 1623, Henry Cockeram followed with *The English Dictionarie; or, An Interpreter of Hard English Words*; in 1656, Thomas Blount published *Glossographia*. By the end of the seventeenth century, it was possible to fill bookshelves with English dictionaries.

But even after the first English lexicons had been written, the public wasn't satisfied—there may have been English dictionaries, but there was still no *authoritative* English dictionary. These new books did nothing to settle disputes, and to many the language still seemed frustratingly chaotic. The diarist John Evelyn, for instance, wrote in 1665, calling for "a Lexicon or collection of all the pure English words," sorted into literal and figurative meanings. He was hopeful that such a lexicon would arrest linguistic decay. The lexicographers would run the show; it would be their job to produce "a full catalogue of exotic words, such as are daily minted by our *Logodædali*"—and not only to produce such a list, but also to pass judgment on all the words in it.[2]

Evelyn was only one voice among many in the seventeenth century. When John Dryden adapted Shakespeare's *Troilus and Cressida* in 1679, he commented on the state of linguistic affairs when Shakespeare was writing his version of the play: "he began it without a *Grammar* and a *Dictionary*." True enough—Shakespeare's *Troilus* was probably written a few months before Cawdrey's *Table Alphabeticall* appeared—but Dryden insisted things still hadn't gotten better in the intervening decades: "how barbarously we yet write and speak."[3] In his essay "Of the Original and Progress of Satire," Dryden was even more direct: "we have yet . . . not so much as a tolerable Dictionary, or a Grammar; so that our Language is in a manner Barbarous."[4] Even after a dozen dictionaries had appeared, people were still repeating Dryden's complaint. In 1741, philosopher and historian David Hume regretted that the "Elegance and Propriety of Stile have been very much neglected among us. We have no Dictionary of our Language, and scarce a tolerable Grammar."[5] Six years later, Bishop William Warburton noted that "we have neither GRAMMAR nor DICTIONARY, neither Chart nor Compass, to guide us through this wide sea of Words."[6]

SUCH WAS THE state of affairs in the mid-1740s, when a group of printer-publishers came together to collaborate on a major new dictionary. Working in a cartel made good financial sense: although it meant sharing the profits if the resulting book was a success, it also meant sharing the start-up costs and, more important, sharing the risk if the book was a flop. But whom should the publishers tap to write the book?—who was qualified to give the country its standard dictionary? Several big names in English literature had already considered projects like this; Joseph Addison, the great essayist, toyed with the idea of a dictionary, as did Alexander Pope, the most successful poet of the eighteenth century. But none came to fruition.

For reasons that are still unclear, the booksellers turned to a comparative unknown—a sometime poet, a minor scholar, and a man of bizarre appearance, uncouth habits, and minimal qualifications. Samuel Johnson was a strange choice on many counts. He was a bizarre physical specimen—his large, gangly body housed a disturbed mind. Sometimes his physical and mental maladies came together, as when he obsessively rolled his head from side to side and muttered under his breath. (Some modern physicians have identified his ailment as Tourette's syndrome, compounded by obsessive-compulsive disorder.) He was a chronic depressive, and several times suffered near-complete mental breakdowns. His manners were appalling—he spat as he talked; he sweated as he ate. The artist William Hogarth described his first encounter with the legendary critic at the house of the novelist Samuel Richardson, as Hogarth and Richardson were debating the policies of George II: "While he was talking, he perceived a person standing at a window in the room, shaking his head, and rolling himself about in a strange ridiculous manner. He concluded that he was an ideot, whom his relations had put under the care of Mr. Richardson, as a very good man." But despite all appearance to the contrary, Richardson wasn't taking care of a mentally challenged relative:

> To his great surprize . . . this figure stalked forwards to
> where he and Mr. Richardson were sitting, and all at once

took up the argument, and burst out into an invective against George the Second. . . . In short, he displayed such a power of eloquence, that Hogarth looked at him with astonishment, and actually imagined that this ideot had been at the moment inspired.[7]

What made the booksellers' choice even stranger is that Johnson had no university degree. He had been a student at Pembroke College, Oxford, but his family was unable to pay his tuition and fees after just thirteen months. Johnson's biographer James Boswell told the story about this difficult era of his life: "his poverty being so extreme, that his shoes were worn out, and his feet appeared through them, he saw that this humiliating circumstance was perceived by the Christ-Church-men, and he came no more. He was too proud to accept of money, and somebody having set a pair of new shoes at his door, he threw them away with indignation."[8] Johnson's determination not to take charitable donations meant that he never completed his undergraduate education. He had to wait until the *Dictionary* was nearly finished before he received his first honorary master's degree, and even longer for his first honorary doctorate. The famous "Doctor Johnson" never even earned a B.A.

After his finances forced him to leave Oxford, he returned to his hometown and started a school, though it never had more than a few pupils. A few years later he came to London hoping to make it big as an author, but found himself reduced to hack writing. His early publications were anonymous: the first of his works to bear his own name was his great poem, *The Vanity of Human Wishes*, which appeared in 1749, several years after he signed the *Dictionary* contract. It's odd, then, that the booksellers settled on Johnson as the man to write the long-expected dictionary. But in 1746 Robert Dodsley, serving as facilitator for the project, asked Johnson if he might be persuaded to take on the task. Johnson later recollected that he "had long thought of it."[9]

Johnson's first concern was to get the money to support himself through the project. He needed a regular income for the years it would take him to produce his dictionary. Patronage was the usual way projects like this were undertaken in the seventeenth and eighteenth centuries. Before Johnson's day, few authors were able to make a living by selling their books—the royalty system that supports writers today didn't exist, and the lack of an enforceable copyright system made it almost impossible for authors to make money on book sales.

Noble authors, of course, didn't mind; they could afford to take a few years to write a book without worrying about feeding their families. And successful playwrights could take a fraction of the house receipts. But the rest of the writers had to find some means of support. The patronage system was a clever way of putting authors with too little money in touch with nobles with too much money, and it usually made both parties happy. Typically an author would approach a wealthy person and seek permission to dedicate a book to him or her. The patron would provide financial support while the author was at work; the writer, in return, would preface the book with a dedication that praised in glowing terms the patron's virtue, knowledge, wisdom, taste, beauty, fashion sense, punctuality, penmanship, or whatever else needed praising.

Some of these dedications are hard for modern readers to swallow—so over-the-top that we can't believe they were meant to be taken seriously. Aphra Behn, for instance, a playwright and novelist from the end of the seventeenth century, addressed one of her plays to Nell Gwyn, the king's mistress:

> I make this Sacrifice with infinite fear and trembling . . .
> for besides Madam, all the Charms and attractions and
> powers of your Sex, you have Beauties peculiar to your
> self, an eternal sweetness, youth and ayr, which never
> dwelt in any face but yours; . . . so Natural and so fitted
> are all your Charms and Excellencies to one another, so
> intirely design'd and created to make up in you alone the
> most perfect lovely thing in the world, you never appear

but you glad the hearts of all that have the happy fortune
to see you. . . . [10]

So it goes, for page after nauseating page. John Dryden's fawning
dedication to the Duchess of York was little better:

> Beauty is [the poets'] Deity to which they Sacrifice, and
> Greatness is their Guardian-Angel which protects them.
> Both these are so eminently join'd in the Person of Your
> Royal Highness, that it were not easie for any, but a Poet,
> to determine which of them out-shines the other.[11]

Johnson found Dryden's dedication particularly distasteful, calling it "a strain of flattery which disgraces genius. . . . It was wonderful that any man that knew the meaning of his words could use
[them] without self-detestation." Dryden "made flattery too
cheap," with "the meanness and servility of hyperbolical adula-
tion."[12]

But, tasteless as Johnson found dedications, there was no alternative in the publishing world of the eighteenth century, and so he
held his nose and approached a potential patron. This was Philip
Dormer Stanhope, 4th Earl of Chesterfield, who had supported
several other high-profile literary projects. Johnson drafted a document describing his intentions, *The Plan of a Dictionary of the
English Language*, and addressed it to Chesterfield. He stopped
shy of the revolting flattery used by other authors, but he did speak
of "you, whose authority in our language is so generally acknowledged," and begged for the chance to be considered "the delegate
of your Lordship" in his book.[13] Then it was just a matter of waiting for the money to roll in, allowing him to devote all his time to
the *Dictionary*.

CHESTERFIELD'S REACTION, THOUGH, wasn't what Johnson hoped
for. An advance of ten pounds was a decent start, but Chesterfield lost interest in the project and eventually brushed him off.

Johnson apparently tried several times to get his attention, but to no avail. He was forced to go it alone. He did receive a big advance from his publishers: £1,575, perhaps equivalent to £100,000, or $200,000, today. It may sound like an impressive amount—many first-time authors would be delighted with a figure like that—but the money had to support not only Johnson but also six assistants through years of work. And so he was obliged to take on many other writing projects at the same time. He composed some of his most famous poems during this period, including "Prologue at Drury Lane" and *The Vanity of Human Wishes*. He turned out dozens of book reviews. He had been working on his play, *Irene*, for a decade; it finally appeared while he was working on the *Dictionary*. Most important, he began a series of essays, *The Rambler*, that appeared twice a week for two years—in the modern edition, the 208 *Rambler* essays fill three thick volumes. These projects alone would be more than full-time work for any professional writer; but somehow, in his spare time, Johnson also managed to write forty-three thousand dictionary entries. The sheer size of the book is a testimony to the labor he put into it. The full text of the *Dictionary* is more than three million words, thirty-seven times the length of *Paradise Lost*, and five and a half times the length of *War and Peace*. And he did it not in the hallowed halls of a university, an academy, or a nobleman's library, but in the attic of his modest house at Gough Square in London.

Where do you begin in writing a dictionary? The first challenge is to come up with the list of words. It's clearly not efficient to brainstorm in alphabetical order (*aardvark, abacus, abandon, abase . . .*); that would make it far too easy to miss important words. Johnson instead decided to read through the great works of English literature—the complete plays of Shakespeare, Milton's *Paradise Lost*, the poems of John Dryden, the essays of Joseph Addison—as well hundreds of more mundane works, like George Abbot's *Briefe Description of the Whole Worlde*, Richard Allestree's *Causes of the Decay of Christian Piety*, John Arbuthnot's medical textbooks, Roger Ascham's educational treatises, John Ayliffe's legal writings, all the way to John Woodward's research on fossils and Sir Henry Wotton's poems. As he read through these books, Johnson kept his eyes open for interesting words and passages, marking them with a vertical line at the beginning and end of each passage he wanted to quote. He then underscored the words he wanted to illustrate, and put the first letter of those words in the margin of the books. As he finished each volume, he passed it to one of his copyists, who transcribed the quotation onto a slip of paper and crossed out the letter in the margin. This database of hundreds of thousands of slips, arranged alphabetically, provided him with the raw material for his dictionary.

Johnson admitted frankly that some words wouldn't make it into his book. He decided that very old and very new words didn't belong. Technical terms and specialized jargon, too, are poorly represented. "That many terms of art and manufacture are omitted," he wrote in his preface, "must be frankly acknowledged; but for this defect I may boldly allege that it was unavoidable: I could not visit caverns to learn the miner's language, nor take a voyage to perfect my skill in the dialect of navigation."[14] He also admitted he wasn't going to try to keep track of slang and nonstandard English. And of course there were plenty of oversights. In the preface he admitted that after he spent years collecting quotations, he discovered he didn't have a single one for the word *sea*. He fixed that omission in time, but many other words never made it. Still, even with all these exceptions, he included a greater proportion of the "real" vocabulary than any of the lexicographers who came before him.

Then came the business of providing definitions. It wasn't easy. "That part of my work on which I expect malignity most frequently to fasten," he wrote, "is the *Explanation*"—the definition—"since I have not always been able to satisfy myself." Johnson saw the problem more clearly than any earlier lexicographer. "To interpret a language by itself," he admitted, "is very difficult." Not every word has synonyms, and "simple ideas cannot be described."[15]

These "simple ideas" have plagued lexicographers for generations. It's not difficult to define, say, *bookcase* or *knapsack*, since we can describe their functions or break them down into their components. We can define *rich* as "having a lot of money." But how do we define *sour* or *green*? What about *light* or *time*? What about function words like *if* and *then* and *whether* and *but* and *from*? And what about words like *geology* or *law* or *barometer*—can we define them without writing long essays on those subjects?[16] We all know what they mean, but trying to put it into words, trying to say anything useful about them, is no mean feat.

One of Johnson's most important achievements was the minute discrimination of senses, something he developed far beyond what any previous English lexicographer had done before. The earliest dictionaries usually provided nothing more than a synonym for the word they were defining: Cawdrey's *Table Alphabeticall*, for instance, includes definitions like "*Baud*, whore. . . . *Magistrate*, governour. . . . *Maladie*, disease." Definitions grew more expansive and precise over the next century, but even Nathan Bailey, whose dictionary was the most thorough before Johnson's, still skimped on elaborate definitions and careful discrimination of senses. Bailey defined the word *take*, for instance, as simply "to lay hold on, to seize; also to receive from another, likewise to succeed and to believe," with similarly curt descriptions of a few phrases like *take your will*, *take heed*, and *take root*. Johnson, on the other hand, identified fully 133 distinct senses, and offered precise definitions and examples of every one of them.

Many people assume the hardest words to define are the obscure ones—words like *ruderary* or *fabaceous* or *anatiferous*. But these so-called inkhorn terms, named for the inkwells used by scholars, are actually some of the easiest to define, because a Latin or Greek dictionary will give the answer. (For the curious: *ruderary* means "belonging to rubbish"; *fabaceous* means "having the nature of a bean"; *anatiferous* means "producing ducks.") Infinitely more challenging are the simple words like *take*. "To assume possession of" may seem a good start for a definition of *take*, but when we say that something *takes* three hours, we don't mean that it "assumes the possession of three hours." There should probably be another sense of *take*, perhaps labeled number 2, with a definition like "to occupy a period of time." But *taking your time* is different still, and needs another definition: there's number 3. You can *take a bus*, you can *take comfort*, and you can *take a nap*. *Taking a bath* and *taking a vacation*—these probably need separate entries too. What about *taking a break*, or *taking a lap* around a field, or *taking something for granted*? And sometimes we have to make judgment calls. Should *taking a drink* and *taking medicine* be treated as one sense—say, "to consume"—or should we distinguish them with two definitions? (When you *take a bite*, you're not "consuming" a bite.) What about *taking tea*, which seems subtly different from *taking a drink*, or *taking milk* with your tea? Can we lump them into a more general sense, or does each one need its own definition? Defining words like *galericulate* ("covered as with a hat") is trivial compared with providing a useful definition of a word every English speaker already knows.

Johnson probably had little idea of the scope of his project when he began. He first vowed that he could do the entire job, from start to finish, without substantial assistance, in a mere three years—where it took a team of forty professional lexicographers forty years to complete the equivalent job in France. Among English dictionaries, the scale of the work was unprecedented. Although other eighteenth-century lexicographers included more words than Johnson, none of them came close to him in terms of scope, of detail, of depth. Cawdrey's *Table Alphabeticall*, for instance, fit comfortably in a compact book of 130 pages. His successors' versions got more expansive over the years, but next to Johnson's 2,300 huge, double-columned pages, they all look skimpy. If we were to put the first seven major English dictionaries together in one great pile—those by Cawdrey, John Bullokar, Henry Cockeram, Thomas Blount, Edward Phillips, Elisha Coles, and John Kersey—they'd still be shorter than Johnson's. No English lexicographer had anything like his range.

ALL THE LITERARY work Johnson was doing in the meantime had turned him from a nobody into a somebody—a somebody with a reputation as a serious writer and scholar. The word on the street

was that Johnson's *Dictionary* was going to be a major achievement. This buzz must have reached Lord Chesterfield: at the end
of 1754, in a magazine called the *World*, His Lordship published a
two-part preview of the forthcoming work. The notice was published anonymously, but there was little doubt who was behind it.
"I think the public in general," he wrote, "and the republic of letters in particular, greatly obliged to Mr. Johnson, for having undertaken and executed so great and desirable a work." He knew
the world longed for a reliable standard dictionary, and so, worried that "Our language is at present in a state of anarchy," he advised, "The time for discrimination seems to be now come.
Toleration, adoption and naturalization have run their lengths.
Good order and authority are now necessary."[17]

So far, so good; many English writers had insisted that the language needed a reliable standard. But Chesterfield crossed the
line from decent compliments to tasteless toadying:

> I hereby declare that I make a total surrender of all my
> rights and privileges in the English language, as a free-
> born British subject, to the said Mr. Johnson, during the
> term of his dictatorship. Nay more; I will not only obey
> him, like an old Roman, as my dictator, but, like a modern
> Roman, I will implicitly believe him as my pope, and hold
> him to be infallible while in the chair.

These are grand claims. Chesterfield crowns Johnson emperor and
pontiff at once, granting him papal infallibility in all matters linguistic. Who wouldn't be flattered?

Johnson wasn't. He saw through the ploy—Chesterfield was
fawning over Johnson because he wanted Johnson to fawn over him
in return. And Johnson's pride—the same pride that led him to
reject the free shoes—led him to reject Chesterfield's proffered
kindness.

Chesterfield wanted to be known as the man who made the new
Dictionary possible. It didn't work, because Johnson knew all too
well that Chesterfield had actually done nothing toward the

completion of the book. As Boswell wrote, "This courtly device failed of its effect. Johnson, who thought that 'all was false and hollow,' despised the honeyed words, and was even indignant that Lord Chesterfield should, for a moment, imagine, that he could be the dupe of such an artifice."[18] And so, on February 7, 1755, Johnson replied with one of the most devastating poison-pen letters ever written. "My Lord," he began; "I have been lately informed . . . that two Papers in which my Dictionary is recommended to the Public were written by your Lordship. To be so distinguished is an honour which, being very little accustomed to favours from the Great, I know not well how to receive. . . . When upon some slight encouragement I first visited your Lordship I was overpowered like the rest of Mankind by the enchantment of your adress." It's easy to imagine Chesterfield's reaction to this point: a warm smile of satisfaction as he accepted the flattery he knew he deserved.

Then, however, came an important turn: "But I found my attendance so little incouraged, that neither pride nor modesty would suffer me to continue it." Perhaps Chesterfield's brow wrinkled at this point. "When I had once addressed your Lordship in public," Johnson continued, "I had exhausted all the Art of pleasing which a retired and uncourtly Scholar can possess. I had done all that I could, and no Man is well pleased to have his all neglected, be it ever so little." Then came Johnson's list of grievances, followed by his declaration of independence: "Seven years, My lord have now past since I waited in your outward Rooms or was repulsed from your Door. . . . [I] have brought it at last to the verge of Publication without one Act of assistance, one word of encouragement, or one smile of favour. Such treatment I did not expect," he added wickedly, "for I never had a Patron before." Then, finally, the knockout punch: "Is not a Patron, My Lord, one who looks with unconcern on a Man struggling for Life in the water and when he has reached ground encumbers him with help. The notice which you have been pleased to take of my Labours, had it been early, had been kind; but it has been delayed till I am indifferent and cannot enjoy it, till I am solitary and cannot impart it, till I am known, and do not want it."[19]

This masterpiece of invective is one of the greatest literary obscene gestures ever composed. In his study of Johnson and author-
ship, critic Alvin Kernan calls this letter "the Magna Carta of the
modern author, the public announcement that the days of courtly
letters were at last ended."[20] This is an exaggeration; the patronage system was already waning in the years before Johnson published his *Dictionary*. But if we need a single moment to mark the
effective end of patronage, this letter is as good as any.

THE PERSONAL RANCOR in this letter is remarkable, and often discussed in biographies of Johnson. At least as important, though,
is the insight it gives us into Johnson's conception of the role of
the lexicographer. In the earliest sketches of the *Dictionary*, Johnson seems to have hoped for something like the dictatorial authority that Chesterfield wanted to give him. In the *Plan*, the original
proposal for the *Dictionary* that he dedicated to Chesterfield in
1747, he imagined himself surveying the English language and
preparing for an invasion: "I am frighted at its extent," he confessed, "and, like the soldiers of Cæsar, look on Britain as a new
world, which it is almost madness to invade." But invade it he will,
hoping that "I shall at least discover the coast, civilize part of the
inhabitants, and make it easy for some other adventurer to proceed
farther, to reduce them wholly to subjection, and settle them under laws."[21] Early in his work on the *Dictionary*, Johnson pictured
himself as a literary conqueror, a champion of linguistic regime-
change who was going to civilize a barbarous language.

Chesterfield therefore had good reason to think of Johnson as a
would-be dictator—Johnson himself had told him as much in his
Plan. By the time he had finished his *Dictionary*, though, Johnson
had reconsidered. To put it in modern terms, he became a less prescriptive and more descriptive lexicographer, concerned less with
declaring laws than with describing the language as it is. The
whole idea of being a literary dictator had come to seem naive at
best and offensive at worst. What's more, it was futile. As Johnson's friend Thomas Warton put it, "To fix a language has been

found, among the most able undertakers, to be a fruitless project."[22] Like Warton, Johnson knew he could issue all the edicts he wanted—the language would continue to change without him. That's why, in the end, he rejected any proposals for a linguistic academy to regulate the language. "*Swift*," he wrote, "in his petty treatise on the *English* language"—he meant *A Proposal for Correcting, Improving and Ascertaining the English Tongue*—"allows that new words must sometimes be introduced, but proposes that none should be suffered to become obsolete. But what makes a word obsolete, more than general agreement to forbear it? and how shall it be continued, when it conveys an offensive idea, or recalled again into the mouths of mankind, when it has once by disuse become unfamiliar, and by unfamiliarity unpleasing."[23]

SOME OF THE most familiar entries in Johnson's *Dictionary* are the funny ones. Johnson made a little joke at his own expense, for instance, in his definition of *lexicographer*—"A writer of dictionaries; a harmless drudge"—and he took another swipe at his profession when he defined the word *dull* this way: "Not exhilarating; not delightful; as, *to make dictionaries is* dull *work*." Not all the jibes were directed at himself, though; he nearly got into serious legal trouble when he defined *excise* as "A hateful tax levied upon commodities, and adjudged [by] . . . wretches." And he was famous for making fun of the Scottish, and knew he'd irritate them with his definition of *oats*: "A grain, which in England is generally given to horses, but in Scotland supports the people."

Other entries weren't meant to be funny, but they may strike modern readers that way. The word *vaulty*, for instance, was defined as "Arched; concave," followed by a usage note: "A bad word." There is something defiant in Johnson's tone—a man who takes no guff, wagging his finger disapprovingly at a naughty word. Oh, the cheek! Such opinionated usage notes are scattered throughout the *Dictionary*: *ruse*, for instance, is "A French word neither elegant nor necessary"; and *scomm*, which means "A buffoon," is "A word out of use, and unworthy of revival." But these usage notes make up a small part of the whole *Dictionary*; just a few dozen entries out of more than forty thousand lay down the law like this. Most of the time he offers simple, straightforward definitions.

In a way, though, those forty thousand straightforward definitions are just as presumptuous—maybe more so. Even when he wasn't passing judgment on virtuous and vicious words, separating the sheep from the goats, he was still defining the entire English language. Who did this Samuel Johnson think he was, anyway? Writing a dictionary all by himself—it's an act of epic-scale vanity. Who has the chutzpah to tell the rest of the world what all the words in the language mean? No one today. Language mavens like William Safire and John Simon imagine themselves as a citizen's militia policing the borders, trying to drive out a few illegitimate interlopers. They rail against people who use *irregardless* in decent company, but they don't have the gumption to issue a ruling on every word in the language. Johnson did.

This presumption wasn't entirely unheard of. Once upon a time dictionaries were the work of individuals; many English dictionaries before Johnson's were one-man shows. But Johnson's project was infinitely more ambitious and demanding. The only earlier works with a comparable scope and ambition were those of the Continental academies, the Accademia della Crusca and the Académie Française. Both were monuments to the nations that produced them, embodiments of the collective wisdom of the country's greatest scholars. They weren't the work of single writers; they were the intellectual equivalent of public works projects, managed by dozens of professional academics who had access to all the scholarly resources their countries could muster. With his usual bravado, Johnson enjoyed comparing his solitary labors to those of the academies. His plan, after all, was to write the entire thing by himself in three years, assisted only by five or six scribes who would copy out the passages he marked. When doubters pointed out that the Académie Française, with its staff of forty of the nation's greatest scholars, took forty years to compile a similar dictionary, he replied with one of his best zingers: "This is the proportion. Let me see; forty times forty is sixteen hundred. As three to sixteen hundred, so is the proportion of an Englishman to a Frenchman."[24] (The boast loses very little of its force when we discover he took not three years but nine: sixteen hundred to nine is still a pretty good proportion.)

JOHNSON DID HIS work virtually single-handed, but he was also offended when Chesterfield proclaimed him a lawgiver. If you write a dictionary all by yourself, how can you avoid being the sole arbiter of the language? Johnson's answer to this conundrum determined the character of his book. It's one of the most important things that distinguishes his *Dictionary* from all those that came before it. The difference is visible at once in Johnson's book—definitions, the usual business of a dictionary, occupy just a small part of it. The majority is actually quotations, around 114,000 of them, from the greatest writers in the English language. And it's the quotations that do the serious business of the *Dictionary*. Johnson's greatest achievement was not dictating to the great writers in the language but *listening* to them.

Johnson insisted that a word means whatever the best writers say it means. He was convinced that no one—no scholar, no emperor, no pope even—had the authority to rule on meanings. English simply doesn't work that way. Our language is the common property of all those who've used it—it's exactly what Horace had in mind when he called usage the basis of *norma loquendi*. So before writing his definitions, Johnson spent most of his nine years reading the great authors in the English language, and it's these authors in their hundreds who do the real work. They tell Johnson what the words mean, and Johnson in turn tells us.

Shakespeare was at the head of the pack: Johnson drew quotations from all his plays. He was a remarkably sensitive reader of Shakespeare, alive to many meanings and connotations that had escaped his predecessors and contemporaries; after he finished his *Dictionary*, his next big project was an eight-volume edition of Shakespeare's collected works.[25] Some of Johnson's notes are still quoted in Shakespeare editions today. Johnson took thousands of other quotations from the greatest writers in English—poets like Spenser, Donne, Milton, Dryden, Swift, and Pope; playwrights like Ben Jonson and William Congreve; fiction writers like Sir Philip Sidney, Daniel Defoe, and Samuel Richardson; prose writers like Sir Walter Ralegh, Francis Bacon, and Joseph Addison. He used the Bible in its majestic King James Version. Not all the quotations, though, come from big names. He relied on theologians like Richard Hooker, classical scholars like Richard Bentley, politicians like the Earl of Clarendon, physicians like Gideon Harvey, and economists like Sir Josiah Child. When he wrote about science, he often went right to the source: under *alcohol* and *laboratory*, he quoted the chemist Robert Boyle, whose gas laws tenth graders still have to memorize; under *light* and *gravity*, he quoted Sir Isaac Newton. He read through histories, sermons, philosophical treatises, cookbooks, agricultural handbooks, even mathematics textbooks and schemes for building flying machines. And though the eighteenth-century canon was pretty solidly masculine, Johnson's library wasn't an all-boys club. The Johnson of legend is a blustering misogynist, but the Johnson of real life was one of the most dedicated supporters of women intellectuals of his day. He quoted Jane Collier's wicked little satire *The Art of Ingeniously Tormenting* and Charlotte Lennox's novel *The Female Quixote* in his *Dictionary*. That's an impressive library, and it's only a small fraction of the books he read. These authors are the ones who fix the language, not Johnson: what looks like a tremendous act of egotism in fact turns out to be a tremendous act of humility, because he allows them to define every word in the language. After all, meanings come not from fiat but from precedent.

It sounds very much like the English common law, which comes not from proclamations, not even from legislatures, but from tradition. That's all the English constitution is—precedents. And the similarity is more than coincidental. Johnson wasn't a lawyer, but he knew the common law intimately. He surrounded himself with practicing attorneys and scholars, including his friend and biographer James Boswell. So great was Johnson's legal knowledge that the lawyers often turned to *him* for advice. Boswell's *Life* describes many instances when the layman dictated arguments to the lawyer. Even more remarkable, Sir Robert Chambers, Vinerian Professor of Law at Oxford University, sought out Johnson's advice in composing his lectures on the common law. Chambers's name isn't familiar now, but many lawyers still know the name of his predecessor, Sir William Blackstone, whose *Commentaries on the Laws of England* is one of the most famous works on law ever written. After Blackstone retired, Chambers was named to the most distinguished legal professorship in Britain and charged with the task of lecturing to Oxford's students. But he used Johnson as a ghostwriter on most of his lectures. This fact is worth a moment's pause: one of the most celebrated legal scholars in the country had to spell out the principles of the common law, and he needed help. Did he consult with other legal scholars?—other lawyers? No; he turned to someone who had never formally studied the law. It's no surprise, then, that Johnson used the same notion of precedent in compiling his *Dictionary*.

IN A CONVERSATION with Boswell, Johnson once talked about the difficulties of defining common words. "We all *know* what light is," he said, "but it is not easy to *tell* what it is."[26] But when he wrote his *Dictionary*, he had to tell what it is. So how did he define *light*? He distinguished seven senses of the word and backed them up with two dozen quotations. That may sound like overkill; "authorities," Johnson noted in his preface, "will sometimes seem to have been accumulated without necessity or use." But they were chosen with care, and "those quotations which to careless or unskilful perusers appear only to repeat the same sense, will often exhibit, to a more accurate examiner, diversities of signification."[27]

His first definition of *light* was the most obvious one: "That quality or action of the medium of sight by which we see." This represents what was in 1755 a cutting-edge scientific understanding of *light*, because his quotation comes from Sir Isaac Newton's *Optics*, the work that first explained the separation of white light into various colors. "*Light*," said Newton, "is propagated from luminous bodies in time, and spends about seven or eight minutes of an hour in passing from the sun to the earth." (This is, by the way, a remarkably accurate estimate for 1704; it actually takes about eight and a quarter minutes for the sun's light to reach the earth.)

That's *light*; there's also *a light*, "Any thing that gives light," especially a candle or a lamp. The first illustration for this sense, from Shakespeare, not only showed the word in use but also let Johnson deliver a miniature sermon by quoting Portia in *The Merchant of Venice*: "That *light* we see is burning in my hall; / How far that little candle throws his beams, / So shines a good deed in a naughty world." God himself uses lights, for as Milton's *Paradise Lost* explained, God placed the stars above, declaring, "let them be for *lights*, as I ordain / Their office in the firmament of heav'n, / To give *light* on the earth." This sort of light can also be metaphorical, as Paul and Barnabas deliver God's word to the masses: "I have set thee to be a *light* of the Gentiles, for salvation unto the ends of the earth."

Light can also mean "Illumination of mind; instruction; knowledge." This is a more subtle meaning and needs to be pinned down more carefully, so Johnson turned to writers in different fields. One was an important scientist, the father of modern scientific method, Sir Francis Bacon, who explained how a medical experiment can provide light for the mind. Another was a theologian, Richard Hooker, the most important religious writer from the reign of Queen Elizabeth, who described how some facts require study while others can be learned simply with "the *light* of nature." This kind of light is intimately bound up with the philosophy of mind, so Johnson provided a pair of quotations from the age's most important philosopher, John Locke, who echoed Hooker in speculating on what can be known strictly through the "internal *light*." Two poetic quotations, from Milton's *Paradise Lost* and from John Dryden, rounded out the illustrations of this meaning.

A related definition is "Reach of knowledge; mental view." For this sense Johnson quoted the passage in the Book of Daniel where the queen interprets for Belshazzar the mysterious handwriting on the wall, explaining that there was once a holy man, and "*Light*, and understanding, and wisdom, like the wisdom of the gods, was found in him." This meaning isn't always so sanctified; Francis Bacon's *Natural History* talked about the great voyages of discovery reaching the South Sea, and bringing new islands and whole continents to light. *Light* can also mean "Explanation," as in "shedding light on a question." Hooker was once again pressed into service for this sense, as was John Locke—not, this time, as a philosopher, but as a commentator on the Epistles of St. Paul, offering a valuable bit of exegetical wisdom: "We should compare places of scripture treating of the same point: thus one part of the sacred text could not fail to give *light* unto another."

Light is also an artist's term—"The part of a picture which is drawn with bright colours." To illustrate this, Johnson drew on Charles-Alphonse Dufresnoy, painter and art theorist, who warned painters that they should "Never admit two equal *lights* in the same picture; but the greater *light* must strike forcibly on those places of the picture where the principal figures are." *Light* can also mean "Point of view; situation"; for this sense, Johnson quoted the great Anglican theologian Robert South: "Frequent consideration of a thing wears off the strangeness of it; and shews it in its several *lights*." And the great essayist Joseph Addison, whose *Spectator* papers provided one of the most important models for Johnson's own *Rambler*, advised that "It is impossible for a man of the greatest parts to consider any thing in its whole extent, and in all its variety of *lights*."

This final example neatly embodies Johnson's method. He was certainly "a man of the greatest parts"—one of the most wide-ranging intellects who ever lived—but even he couldn't hope to consider the English language "in its whole extent, and in all its variety of lights." For that he depended on hundreds of the best writers, drawn from many fields: poets, novelists, philosophers, theologians, scientists, artists, politicians. He knew that even a simple word like *light* was beyond the powers of any one man, and so he called in Shakespeare, Milton, Locke, Bacon, and Newton to lend a hand.

MANY MODERN READERS of Johnson's *Dictionary* gravitate toward the quirky and opinionated definitions where his personal voice comes through most clearly, and they skip over the quotations that constitute the bulk of the book, turning it into a collection of imperial declarations. If we think of the *Dictionary* that way, it's certainly a tremendous act of vanity. But that is to make the same mistake as Chesterfield, turning Johnson into a dictator. He refused the emperor's laurels. He laid down the law, but it was the common law, where no one is qualified to speak as a tyrant.

Even if someone were qualified to speak as a tyrant, Johnson knew that no one would listen. The preface to his *Dictionary*, one of the greatest considerations of the problems of lexicography ever written, is perhaps most acute when it takes on the problems of standardizing the language. Johnson looked at the European academies' attempts to stop their languages from changing, and admitted he entertained thoughts of doing the same with English. By the time he finished, though, he feared that he had "indulged expectation which neither reason nor experience can justify." Any lexicographer who thinks "his dictionary can embalm his language, and secure it from corruption and decay" is simply deluded. "To enchain syllables," he wrote, "and to lash the wind, are equally the undertakings of pride."[28] This insight is what led Johnson to reject the idea of an academy, and what led him to ground his *Dictionary* in *norma loquendi*.

In one sense, then, Johnson's *Dictionary* is indeed a one-man production; but in another, more important, sense, it's one of the greatest collaborative works ever written, and his collaborators are the entire canon of great writers. The *Dictionary* isn't just a dictionary; it's also one of the largest anthologies of English literature ever published, and one of the largest dictionaries of quotations. To skip over these quotations is to miss some of the most enjoyable and enlightening parts of the book. It's also to miss a valuable lesson on how best to think about our own language, and where words get their meanings. Unlike France and Italy, no English-speaking country has an academy to issue decrees on what words *really* mean: English words mean what previous English speakers and writers have said they mean. Johnson knew that—something it's impossible to forget if you look at his *Dictionary* in the form in which he originally published it. The *Dictionary* is a monument to a great writer, but more than that, it's a monument to a great reader—one of the best readers English literature has ever had. And this remarkable three-million-plus-word dictionary-cum-anthology-cum-reading notebook, even though it has passed its 250th birthday, gives us a chance to understand how our language works, even today.

CHAPTER 5

The Art of Using Words Properly

JOSEPH PRIESTLEY SEEKS GENUINE
AND ESTABLISHED PRINCIPLES

HISTORY HAS RENDERED ITS VERDICT: guilty. They're the bad guys in the story of the English language. They're an unholy hybrid of dastardly, mustache-twirling villains and mouth-breathing, knuckle-dragging morons, and they stand convicted of vandalizing the mother tongue. The eighteenth-century grammarians are now remembered, if they're remembered at all, as meddlesome bugbears responsible for everything wrong with the language. *Merriam-Webster's Dictionary of English Usage* sports ten references to "the 18th-century grammarians," not one of them even close to complimentary, as when the compilers write of "The Latin grammar that was all the 18th-century grammarians knew."[1] The usual story is that English speakers were happily speaking confidently, without the least hint of self-consciousness. Then along came the grammarians, who ruined it for the rest of us ever since. They foolishly imposed Latin rules on a recalcitrant language; they made people ashamed of the way they spoke; they imposed whippings on schoolboys who dared to split their infinitives. A Web search for "18th-century grammarians" reveals the phrase is rarely far from words like "prejudice," "ignorance," and "arbitrary."

Were they really the supervillains that appear in so many descriptions? It turns out that many of the rules routinely attributed to the eighteenth-century grammarians were never discussed by anyone in the eighteenth century. The split infinitive is a favorite example, perhaps *the* paradigmatic rule: many people with an interest in the language know that it's wrong to split infinitives, even if they're a little vague on what an infinitive is or how it might be split. And many modern sources tell us that it was the wicked eighteenth-century grammarians who brainwashed us into this bizarre superstition.

WHAT, EXACTLY, IS a split infinitive? The word *infinitive* means "unlimited" or "indefinite." *She writes, they believe, he went* are "limited" to one person and number; the infinitive, on the other hand, is the base form of the verb, which appears after the particle *to*, as in *to speak, to go, to have*. The *to* isn't always part of the infinitive; after auxiliary verbs, it's common to have the "bare infinitive." In a clause like *She can sing*, for instance, the word *sing* is an infinitive, but bears no *to*; likewise *They will arrive*. The same applies to a few other verbs: *let me go* and *have her call me* are examples of clauses with infinitives not marked by *to*. (A very few verbs can go either way: *help*, for instance, can be followed by an infinitive either with or without the *to*. *She helped him set up the new shop* and *She helped him to set up the new shop* are both idiomatic English.)

While *to* is not always required, it usually appears with the infinitive, and it's the relationship between this "particle" and the following verb that causes all the trouble. In many languages, including Latin and Greek, the infinitive is a single word with its own distinctive form: the two-word English phrase *to love*, for instance, is *amare* in Latin and *philein* in Greek. Since Latin and Greek infinitives are single words, it's impossible to "split" them. And it was once the same in English. In Old English the infinitive was usually a single word ending in *-an*, as in *lufian*, the origin of our verb *love*. If you wanted to modify the infinitive with an adverb, the adverb would have to come before or after.

In the eleventh and twelfth centuries, though, the Old English single-word infinitive began to give way to the two-word version, as the preposition *to* became a "marker" of the infinitive. This development made it possible for a word to come between the two halves. *The Oxford English Dictionary* notes, "Occasionally an adverb or advb. phr. [adverbial phrase] . . . is inserted between to and the infinitive, forming the construction now usually (but loosely) called 'split infinitive.' " When we say *to quickly read*, *to never part*, or *to boldly go where no man has gone before*, we're taking the halves of the infinitive and inserting an adverb between them. The infinitive has been split.

Why, if people had been content to put adverbs before or after the one-word infinitive, did they begin putting them in the middle of the two-word one? It probably comes from a change in how native speakers analyzed the sentences they were using—how they formed mental models of the grammar. Historical linguists know where the two-word infinitive came from, but the overwhelming majority of speakers have never thought about the question, and probably wouldn't care if the answer were offered. But every speaker has at least an unconscious sense of how the parts of a sentence fit together, and they don't always correspond to the historical account.

In a simple sentence like *I want to go*, the subject is the pronoun *I*; the main verb is *want*; and what do I want?—*to go*. The two-word infinitive functions grammatically like a noun, so it can be the object of a transitive verb like *want*. That's the way a sentence like that was analyzed for centuries, and as long as that was the case, there was little or no reason to stuff an adverb in the middle of the two-word infinitive. Eventually, though, English speakers and writers came to analyze that same sentence differently, treating the word *to* as a trailing part of the main verb *want*, not as the leading part of the object *go*. In other words, the sentence is mentally modeled not as *I want to-go*, but as *I want-to go*. The habit is clear in the informal, usually spoken form of *want to* as *wanna*, and in our habit of ending clauses with *to* and no following verb, as in *I don't want to*. This *want-to* or *wanna* is then treated as a verb that takes a "bare infinitive," one without the *to*, making it possible— easy, even—to put words between the *verb* and the infinitive. It's not limited to *want;* many other common verbs have their own informal spoken versions—*hafta, gonna, oughta.*

The split infinitive has come and gone through the history of the language. In Middle English it wasn't unusual for the direct object of a verb to appear between *to* and the verb. An anonymous work called *Cursor Mundi,* for example—a long, influential poem of the thirteenth or fourteenth century—provides several examples: "To temple make he sal be best" ("He shall be best to make [the] temple"), and "He sal þe send Angels for to þe defend" ("He shall send thee angels for to defend thee"). Adverbs also sometimes appeared in the middle of the two-word infinitive, as in *to ever want.* These constructions, however, all but disappeared a little before 1500: Shakespeare, for instance, has only one split infinitive in his entire body of work, "thy pity may deserve to pitied be."[2]

The split infinitive didn't vanish because grammarians set people straight: it simply faded away. No one took a vote, passed a law, or issued a memo. It just disappeared over time. No one had any sense that it was forbidden; it simply sounded wrong. For the next two or three hundred years, the split infinitive remained extremely rare. But then, for no particular reason, it started to become common again in the middle of the eighteenth century. There's no evidence that its popularity was owing to ignorance or illiteracy, since even the most educated used it occasionally. Samuel Johnson, for instance, in his career-topping work, *Lives of the Most Eminent English Poets* (1779–81), noted that "Milton was too busy to much miss his wife," inserting the adverb *much* in the middle of *to miss.* By the end of the eighteenth century, the split infinitive was becoming common again.

Only in the nineteenth did anyone bother to single it out for blame. The earliest example of the prohibition that has yet turned up is from an 1834 magazine article, signed only with the initial "P." This "P" commented on the common "practice of separating the prefix of the infinitive mode from the verb, by the insertion of an adverb," and realized that no one had yet spelled out a rule. He therefore volunteered to supply the omission:

The rule which I am about to propose will, I believe,
prove to be as accurate as most rules, and may be found
beneficial to inexperienced writers. It is this:—*The particle,* TO, *which comes before the verb in the infinitive
mode, must not be separated from it by the intervention
of an adverb, or any other word or phrase; but the adverb
should immediately precede the particle, or immediately
follow the verb.*[3]

Over the course of the next few decades, more and more grammarians tried to enforce this new rule—though why they tried so
hard is difficult to say. The influence of classical grammar, with its
one-word infinitives, must have played a part. There were probably
also concerns about social class: perhaps the split infinitive became
more common among the working classes than among the rich and
educated. Whatever the reason, the prohibitions against it grew
and grew until, by the early twentieth century, it was among the
most reprehensible of verbal crimes.

WHEN THE DESCRIPTIVE linguists arrived on the scene and started
questioning the traditional prescriptive pieties, they regarded this
strange prohibition as the paradigmatic example of a misguided,
even stupid, principle. One critic—apparently the first to use the
term *split infinitive*—reminded readers in 1897 that "Byron is
the father of their split infinitive. . . . 'To slowly trace,' says the noble poet, 'the forest's shady scene.' "[4] Even some fairly strict academic grammarians insisted there was no reason to avoid it. George
O. Curme maintained that "the split infinitive is often a clearer
means of expression than the older form of statement," and he
backed up his claim with an example: "In 'He failed *completely* to
understand it' *completely* belongs to *failed*, but in 'He failed to
completely understand it' *completely* belongs to *understand*. . . .
the split infinitive evidently enables us here to express ourselves
more accurately than is possible in the older form of statement."[5]
    When criticizing the eighteenth century became the norm with

the rise of descriptive linguistics around 1900, the never-split-an-infinitive rule was predictably attributed to those eighteenth-century grammarians, the source of every foolish regulation. A recent book titled *Legal Writing Advice*, for instance, considers "the status of the grammatical rule: never split an infinitive," declaring, "the rule does not exist. Its promulgators were 18th century prescriptivist grammarians who believed that English should follow the Latin paradigm."[6] Another book notes, "There have been periods in English literary history when splitting infinitives was very fashionable. However, 18th century grammarians noticed that Latin infinitives were never split. Of course, it was impossible to split a Latin infinitive because it was a single word. . . . But that fact did not prevent the early grammarians from formulating another prescriptive rule of English grammar."[7] Even Steven Pinker, usually careful with his facts, writes, "Most of the hobgoblins of prescriptive grammar (don't split infinitives, don't end a sentence with a preposition) can be traced back to these eighteenth-century fads." This is what leads him to declare, "The scandal of the language mavens begins in the eighteenth century."[8]

Never mind that the split infinitive is nowhere even mentioned, let alone forbidden, by any eighteenth-century English writer; never mind that eighteenth-century writers actually brought the split infinitive *back* after a long period of disuse. Eighteenth-century grammarians are convenient villains, and to them can be attributed every half-witted attempt to meddle with the language. Of course they made their share of mistakes and took on their share of quixotic causes, but in no greater numbers than any other generation, including our own. They are not above reproach, but they certainly don't deserve all the opprobrium that has been heaped on them.

SO WHO WERE these dastardly eighteenth-century grammarians? The three most important British writers on English grammar in the eighteenth century were Joseph Priestley, Robert Lowth, and Lindley Murray. Since they've been accused of the most egregious crimes, it's only fair to pay attention to who they were and what they said.

The first, Joseph Priestley, was a political, religious, educational, and social radical with an astonishingly wide-ranging mind. He is most famous today for his work in the sciences, what contemporaries would have called natural history or natural philosophy. In performing one of his famous scientific investigations, he discovered that "atmospherical air is not an unalterable thing"[9]—that the air we breathe is actually made up of several gases, one of which he called "dephlogisticated air." (The word *gas* wouldn't get its modern meaning until 1779.) This discovery makes Priestley one of three or four people with a legitimate claim to having discovered oxygen—no small feat. But Priestley was plenty busy with his nonscientific pursuits as well. As his biographer notes, "An early nineteenth-century edition of his collected works, minus the science, filled twenty-six octavo volumes and the science would have added at least five more."[10]

Even as a young man, he was remarkably prolific. Born to a middle-class Yorkshire family in 1733, Priestley, a Unitarian, was excluded from Oxford and Cambridge for his religious heterodoxy. This led him to the Dissenting academies, the same sort of institutions where Daniel Defoe had studied a few decades earlier. Priestley attended Daventry Academy, which provided him with a sound knowledge of Latin and Greek, ancient history, theology, metaphysics, mathematics, anatomy, chemistry, and physics. As a child of thirteen he began to study Hebrew, and he soon added some proficiency in other Middle Eastern languages, including Chaldee, Syriac, and Arabic. Along the way he taught himself French and German.

Priestley eventually became a Unitarian preacher. But his contemporaries noted—and often were unhappy about—his Yorkshire accent and his habit of stammering, two facts that may have contributed to his interest in the way the language works. Priestley himself acknowledged that "this *impediment in my speech* . . . was the cause of much distress to me." At the same time, he hoped that "it has not been without its use."[11] He put that distress to good use in 1758, when he moved to Nantwich, in Cheshire. There he not only preached regularly; he also opened a grammar school, where he taught Latin, Greek, English, geography, history, science, and mathematics to boys and girls. He bought some scientific equipment, including an air pump and various electrical machines, for in-class demonstrations. It was an exciting time for scientific discovery, especially with electricity. Benjamin Franklin's famous kite-and-key experiment took place not long before, in the early 1750s, and with each passing month the "electrical fluid," or "electrical fire," seemed to have new miraculous powers. (Priestley and Franklin would later become friends.) Priestley's *History and Present State of Electricity, with Original Experiments* was published in 1767 and appeared in five English editions as well as French and German translations before the century's end.

While still at Nantwich he prepared a short English grammar for the use of his own students. A few years later, when he moved to Warrington, he was named tutor in languages and belles lettres. There he taught Greek, Latin, French, and English. "Grammar schools" earned the name because they taught grammar—Latin grammar, of course—and in virtually all schools an education in languages meant the study of Latin and Greek, and sometimes Hebrew. Even tradesmen might benefit from studying the classical languages, said Priestley, since "There is so much of Latin in the English tongue." Schools should therefore teach Latin alongside more practical sciences; he hoped that "all boys at grammar schools might have access to a good collection of objects of *natural history.*"[12] And while he was at Warrington, the notes on grammar he had compiled for his students in Nantwich appeared in print: *The Rudiments of English Grammar* was published in 1761, followed a year later by *A Course of Lectures on the Theory of Language and Universal Grammar.*

PRIESTLEY OPENED HIS *Rudiments* by stating his plan: "The following performance is intended to exhibit, *A View of the genuine and established principles of the English language; adapted to the use of schools.* For this purpose, care hath been taken to omit nothing that properly falls within the province of the *Grammarian*." He settled on a question-and-answer format: the style of the catechism would be "both the most intelligible to the scholar, and the easiest for the master."[13]

The very first question and answer made it clear that Priestley had a normative conception of grammar: "*Q.* What is GRAMMAR?" "*A.* GRAMMAR is the art of using words properly."[14] Here he was echoing what had appeared in many previous Latin grammars, as when William Lily, in one of the most influential grammars ever printed, wrote in 1540, "Grammatica est recte scribendi atque loquendi ars"—grammar is the art of writing and speaking correctly.[15] Priestley's echo is significant: grammar was, for many, a matter of getting the language right. This makes good sense when an English speaker is trying to learn Latin—English speakers don't have an intuitive feel for what's right or wrong in another language. It's more controversial, though, when an English speaker is studying English. Every speaker has already learned thousands of rules about how to speak the language.

Sometimes Priestley's book took the form of a grammar for nonnative speakers, and in such cases he was the model descriptivist. Here, for instance, is his paradigm for a common English verb:

PRESENT TENSE,

Singular.	Plural.
I love.	*We love.*
Thou lovest.	*Ye love.*
He loveth, or *loves.*	*They love.*

PRETER TENSE,

I loved.	*We loved.*
Thou lovedst.	*Ye loved.*
He loved.	*They loved.*[16]

This is all descriptive enough, albeit a little old-fashioned; the *-eth* ending and both *thou* and *ye* were on their way out in the mid-eighteenth century. At times, though, he abandoned objective description for unabashed prescription. In the second edition of the *Rudiments*, for example, he noted, "Adjectives are often put for adverbs"—as when people said *near* for *nearly* or *exceeding* for *exceedingly*—"but the practice is hardly to be approved."[17] And sometimes he offered nothing more than subjective preferences: "A *Metaphor* should not be very far fetched. It is sufficient that the resemblance hold in the point of light in which the objects are placed."[18]

And yet, even though he is one of the eighteenth-century grammarians who have been blamed for everything bad about the teaching of grammar, Priestley's ideas about proper English could be surprisingly enlightened. His preface began by suggesting that "*Grammar* may be compared to a treatise of *Natural Philosophy*," which is to say natural science. But there were differences between the natural realm of physics and the messy human institution of language: "were the language of men as uniform as the works of nature," he wrote, "the *grammar of language* would be as indisputable in its principles as the *grammar of nature*." He knew better: the language of men is *not* uniform, but often illogical and inconsistent. Even "good authors have adopted different forms of speech," he observed, "and in a case that admits of no standard but that of *custom*, one authority may be of as much weight as another."[19] This is an important passage:

> By an attention to these maxims hath this grammatical performance been conducted: the best and most numerous authorities have been carefully followed. Where they have been contradictory, recourse hath been had to analogy, as the last resource: For if this should decide for neither of two contrary practices, the thing must remain undecided, till all-governing custom shall declare in favour of the one or the other.[20]

"All-governing custom"—it's not a bad translation of Horace's ancient phrase *norma loquendi*. It's custom, or usage, that determines what's right in the language.

Priestley could therefore be forgiving of some supposed violations of grammar, even as he prescribed what he said were the correct forms of the language. In casual conversation, for instance, he advocated "a relaxation of the severer laws of Grammar." There's nothing wrong with "who is this for" instead of "for whom is this," and some of the obsolescent verb endings (*learnedst*) could be dropped in good conscience, however much the textbooks insisted the traditional forms were correct.[21] He also believed—crucially—that variety is a good thing, and that not every linguistic question has a single answer. "In style, as in every other production," he wrote, "there is room for infinite diversity, where the degrees of excellence may be the same." Diversity, far from being a fault, is actually one of the glories of language. Because earlier critics had neglected diversity, they were "too hasty in establishing general laws of writing"—rules that no good writer could follow all the time. Priestley was ready to allow for some inconsistency. When the tutor asked the question "Suppose the noun be a *collective*, or one that signifies many particulars under a singular form?" the student was to answer, "The verb, in that case, may be either singular or plural; as *the people says, or the people say*."[22]

PRIESTLEY'S POLITICAL RADICALISM caused him much trouble in the following years. His *Essay on the First Principles of Government*, which appeared in 1768, earned him enemies in political circles; he argued publicly with William Blackstone, the most prominent legal scholar of the century, over the rights and legal status of Dissenters. His reputation as a political reformer and his support of the French Revolution led to violence. The brouhaha—known as the Birmingham Riots, the Church and King Riots, or the Priestley Riots—forced Priestley and his family to flee their house, which was burned to the ground, along with his scientific laboratory. The riot was put down, though not in any great hurry, by royal troops after three days. Feeling unwelcome at home, Priestley sailed for the United States in 1794. He died in Pennsylvania in 1804.

THE SECOND OF the big three eighteenth-century grammarians, on the other hand, was as much a child of the establishment as Priestley was a radical. Robert Lowth, son of a senior church official in Winchester, was born in 1710. After receiving a first-rate education at Winchester College and Oxford University, he became a fellow of New College, Oxford. His reputation for learning and literature was great, and in June 1741, he was elected to the Professorship of Poetry at Oxford. This was a signal honor; even today it remains one of the most distinguished academic posts in the nation. It has been held over the last three centuries by a procession of worthies including Thomas Warton, Matthew Arnold, Francis Turner Palgrave, A. C. Bradley, C. Day Lewis, W. H. Auden, Robert Graves, Edmund Blunden, Seamus Heaney, Paul Muldoon, and Christopher Ricks.

A few months after becoming Oxford Professor of Poetry, Lowth was ordained as a deacon, and a year later, in December 1742, he became a priest, beginning his steady movement through the ecclesiastical ranks. In 1750 he became Archdeacon of Winchester; he received his doctorate of divinity from Oxford in 1754; he was created Bishop of St. David's in 1766 and Bishop of London in 1777. Along the way he picked up other honors, such as a fellowship in the Royal Society.

Lowth had an expansive mind and was one of the first Westerners to understand ancient Hebrew poetic forms without forcing them into Greek or Latin molds. While at Oxford, Lowth delivered a series of lectures titled *Prælectiones de sacra poesi Hebræorum*, "Lectures on the Sacred Poetry of the Hebrews." They were published in Latin in 1753, with a second expanded edition a decade later and a third in 1775. A five-hundred-page collection of Latin lectures on ancient Hebrew poetry hardly seems destined for a bestseller list, and even in English translation (a two-volume set was published in 1787, the year of Lowth's death) it can be slow going. But Lowth's book was a milestone in understanding the poetry of the Hebrew Bible—what made it poetry at all, since it didn't rhyme or have the same number of syllables per line. Lowth's breakthrough was insisting on the importance of understanding Hebrew poetry in an "Oriental" context, rather than a classical one—that is, recognizing the difference between the ancient biblical poetic tradition and the Western tradition that Englishmen had come to assume was poetry. All this made him an interesting candidate to write a serious grammar of English. The usual accusation leveled at the eighteenth-century grammarians is that they thought only in terms of classical grammar, but Lowth's strength consisted in shaking off the classical chains that had restricted others before him.

Lowth opened his *Short Introduction to English Grammar*, published just a few weeks after Priestley's, by recalling Jonathan Swift's proposal for an academy:

> It is now about fifty years since Doctor *Swift* made a public remonstrance . . . of the imperfect State of our Language; alledging in particular, "that in many instances it offended against every part of Grammar." . . . Indeed the justness of this complaint, as far as I can find, hath never been questioned; and yet no effectual method hath hitherto been taken to redress the grievance of which he complains.[23]

By this time, most English writers had given up on the idea of an academy. For some it was desirable but impractical; for many others, the very thought of an academy was offensive. Perhaps an academy was suitable for the slavish, rule-bound French, they argued; the English, though, prided themselves on their liberty. Samuel Johnson worried about the prospect that "an academy should be established for the cultivation of our stile," and said that he could "never wish to see dependance multiplied" and that he hoped "the spirit of *English* liberty will hinder or destroy" any such scheme.[24]

It's appropriate that this call for self-regulation was emerging in Britain in the second half of the eighteenth century, because many similar things were happening in the country at the same time. This was the age of the economist Adam Smith, who in 1776 laid out the theoretical basis of capitalism. His contemporary Priestley was clearly thinking about what would come to be known as laissez-faire economics: he thought "a publick *Academy*, invested with authority to ascertain the use of words," would be "unsuitable to the genius of a *free nation*." Besides, he argued, "the best forms of speech will, in time, establish themselves by their own superior excellence."[25] The servile French may need an authoritative voice to tell them how to behave, but liberty-loving and industrious Britons will sort out their own language without submitting to dictators.

And so, since an academy didn't seem practical, Lowth did his best to clean up his countrymen's offenses against grammar. Like Priestley (and Lily before him), Lowth thought that the purpose of grammar was to issue decrees, "to teach us to express ourselves with propriety." He therefore highlighted a number of common errors, such as *you was*: "*You was*, the Second Person Plural of the Pronoun placed in agreement with the First or Third Person Singular of the Verb, is an enormous Solecism"—this even though, as he acknowledged, "Authors of the first rank have inadvertently fallen into it." He also looked at verbs like *drive, drove, driven* and *ride, rode, ridden*, and argued that analogy demanded *sit, sat*, and *sitten*. A good thing, then, that Conyers Middleton, an English clergyman and biographer, "hath with great propriety restored the true Participle."[26]

There's no question that Lowth was more prescriptive than Priestley. Lowth rejected the common assertion that "our Language is in its nature irregular and capricious; not subject, or not easily reduceable, to a System of rules," but in order to do so, he had to convict a number of great authors of violating the system of rules he imagined: "the *English* Language as it is spoken by the politest part of the nation, and as it stands in the writings of our most approved authors, oftentimes offends against every part of Grammar." And yet even Lowth was not the monomaniacal linguistic despot some have imagined. Swift railed against the ugliness of contractions, but Lowth found them a perfectly natural part of English: "The nature of our language, the Accent and Pronunciation of it, inclines us to contract even all our Regular Verbs: thus *loved*, *turned*, are commonly pronounced in one syllable, *lov'd*, *turn'd*. . . . we generally throw the accent as far back as possible towards the first part of the word."[27] This sense of "the nature of our language" informs many of his proclamations.

Another example of the way he qualified his rules shows up in his opinion on the sentence-ending preposition, perhaps his most influential contribution to discussions of English grammar:

> The Preposition is often separated from the Relative
> which it governs, and joined to the Verb at the end of the
> Sentence, . . . as, "Horace is an author, *whom* I am much
> delighted *with*." . . . This is an Idiom which our language
> is strongly inclined to; it prevails in common conversa-
> tion, and suits very well with the familiar style in writing;
> but the placing of the Preposition before the Relative is
> more graceful, as well as more perspicuous; and agrees
> much better with the solemn and elevated Style.[28]

Many readers have taken from this only the fact that Lowth was prohibiting sentence-ending prepositions. But when examined more closely, Lowth's decree turns out to be a model of descriptivism— one related to different levels of diction, with "common conversation" contrasted with "the solemn and elevated Style." Lowth acknowledged that the sentence-ending preposition is common in English and perfectly appropriate to the "familiar style"; more formal writing, though, benefits from a different placement of the preposition, which is "more graceful." Lowth made clear that this "more graceful" version isn't the only acceptable one, because he himself ended a clause with a preposition: "This is an Idiom which our language is strongly inclined to."[29]

LOWTH'S *GRAMMAR* WAS a phenomenon: more than thirty-four thousand copies were printed in the first twenty years, and dozens of editions appeared over the next century. And yet even Lowth couldn't rival the popularity of the last member of the triumvirate of major eighteenth-century English grammarians. Lindley Murray may have been the least sophisticated thinker of the lot, but he was certainly the most influential.

Murray was the only member of the big three to hail from the Americas: he was born in 1745 near Lancaster, Pennsylvania, and began his education at a school founded by Benjamin Franklin in Philadelphia. Though brought up to be a merchant, he convinced his father to allow him to study law and spent the late 1760s and early 1770s as a lawyer in London. His loyalist sympathies during the American Revolution made it prudent for him to stay in the mother country, and so he settled in York in 1784.

In 1795, teachers at a nearby Quaker school for girls asked him for help teaching their pupils to speak with more elegance. Murray obliged with a set of short books designed to teach young people proper English: a grammar, a reader, and a book of exercises. These books ended up being fantastically influential and long-lasting: a book calling itself a "sixty-fifth edition" of his grammar was published in 1871, and at least 259 separate editions of his reader were printed between 1815 and 1836. A strange Murraymania led to an edition for the blind (almost unheard-of in the nineteenth century) and even a board game, "A Journey to Lindley Murray's." His work was published around the English-speaking world—not only in England but also in the United States, Ireland, Canada, and India, as well as in Germany, France, and Portugal in English editions, and in translation in Germany, France, Holland, Sweden, Spain, Russia, and Japan. Together they earned him the title "father of English grammar." Linguist Ingrid Tieken-Boon van Ostade notes in a brief biography of Murray, "This worldwide popularity of the work marks the beginning of the development of English as a world language." Tieken explains part of the attraction of Murray's grammars: "In their clarity and succinctness the rules set out by Murray are eminently learnable . . . and the material is presented in gradable form, with the basic rules in the main text and further explanations in footnotes."[30]

Murray shared Lowth's conviction that English was, or at least was supposed to be, a logical and systematic language; when he saw people, even great writers, departing from his notion of propriety, he took it as prima facie evidence that they were wrong. Much of his grammar was concerned with singling out published examples of bad English—or at least English that didn't live up to his standards. That's because "a proper selection of faulty composition is more instructive to the young grammarian, than any rules and examples of propriety that can be given": to teach people to use the language properly is to show them how others have messed up.[31]

And of the three major linguists of the day, Murray was the one who most enjoyed legislating: a greater proportion of his grammar is devoted to prescription than either Priestley's or Lowth's. Murray, for instance, was among the first to formulate a rule that was much taught even into the twentieth century, though few know it now: "*Will*, in the first person singular and plural, intimates resolution and promising; in the second and third person, only foretells. . . . *Shall*, on the contrary, in the first person simply foretells; in the second and third persons, promises, commands, or threatens."[32] Many a schoolchild has been scolded for getting this wrong, even though only a tiny portion of the English-speaking world now routinely uses *shall* in casual speech. Outside legal documents, in which *shall* sometimes carries a specific meaning, and a few common phrases like "Shall we?" the word sounds irredeemably stuffy to most of today's English speakers.

Murray didn't make up this rule by himself. He was actually reporting on the usage of one class of late eighteenth-century English speakers, who naturally distinguished *shall* from *will* more or less according to the rule he spelled out. The very fact that the rule appears in Murray's *Grammar*, though, tells us that the distinction wasn't familiar to many speakers even in 1795—had everyone made the distinction, there would have been no need to issue the legislation. Murray studied the habits of those he considered the best writers and speakers and declared to the world that their habits were the right ones. He did the same thing when he claimed, "Adjectives are sometimes improperly applied as adverbs; as, 'Indifferent honest; excellent well; miserable poor'; instead of 'Indifferently honest; extremely well; miserably poor.'"[33] People are still scolded for using adjectives to modify verbs, as in "I can run fast" (some sticklers call for *quickly*, unaware that *fast* can be both an adjective and an adverb). But Murray's real objection was that forms like *excellent well* and *miserable poor* were, by the 1790s, used almost exclusively by the wrong kind of people. If people wanted to sound like their social superiors, and Murray took it for granted that everyone would, they should follow his orders.

But even Murray, for all his finger-wagging at supposed illiteracies, was not quite the bogeyman he's been made out to be. Many of his rules are really expressed in descriptive terms. Here, for instance, is his discussion of what some call the "double genitive," that is, a possessive formed both with the usual apostrophe and *s* (*my friend's book*) and a construction with *of* (*book of my friend*):

> In some cases we use both the genitive termination and the preposition *of*; as, "This book of my friend's." Sometimes indeed this method is absolutely needful, in order to distinguish the sense, and to give the idea of property, strictly so called, which is the most important of the relations expressed by the genitive case; for the expressions "This picture of my friend," and "This picture of my friend's," suggest very different ideas. The latter only is that of property in the strictest sense.
>
> Where this double genitive, as it may be called, is not necessary to distinguish the sense, and especially in a grave style, it is generally omitted.

Notice the way he expresses it: "in a grave style, it is generally omitted." As with Lowth's comment on the sentence-ending prescription, it's a model of descriptivism. Murray explicitly refuses to declare it wrong: "we say, 'It is a discovery of Sir Isaac Newton'; though it would not have been improper, only more familiar, to say, 'It is a discovery of Sir Isaac Newton's.'"[34] Murray here is talking about what's *appropriate* rather than what's *right*.

WE WOULD ALL be happier had Murray and his followers paid even more attention to questions of appropriateness rather than correctness. At their worst, the eighteenth-century grammarians were concerned with English as they thought it *should* be; at their best, they took the language as it was. Not everyone was a narrow-minded prescriptivist grammarian; there were people saying surprisingly modern things even in the eighteenth century. "It is not the business of grammar," wrote the clergyman and educator George Campbell in 1776, "as some critics seem preposterously to imagine, to give law to the fashions which regulate our speech. On the contrary, from its conformity to these, and from that alone, it derives all its authority and value." Others occasionally had the same insight: that *norma loquendi* was the only true standard by which language could be judged. As we'll see, the better authorities on the language never forgot that lesson. Too many, though, were convinced that the masses were wrong—that they alone knew the secret that the rest of the English-speaking world neglected—and had to be chastised for it. The world is probably poorer for it.

Murray's descendants are still with us. Lynne Truss's *Eats, Shoots & Leaves* is only the latest bestseller in a long line of unexpectedly successful books on the language. Since the late 1950s, grammarians have made explicit the connection between preserving the English language and preserving a way of life. We live in the age of the mavens.

Maven—a Yiddish word meaning "expert"—is the title adopted by William Safire; it has caught on in the United States, occupying the place held in Britain by *language pundit* (from the Sanskrit *pandita* 'learned man'). Prominent examples include Theodore Bernstein, who published *Watch Your Language* (1958), *More Language That Needs Watching* (1962), *The Careful Writer* (1965), *Miss Thistlebottom's Hobgoblins* (1971), and *Dos, Don'ts & Maybes of English Usage* (1977); Edwin Newman, who began his series with *Strictly Speaking* (1974) and went on to publish *A Civil Tongue* (1976) and *I Must Say* (1988); the "Underground Grammarian," Richard Mitchell, who published *Less than Words Can Say* (1979) and *The Leaning Tower of Babel and Other Affronts* (1984); the sharp-tongued film and drama critic John Simon, who published a witty threnody-cum-call-to-arms in *Paradigms Lost* (1980); Jacques Barzun, who weighed in with *A Word or Two Before You Go* (1986); and Safire, of the *New York Times*, who can fill several shelves with collections assembled from his "On Language" column. Virtually all these books spent time on the best-seller list.

Bernstein, Newman, Mitchell, Simon, Barzun, and Safire have a number of things in common. They're all fine writers; their books are enjoyable to anyone with an interest in the language. They're all culturally conservative, and that often (but not always) comes through in their political-party affiliations.[35] But they're also the same in that they're not linguists—they all have a good practical grasp of the language, but they don't know much about the history of English or its underlying structures. And so a turf war between two groups of putative language experts has broken out. On one side are the professional linguists, who have had limited success in writing for a popular audience: most linguists, to be frank, are simply not very capable writers. Only an exceptionally talented few—David Crystal, Steven Pinker—have managed to find readers outside academia. The mavens, on the other hand, usually have very limited knowledge of the research of professional linguists; worse, they are often openly hostile to the academics.

Usually the journalists dismiss the professional linguists as incompetent tin-eared hacks, the linguists dismiss the journalists as ignorant know-nothing meddlers, and both sides exude smug self-satisfaction at having nothing to do with the other. One of the journalists, Dwight Macdonald, explained, "The academic establishment has gone overboard for Structural Linguistics—nothing an American scholar likes more than a really impressive system with scientific pretensions."[36] The linguist and neuroscientist Steven Pinker, on the other hand, curses the whole tribe of mavens: "Maven, shmaven!" he fulminates. "*Kibbitzers* and *nudniks* is more like it. . . . Most of the prescriptive rules of the language mavens are bits of folklore that originated for screwball reasons several hundred years ago."[37] Sometimes their quarrels can get downright nasty. For John Simon, the scholars "masquerading under the euphemism 'descriptive linguistics'" are guilty of "a benighted and despicable catering to mass ignorance under the supposed aegis of democracy, of being fair to underprivileged minorities, and similar irruptions of politics where it has no business being. . . . Demotic ignorance plays into the hands of pseudoscientific mumbo jumbo, and structural linguistics rushes to the defense of every popular distortion or misconception."[38] Pinker is ready with a comeback: "It is ironic that the jeremiads wailing about how sloppy language leads to sloppy thought are themselves hairballs of loosely associated factoids and tangled non sequiturs."[39]

It may seem impossible to achieve detente between the mumbo jumbo and the hairballs; too much seems to be at stake. And yet it's possible to find a modus vivendi. The academics have to remember—and be willing to admit—that there are times when prescription is just the thing. Too many descriptive linguists forget, or pretend to forget, that certain social contexts (business writing, magazine and newspaper publishing, among others) call for a distinctive register of the language that most people haven't mastered on their own. The descriptivists assume that a statistical report on prevailing habits in the whole population can take the place of a sharp ear and a sensitive spirit. They also sometimes hint that no one is qualified to offer an opinion on the language without a doctorate in linguistics.

But prescription without a sound knowledge of the actual practice of the majority of a language's speakers is not merely misguided; it's actually destructive. Too often the mavens and pundits are talking through their hats. They're guilty of turning superstitions into rules, and often their proclamations are nothing more than prejudice representing itself as principle. Of course there's something satisfying about imagining yourself the only righteous person preaching the gospel of good English in a wicked world. "I have done judgment and justice," the traditional grammarians say: "leave me not to mine oppressors."[40] And too often readers respond to the mavens' passion more than their knowledge. There's a strange phenomenon, little commented on by people who study the language: the rules we learn as children often stick with us, no matter how absurd, long after we should know better.[41] The key is to find the right balance of academic knowledge and writerly panache. Of course everyone thinks he or she has already found that balance. If others observe fewer rules than we do, they're dullards; if they observe more, they're pedants. Nearly all the people who care about language are convinced they've found the sweet spot between the know-nothings and the know-it-alls. Both sides, though, would do well to be a little more willing to examine their own preconceptions from time to time.

CHAPTER 6

The People in These States

NOAH WEBSTER AMERICANIZES
THE LANGUAGE

ENGLISH, FOR A VERY LONG TIME, belonged to the English. And not to all the English, but to the inhabitants of a single metropolitan area. It's hard for moderns to appreciate just how much London dominated the English-speaking world in the seventeenth and eighteenth centuries.

London wasn't always the capital of the Anglophone world. During the Old English period—circa 500 to 1100—several English dialects from different parts of the island were accorded equal respect. In the Middle English period there were still many regional linguistic centers throughout England (as well as Scotland, Wales, and Ireland), and none dominated the others. The English of York was as important as that of London. In the fifteenth century, though, London began to assume greater importance as a commercial, political, intellectual, and spiritual center, not only of England but of English as well. London (including Westminster) was the site of the royal court and of Parliament, where the English language took over from French as the official language of government early in the fifteenth century. The legal profession also did much to make London's dialect the norm, for it was fifteenth-century London scribes who worked in the Chancery court and helped to establish a kind of "standard" English.

Perhaps most important for the fate of the language, though, is that London was the home of the most important writers, the ones who would provide the most highly praised examples of English style for centuries. Geoffrey Chaucer, for instance, was a Londoner who served in the royal court in the late fourteenth century; William Shakespeare left provincial Stratford around 1590 to make it big in London; John Milton was born in London in 1608 and, apart from a stint at Cambridge University and a tour of the Continent, spent his whole life there. John Dryden, Alexander Pope, Joseph Addison, Richard Steele, Daniel Defoe—all were Londoners, whether by birth or by choice. Virtually all the major English writers made it their home from the end of the fourteenth century to the middle of the eighteenth. The canon of great English writers was really a canon of great London writers, and the English language, with all its dialect diversity across the British Isles, was supposed to have found perfection in the form spoken in London.

London was also the home of the publishing business. A database called the English Short Title Catalogue contains information on every early English printed book, and the statistics there show London's unrivaled importance in the literary culture of the English-speaking world. If we examine the quarter millennium from 1500 (shortly after the rise of printing in England) to 1750 (probably the peak of London's dominance over the language), it becomes evident just how much the metropolis overshadowed the provinces. Over those 250 years, for example, a mere 44 books were published in the city of Manchester, and Birmingham produced only 67. Bristol, which would become a center of print culture early in the nineteenth century, produced only 428 titles, and Newcastle just 470. Even York, the biggest city in the north of England, released only 574 printed books in a quarter of a millennium.

Oxford and Cambridge were important publishing cities then as now, but their real work was supporting the scholars in the universities. Oxford turned out more than 5,300 books and Cambridge more than 4,000 before 1750, but more than a third of them were in Latin or Greek. The Irish publishing business was centered in Dublin, but it produced just over 10,000 titles before 1750. Even Edinburgh, the heart of Scottish literary culture, produced just under 15,000 books in the first two and a half centuries of printing.

Things were even more modest across the Atlantic. Printing arrived in what would become the United States in 1640, when Stephen Daye set up a press in Cambridge, Massachusetts, and printed *The Whole Booke of Psalmes Faithfully Translated into English Metre*, better known as *The Bay Psalm Book*. But it took quite some time for America to become a publishing powerhouse. From the beginning of North American settlement through 1750, only 829 books were published in New York. Philadelphia, long the most populous city in British America, printed fewer than a thousand titles. Even Boston—the home of America's early literary and intellectual culture—produced around 4,100. All the presses in the American colonies put together produced fewer than 6,500 titles before 1750.

London over the same period presents a very different picture. Between 1500 and 1750, London publishers turned out more than 190,000 titles—not only more than all the other cities combined, but also nearly four times as many as the rest of the English-speaking world. Four of every five books in English came from one city—a city that, by the middle of the eighteenth century, had become the most populous in all of Europe. Other locations were nothing more than outposts of the language's empire. London English was, as far as most people were concerned, the *real* English, and everything else was an inferior imitation.

This opinion was prevalent even in the more remote corners of the British Isles. Thomas Sheridan, for instance, was an Irish actor who was proud of shaking his native brogue when he arrived in England. He offered lectures on proper pronunciation—of course that meant the courtly pronunciation of London—and middle-class provincials from around the British Isles signed up to learn his lessons, eager not to be dismissed as yokels by sophisticated Londoners. In his *Course of Lectures on Elocution*, Sheridan advised the Scottish or Irish student to "employ his attention in discovering the particular vowels in the sounding of which the provincial manner differs from the polite pronunciation," for "surely every gentleman will think it worth while, to take some pains, to get rid of such evident marks of rusticity."[1] The philosopher David Hume, a Scot who was passionate about his prose style, was determined to remove the regionalisms in his own language and to speak and write like an Englishman. He compiled a list of "Scotticisms" to remind himself of what he should avoid in his writing: "*Notice*," for instance, "shou'd not be used as a verb. The proper phrase is *take notice*," and "*Hinder to do*, is *Scotch*. The *English* phrase is, *hinder from doing*." Scots write *incarcerate*, but the more polite English write *imprison*. Scottish *anent*, *alongst*, and *evite* should be rejected in favor of English *with regard to*, *along*, and *avoid*.[2] And if the list let him down, Hume was glad for help from native-born Englishmen. In a letter to Hume, Lord Lyttelton generously offered, "if I should see that any *Scotticisms* have inadvertently dropped from you, I will certainly take the liberty of marking them for your correction, in the manner you desire."[3] English meant London English, and careful writers and speakers used it as their model.

IT'S ONLY FITTING, then, that the language with its spiritual home in London should have as its most famous guardian a passionate Londoner. In the late eighteenth century "the dictionary" meant *A Dictionary of the English Language* by Samuel Johnson, one of the most famous Londoners who ever lived. Though he was born in the West Midlands, he moved to London at the age of twenty-five and made the city his home for the rest of his life—and no one loved London more. Tourists can still buy T-shirts, mugs, and tote bags emblazoned with one of his more famous bons mots: "Sir, when a man is tired of London, he is tired of life; for there is in London all that life can afford." Similar sentiments crowd Johnson's works and biographies. "London is nothing to some people," he admitted; "but to a man whose pleasure is intellectual, London is the place."[4]

His biographer James Boswell hailed from distant Scotland; Johnson enjoyed lecturing his younger friend on the attractions of the English metropolis. "The happiness of London," he told Boswell, "is not to be conceived but by those who have been in it. I will venture to say, there is more learning and science within the circumference of ten miles from where we now sit, than in all the rest of the kingdom." He also liked taunting those who were unfortunate enough to live in "the rest of the kingdom," and he couldn't resist the urge to ridicule the Scots in particular. One Scottish friend pointed out that "Scotland had a great many noble wild prospects." Johnson couldn't deny there were many beautiful prospects in North Britain, "But, Sir," he replied, "let me tell you, the noblest prospect which a Scotchman ever sees, is the high road that leads him to England!"[5]

And while Johnson enjoyed ribbing his friends from the less desirable corners of the British Isles, he positively relished attacking those from across the Atlantic. Sometimes it was the same sort of lighthearted ridicule that he leveled at his Scottish friends, but he also had a real political animus against Americans. The curmudgeonly Englishman once admitted that he was "willing to love all mankind, *except an American*," and he called the rebellious colonists "a race of convicts, [who] ought to be thankful for anything we allow them short of hanging."[6] In 1775, when the patriotic cry from Boston to Savannah was "Taxation without representation is tyranny," Johnson published a pamphlet called *Taxation No Tyranny*. He despised the Americans for their disrespect for monarchy, their republican principles, their tasteless moneygrubbing, and especially for their slave economy.

So it's no surprise that eighteenth-century Americans had a complicated relationship with Johnson: they were the target of some of his angriest political fulminations, but they had to admire his breadth of knowledge and his magisterial prose style. Though he took Americans to task, they read his works in great numbers. Critic James Basker has examined the catalogs of dozens of eighteenth-century American booksellers and libraries and has found Johnson's works in virtually all of them: "Throughout

America," he writes, "by the 1790s Johnson is not only om-
nipresent but dominant: he is by far the most widely available author, English *or* American, in the American book trade."[7] And the
Dictionary was a particular favorite. Many members of the founding generation owned a copy, and they turned to it when they
worked on the Declaration of Independence, the Constitution, the
Bill of Rights, and the *Federalist*. George Washington's copy of
the 1786 edition survives, his signature prominent on the title
page. Thomas Jefferson also owned one; when, in 1771, he gave a
friend a list of books to "fix . . . the principles and practices of
virtue," the *Dictionary* was on it.[8]

AMERICAN DEFERENCE TO Johnson's *Dictionary* tells us much
about how the colonists saw themselves. Many eighteenth-century
English-speakers in North America recognized themselves as
provincials, and were self-conscious and insecure about their use
of the language. The English language belonged to England; the
Americans were only borrowing it. They sometimes showed their
anxiety when they used what John Witherspoon labeled "Americanisms" in 1781. Witherspoon was a Scottish preacher who ar-
dently advocated the American cause: he was a signer of the
Declaration of Independence and went on to become president of
Princeton University. He was also fascinated by language. "By
Americanisms," he explained, "I understand a use of phrases or
terms, or a construction of sentences, even among persons of rank
and education, different from the use of the same terms or phrases,
or the construction of similar sentences, in Great Britain." He insisted, "It does not follow in every case that the terms or phrases
used are worse in themselves," but most of his countrymen were
less sure about the advisability of departing from the English
norm.[9]

Benjamin Franklin, for instance, wrote to the *London Chroni-
cle* in 1759, praising his countrymen for "speak[ing] the language
with such an exactness both of expression and accent, that though
you may know the natives of the several counties of England, by

peculiarities in their dialect, you cannot by that means distinguish a North American." Notice that he praises Americans for meeting *English* standards of the language, not their own. Being too obviously American was bad form, and Franklin himself sought to eliminate traces of his origins in his own writing. In 1760, when he was drafting a short work, he was glad for a "friendly Admonition" from David Hume about "some unusual Words in the Pamphlet. It will be of Service to me," Franklin said. "The *pejorate*, and the *colonizer*, since they are not in common use here"—that is, in England—"I give up as bad."[10]

Even the first few dictionaries published in the newly independent United States were deferential to the mother country, making few claims about the distinct variety of the language and giving up as bad anything that was not in use in fashionable London. They included some words unique to North America—*tomahawk*, *wampum*—and a few specifically American senses of familiar words, like *Capitol* and *federal*. Only one early American dictionary, though—*The Columbian Dictionary of the English Language* (1800)—even bothered to mention the American words on the title page. Americanisms were not a selling point; some saw them as a liability.

ONLY A FEW experts remember the compilers of these early American dictionaries, but their successor became probably the most famous lexicographer in history, surpassing even Johnson's fame. Noah Webster was born in West Hartford, Connecticut, in 1758, three years after Johnson's *Dictionary* first appeared in London. He would go on to take an utterly different approach to the Americanisms that so offended the British and embarrassed the colonists. Rather than seeking to conceal the American features of the language, Webster trumpeted them. And here he was consciously, even polemically, departing from Johnson's example.

Like other Americans, Webster found much to admire in Johnson's works. He praised the Englishman's "great intellectual powers" and admitted that his own life was changed forever by

Johnson's *Rambler* essays. "When I closed the last volume," he told a friend, "I formed a firm resolution, to pursue a course of virtue thru life—& to perform all moral & social duties with scrupulous exactness—a resolution which I have endeavour'd to maintain."[11] Even some of Johnson's political sentiments appealed to Webster, who was, like his lexicographical predecessor, a committed abolitionist.

But Webster could not abide Johnson's anti-American rancor, and from early in his life he zealously supported the American independence that Johnson had disparaged, even going so far as to march to join a battle in the Revolutionary War in 1777 (though he arrived after hostilities had ended). He attended Yale University, known in the eighteenth century as a hotbed of political radicalism: the loyalist Thomas Jones called the university a "nursery of sedition, of faction, and republicanism."[12] Webster thrived in this environment. He studied law and took his degree in 1778, at the height of the Revolution. In 1785, the year after Johnson's death, he published *Sketches of American Policy*, in which he agitated for a new constitution to take the place of the weak Articles of Confederation. He traveled to Mount Vernon to show the pamphlet to General Washington, and James Madison saw it soon after. He even took credit for prompting the Annapolis Conference of 1786, the first step toward drafting the new federal Constitution in 1787. While the Constitution was being written in Philadelphia, he was nearby, determined to be close to the action.

Unlike earlier American writers on the language, who were conciliatory about their relation to Britain, Webster was a devoted patriot who refused to make nice with the mother country. And it was this linguistic nationalism that led him to write his famous dictionary—a presumptuous plan, because it meant challenging the mighty Samuel Johnson, producing an American answer to the greatest monument to English and to Englishness. Despite his praise for Johnson's intellect, therefore, he had few kind words for the *Dictionary*, which he found "extremely imperfect and full of error." "Not a single page of Johnson's *Dictionary*," he griped on another occasion, "is correct." As he wrote in 1807, "the errors in

Johnson's Dictionary are *ten times* as numerous" as people sus-
pect.[13]

Webster was not the first to challenge the supremacy of Johnson's *Dictionary*, and some of the criticism Johnson had received
was warranted. It's true that Johnson was ill-prepared for some of
the jobs of a dictionary-maker. His etymologies were sometimes
wrong. He could be surprisingly sluggish for such a productive
scholar—though capable of almost superhuman intellectual exertion when the need arose, he was not the sort to work systemati-
cally over long periods, and his designs were often better than his
execution. The grammar and the history of the language that appeared at the beginning of the *Dictionary* were perfunctory and
derivative performances. He probably gave more space to obscure
terms than they deserved, and he certainly didn't give enough attention to the spoken language. What's more, by the time Webster
took on the task, Johnson's *Dictionary* was badly in need of updating. It first appeared in 1755 and was revised by Johnson in
1773, but the language had changed in many ways over the ensuing
quarter century.

All these criticisms are fair, but Johnson also came in for some
less-well-deserved criticism. The cranky and petulant scholar John
Horne Tooke, for instance, published a work known as *The Diversions of Purley* in 1786 that advocated eccentric—or, to use the more
accurate word, crackpot—theories about the nature of the language.
He was convinced every word has one and only one meaning; what
look to us like multiple definitions are really poorly understood
derivative meanings. He also advocated strange ideas about the
parts of speech, arguing, for instance, that English conjunctions
and prepositions were really fossilized nouns and verbs—he
claimed *if* was derived from *give*, and *that* was really a noun, not a
conjunction. He dismissed Johnson's *Dictionary* as "the most imperfect and faulty, and the least valuable of any of his produc-
tions," adding that Johnson himself "possessed not one single
requisite for the undertaking."[14]

Horne Tooke's protégé Charles Richardson wrote a big and influential lexicon in the 1830s, and he too expressed his distaste for

his most distinguished predecessor: "No man," he wrote, "can possibly succeed in compiling a truly valuable Dictionary of the English language, unless he entirely desert the steps of Johnson."[15] Before Richardson put Horne Tooke's theories into practice, he offered a long entry-by-entry commentary on the *Dictionary* of 1755, filling nearly two hundred pages, in which he excoriated Johnson and praised Horne Tooke. But Richardson never achieved the kind of authority he thought was his due, not least because Horne Tooke's theories were too eccentric to produce a useful dictionary. As Sir James A. H. Murray, chief editor of *The Oxford English Dictionary*, put it, Richardson "was impressed with the notion that, in a dictionary, definitions are unnecessary . . . and he proceeded to carry this into effect by making a dictionary without definitions."[16] Small wonder, then, that Richardson is not a household name.

WEBSTER HAD ALL these concerns in mind—he was a partisan of Horne Tooke and took many of his quirky lessons to heart—but it was politics above all that drove his lexicographical rivalry with Johnson. Instead of beginning with a full-scale dictionary, though, he worked his way up, starting with a series of smaller books. His most important early work was the three-part *Grammatical Institute, of the English Language*, made up of a speller, a grammar, and a reader. The title was not Webster's choice, and in subsequent editions he unbundled the parts and gave each its own more patriotic title: the *American Spelling Book*, the *American Grammar*, and the *American Selection of Lessons in Reading and Speaking*, better known as the *American Reader*. Those titles made it clear that he was teaching the language of America, not of the nation America had just defeated. If there was any doubt, the preface to his speller made it unambiguous: "The author," he wrote, "wishes to promote the honour and prosperity of the confederated republics of America and cheerfully throws his mite into the common treasure of patriotic exertion."[17]

Webster's nationalist mission is most obvious in the third part of the *Institute*, the reader. The title page bears a motto from the French writer Mirabeau—"*Begin with the Infant in his Cradle: Let the first Word he lisps be* Washington"—and though Webster could not get his message to infants in their cradles, he could at least teach the American story to beginning readers. The "capital fault in all our schools," he lamented, was that schoolbooks served up "subjects wholly uninteresting to our youth," musty legends drawn from classical or British history. America had produced heroes as great as any from England's past, and the orators of Massachusetts and Virginia were easily the equal of those of Greece and Rome: "the writings that marked the revolution . . . are not inferior in any respect to the orations of Cicero and Demosthenes," and speeches in America's Congress "contain such noble sentiments of liberty and patriotism, that I cannot help wishing to transfuse them into the breasts of the rising generation." He therefore looked closer to home for his selections: schoolchildren were to learn to read by working through Benjamin Franklin's "Way to Wealth," Joel Barlow's "History of Columbus," "General Washington's farewel Orders to the Army," and so on. Webster's headnotes gave these American selections an unmistakable patriotic slant. On the restrictions that followed the Boston Tea Party, for instance, he editorialized, "These rash and cruel measures, gave great and universal alarm to Americans," and he was positively rapturous about Washington, who "seemed destined by heaven to be the savior of his country . . . and by his matchless skill, fortitude and perseverence, conducted America through indescribable difficulties, to independence and peace."[18] He later appended a "Federal Catechizm" in which he explained the various kinds of governments, demonstrating to students that a representative democracy is the ideal form and explaining the branches of America's government, their powers, and the qualifications for voting.

Webster's mission, though, went beyond reprinting patriotic essays: he wanted to rework the fabric of the English language itself. He wrote to Benjamin Franklin that he hoped proud Americans might shake "an implicit adherence to the language and manners of the British nation." A few years later he was clearer about the need for linguistic independence: "Our honor requires us to have a system of our own," he wrote, "in language as well as government." He advised that "Customs, habits, and *language*, as well as government should be national. America should have her *own* distinct from all the world."[19]

He was not the first to call for an American language. Unreliable stories tell us that some hoped to make ancient Greek or biblical Hebrew the official language of the United States. If these schemes were ever seriously offered, though, Webster would have found them impractical: as he wrote in 1790, "The English language . . . is the repository of as much learning, as one half the languages of Europe."[20] It was English—not the Spanish, French, or German spoken in parts of North America—that would dominate the continent. Webster, however, was determined to separate the English language from the English nation, and he believed that a specifically American brand of English was bound to evolve out of the mother tongue. The "new country, new associations of people, new combinations of ideas in arts and science"—all these will inevitably "introduce new words into the American tongue." Given enough time, the result will be "a language in North America, as different from the future language of England, as the modern Dutch, Danish and Swedish are from the German." Webster overestimated the speed of linguistic change, but he was right about the mechanism: centuries of separate development have given us all the now-familiar British–American pairs like *lift–elevator*, *lorry–truck*, *draughts–checkers*, and *braces–suspenders*. And Webster figured that, since the progress of centuries would eventually produce an American language, it only made sense to help it along. "As a nation," he wrote, "we have a very great interest in opposing the introduction of any plan of uniformity with the British language."[21]

Why seek to distance American from British English? It seems only to invite confusion, a step on the way to George Bernard Shaw's famous witticism about two countries separated by a common language. Webster, though, saw not confusion but national and cultural unity. As early as 1783 he was declaring that "America must be as independent in *literature* as she is in *politics*." He hoped his language books would promote American unity and lead to the ratification of a strong national Constitution. "A national language," he wrote to a friend in May 1786, "is a national tie, and what country wants it more than America?"[22]

AFTER THE *INSTITUTE* he turned his attention to dictionary-making. Webster's first foray into lexicography was *A Compendious Dictionary of the English Language*, published in 1806. It was compiled, he wrote, "for my fellow citizens," and he wanted no truck with those readers "whose veneration for trans-atlantic authors leads them to hold American writers in unmerited contempt." He wanted Americans to be proud, and he drew attention to the words that were "either new in the United States" or more familiar "English words" that "have received a new sense" in the New World.

The *Compendious Dictionary* was a useful work for students, but it was hardly a major achievement—it certainly posed no threat to Johnson's dominance of the dictionary market. There were no etymologies or usage notes, and the definitions were skimpy, rarely more than a half-dozen words on a single line: "Language, *n.* all human speech, a tongue, a style"; "Music, *n.* harmony, the science of sound, musicians." Even the complicated polysemous verbs on which Johnson had lavished so much attention were dispensed with quickly: "Get, [g hard] *v.* gat, got, gotten, *pa.* to procure, gain, win, learn, arrive, induce"; "Take, *v.* took, *pret.* taken, *pa.* to receive, seize, trap, suppose, hire, please." A few thousand entries were new to dictionaries and unfamiliar in Britain, but the book wasn't as compendious as its title promised, and the definitions lacked the kind of rigor that Johnson brought to the language. As lexicologist Joseph H. Friend put it in surveying Webster's later achievements, his "reputation would have reached no such heights if it had been based entirely on his *Compendious Dictionary*." But even as the *Compendious* was being compiled, Webster was planning his masterwork, "a magnum opus," in Friend's words, "that would dwarf the *Compendious* and surpass even Johnson." After several decades of labor he finally finished what his biographer Harry Warfel calls "America's first monumental work of scholarship." *An American Dictionary of the English Language* appeared in 1828, and Webster's name has been synonymous with "dictionary" in America ever since.

The feud with Johnson is clear even on the title page of Webster's great work: he simply took Johnson's title, *A Dictionary of the English Language*, and ostentatiously inserted the word *American* at the beginning. And he tried to live up to that title first by adding a slew of distinctively American words to the lexicon— *tomato*, *squash*, *prairie*, *moose*—and German and Dutch words that were current among English speakers in Pennsylvania and New York, like *noodle* and *boss*. English lexicographers had derided many of these Americanisms, but Webster insisted they "form an essential part of our language." It wasn't for him to keep them out: "Such local terms exist, and will exist, in spite of lexicographers or critics. Is this *my* fault? And if local terms exist, why not explain them?"[23]

The preface to the *American Dictionary* even had the temerity to suggest that British readers should turn to Webster, not Johnson and his countrymen, if they wanted to know the true meanings of many words:

> The people of this country should have an *American Dictionary* of the English language. . . . A great number of words in our languages require to be defined in a phraseology accommodated to the condition and institutions of the people in these states, and the people of England must look to an American Dictionary for a correct understanding of such terms.[24]

This is because American and English institutions differed widely, and what made sense in one country was nonsense in another. Words like "*senate, congress, court, assembly, escheat,* &c.," he wrote, "are either words not belonging to the language of England, or they are applied to things in this country which do not exist in that." The British are useless as guides to these American institutions: "No person in this country will be satisfied with the English definitions of the words *congress*, *senate* and *assembly*, *court*, &c."

In practice, Webster owed a huge debt to Johnson, much larger than his rhetoric would suggest. In 1962, critic Joseph W. Reed took a sample of Webster's *Dictionary* and compared it with Johnson's. He found that "of all 4,505 definitions written by Webster" that he examined, "1,481, or about one third, were culled from Johnson or show clear signs of Johnson's influence. Since about 30 percent of Webster's words had not been treated by Johnson at all, the extent of verbal similarity is remarkable."[25] Fully 333 were copied from Johnson word for word, and nearly a thousand more were copied with only slight modifications. Webster also followed Johnson's practice of including short passages from great authors to show how each word was used in context—as Johnson wrote, and as Webster quoted, "The chief glory of a nation arises from its authors." Just as he borrowed definitions, he often lifted quotations from his predecessor: Reed's count shows that nearly two thirds of Webster's citations were taken from Johnson. But he didn't use Johnson uncritically, and in reworking the earlier dictionary he had the glory of his own nation in mind. He argued that too many of Johnson's quotations came from bad authors; in particular, Johnson erred in quoting Shakespeare so often, since "Play-writers . . . use low language, language unfit for decent company." (In a letter to a friend he voiced his objection to two of Johnson's favorite authors even more bluntly: "But Shakespeare and Butler used such words in their writings! ! !") Webster instead went out of his way to choose quotations from American authors. So out went many thousands of Johnson's quotations from Shakespeare, Milton, and Spenser, to be replaced by words of wisdom from American luminaries—he mentions Benjamin Franklin, George Washington, John Adams, John Jay, James Madison, Washington Irving, and others—admitting that "it is with pride and satisfaction, that I can place them . . . on the same page" with British worthies like Milton, Dryden, and Addison.[26]

WEBSTER FOUND ONE other unlikely way to create a distinctively American variety of English—by changing its spelling. Early in his career he toyed with schemes for rationalizing the notoriously quirky spelling of English words. In May 1786, for instance, he sent Franklin a "plan for the purpose of reducing the orthography of the language to perfect regularity," and in 1790 he put his spelling scheme into practice with *A Collection of Essays and Fugitiv Writings*. The several "Peeces," the preface advised, were "ritten at various times." Webster hoped that readers would forgive the "freedom of language," pleading that an impassioned "riter wil naturally giv himself up to hiz feelings, and hiz manner of *riting* wil flow from hiz manner of *thinking*."[27]

"Hiz manner of riting," though, was not received enthusiastically by most readers, and Webster eventually abandoned radical reform. But he never gave up his hope of reforming English spelling and, when he compiled his dictionaries, he introduced several hundred departures from British practice. Often he claimed that his preferred orthography was more ancient, more authentic, than the familiar British spellings. "I do not write *publick, republick*," he explained, "because the introduction of *k* was originally a useless innovation wholly unknown to the primitive English."[28] On other occasions he used etymology and analogy to decide on a spelling. He said that British *colour*, for instance, should be spelled like its Latin root, *color*. Besides, spellings should be consistent across all the forms of the word. The English wrote *honour, rigour*, and *labour* with *u*, but they wrote *honorific, rigorous*, and *laborious* without: in such cases, consistency demands we drop it everywhere. Why did words like *centre* and *theatre* end in *-re* when the pronunciation was clearly *-er*? The last syllable of *travel* is not accented, so the past tense should be *traveled*, not *travelled* as in Britain. And surely there's no need for the silent letters in words like *programme*, *axe*, *catalogue*, and *mould*. So out they went. Americans have been following his example ever since.[29]

Not all of Webster's proposed changes caught on. He had no luck driving the final *e* out of words like *determine* and *examine*. He thought *chemists* should be *chimists*, *porpoises* should be *porpesses*, and *acres* should be *akers*. He snarled that *heinous* is "an incorrect orthography" for the proper *hainous*, and that *island* is "an absurd compound," far from the "genuine English word" *ieland*.[30] And his plan to use U.S. law to enforce his spellings came to nothing. He told his friend John Canfield in 1783 that "the reformation of the language we speak will some time or other be thought an object of legislative importance," and even pleaded with Franklin to present his spelling reforms to Congress.[31] Elected officials, though, chose not to legislate the shape of the language, for Americans were no more ready for an academy than Britons had been. Still, we owe to Webster most of the spellings labeled "chiefly American" in modern dictionaries. Over the last three centuries, thousands of writers throughout the Anglophone world have proposed schemes for spelling reform, some ambitious, some modest. A very few scholars and critics have managed to convince the world to change a spelling or two here and there. No one, though, has had one tenth the lasting success of Noah Webster, to whom we can attribute many hundreds of distinctive spellings.

AND THAT SUCCESS came at an important time, for it was shortly after Webster's death in 1843 that America's population passed England's. Webster may have been born in an unimportant corner of Britain's empire, but America went on to assume its place at the head of what Winston Churchill called "the English-speaking peoples." America, no longer a colonial outpost, has become the center of a new World English. It is now the most populous English-speaking country on earth, with around a quarter of a billion speakers—the United States accounts for two out of every three native English speakers on the planet.

Webster foresaw the inevitability of this development long

before most Britons. As he wrote in a circular letter to "the Governors, Instructors, and Trustees of the Universities and Other Seminaries of Learning in the United States" in 1798, "North America is destined to be the seat of a people more numerous, probably, than any nation now existing with the same vernacular language, unless we except some Asiatic nations." (Here he seems to be echoing his old friend, Yale president Ezra Stiles, who predicted in 1770 that "the English will become the vernacular Tongue of more people than anyone Tongue ever was on Earth, except the Chinese.") Later predictions were even more grand: "The English language," he wrote in 1824, "will prevail over the whole of North America . . . and, according to the regular laws of population, it must, within two centuries, be spoken by three hundred millions of people on that continent."[32] As it happens, his prediction was not far off. The population of the United States recently passed the three hundred million mark, beating Webster's "two centuries" by about twenty years.

An astonishing number of those hundreds of millions read Webster's works. The *American Spelling Book*, known to generations as the "Blue-Back Speller" for the color of its wrapper, is to this day one of the bestselling schoolbooks in history: in 1837, Webster's own estimate put the total sales at around fifteen million copies, and it remained popular for another century. Webster's biographer Harry Warfel estimates a total of around a hundred million copies were sold.[33] The *American Reader* too was influential: even after William Holmes McGuffey's *Eclectic Readers* surpassed Webster's *American Reader* in sales, Webster's use of American history in reading books remained the norm. And if we include the multitudinous versions abridged, adapted, and derived from it, the *American Dictionary* of 1828 is one of the most popular books in the language. There are few literate households in America today without a copy of a dictionary bearing Webster's name. Even those who haven't read Webster's works firsthand have been influenced by him, and reveal that influence every time they put pen to paper. Webster's dictionaries—especially in the versions produced by George and Charles Merriam—continue to define

American English: most newspapers, magazines, and books in the country choose their preferred spellings from a descendant of *An American Dictionary of the English Language*.

It's a commonly held notion that America was founded on the written word. It was the Declaration of Independence—just 1,337 words and fifty-six signatures—that brought the United States into being; it was a written constitution that gave the nation its legal framework; and it was the eighty-five proselytizing essays of *The Federalist* that helped to make that constitution the law of the land. The list could be extended, for many of the founders were capable writers whose words have been scrutinized by generations of jurists, politicians, historians, and literary critics. While it may seem odd to group spelling books and grammars with these founding documents, Noah Webster deserves a place among America's founding writers. We may not be accustomed to thinking of dictionaries and spelling books as founding documents, but whether we like it or not, all Americans now speak what Webster was fond of calling the *American* language.

MANY BRITONS WERE predictably unhappy that colonial barbarians were presuming to teach English to the English. Objections to American style, which go back to the earliest settlements in the New World, became more common after Webster began campaigning for his American language. In an early nineteenth-century review of two biographies of George Washington, for instance, the anonymous reviewer for the *British Critic* groused about "the introduction of several new words," and fretted that this "deviation from the rules of the English language" would eventually "introduce confusion into the medium of intercourse." He encouraged Americans to develop "an entirely separate language as well as a government of their own." In 1810, John Lambert published recollections of his journey through Canada, in which he commented on the "Colloquial barbarisms" among the natives of North America. These verbal blemishes may be excusable among peasants, but "when they are used in composition by writers, they become disgusting." He thought the attempt to frame an American language was doomed: "unless they resort to the *Catabaw*, *Chactaw*, or *Kickapoo* dialects, I am sure they will never accomplish it by *murdering* the English language."[34]

These British complaints lasted long after Webster's death. America's domination of cinema and television helped to spread Americanisms around the world. One English writer deplored the American titles on silent films, dismissing them as "a *lingua franca*, or a *lingua californica*," and it only got worse in the era of talkies and television.[35] The griping goes on even now. When in 2007 London's *Daily Telegraph* asked readers to nominate "the worst phrases in the English language," many of the most galling came from "the incorporation of Americanisms into everyday speech"—and so popular was the contest that the newspaper published a *Dictionary of Annoying Phrases* in book form. A recent review in London's *Times* groans that the book under review is "full of grating Americanisms," and another in the *Guardian* asserts that American words like *helluva* and *goddamn* "infect the whole prose" of the book. And baseball metaphors leave the rest of the world baffled and irritated in equal measure: a recent article in the *Sunday Telegraph* asked, "Does anyone know what, or indeed where, left field is? I thought not. For your information it's a term derived from the American national sport of rounders, and another of those infuriating Americanisms . . . that have crept into our language."

It's not only angry editorial writers who bemoan those insidious American words. Lord Somers addressed the House of Lords in 1979: "If there is a more hideous language on the face of the earth than the American form of English," he demanded, "I should like to know what it is!" In 1995, even the Prince of Wales declared American English a "very corrupting influence." "We must act now," he advised his countrymen, "to insure that English—and that, to my way of thinking, means English English—maintains its position as the world language well into the next century."[36] (American and Canadian newspapers relished the opportunity to needle His Royal Highness with nonstandard English headlines:

BRITANNIA SHOULD RULE THE WORDS, SEZ CHAZ, proclaimed the *New York Daily News*. IT JUST AIN'T PROPER, said the *Courier-Mail*. GO WITH THE FLOW, CHUCK, editorialized the *Toronto Sun*.)

Despite all the complaining—or, to use a sense that first appeared in print in John Farmer's *Americanisms, Old and New* (1889)—despite all the bellyaching about America's baleful influence on proper English, even the most nativist of Britons have adopted a great many Americanisms into their language, though they're often unaware of it. In 1821, an English writer couldn't conceal his revulsion at the barbarisms and solecisms that defaced the language he loved:

> Nor have there been wanting projects among them for getting rid of the English language, not merely by barbarizing it—as when they *progress* a bill, *jeopardize* a ship, *guess* a probability, proceed by *grades*, hold a *caucus*, *conglaciate* a wave, &c. when the President of Yale College talks of a *conflagrative* brand, and President Jefferson of *belittling* the productions of nature—but also by abolishing the use of English altogether, and substituting a new language for their own.[37]

While *conglaciate* and *conflagrative* can hardly be called standard English today, *guessing*, proceeding by *grades*, and *belittling* are now spoken not only by renegade Yankees but by people everywhere. Londoners use them regularly, almost certainly unaware that they are American imports once branded illiterate. H. L. Mencken commented on the popularity of American words in England as early as 1923.[38] And shortly after the Second World War, when thousands of GIs were stationed in Britain—"overpaid, oversexed, and over here," as the usual charge went—London's *Daily Mail* published a list of words that were "positively incomprehensible" to English readers. The list included *commuter*, *seafood*, and *living room*—what were once impenetrable mysteries are now thoroughly naturalized British words.[39] Jonathan Lighter, a linguist, observes that "the common noun *guy* took two or three generations to overhaul the earlier *bloke* in Britain, Australia, and elsewhere, but the American term . . . is now familiar wherever English is spoken."[40]

ONE QUINTESSENTIALLY AMERICAN word may be the most recognized English word on the planet. Theories abound on the origin of *O.K.* or *okay*: it has been traced to the Scottish *och aye*, the French *aux quais*, the Choctaw *okeh*. Some are convinced it is an abbreviation of the Latin *omnis korrecta* or the Greek *ola kala* ("all is good"). Others point to Orrin Kendall, a Civil War–era manufacturer of baked goods whose initials appeared on his packages, or to an abbreviation for "zero killed," supposedly used in the Second World War. But in the early 1960s Columbia University professor Allen Walker Read established that it's a purebred Americanism. Read—who H. L. Mencken said "probably knows more about early Americanisms than anyone else on earth"—demonstrated that, in the late 1830s, newspaper editors in New York and Boston enjoyed reducing expressions to initials—*N.G.* for *no go*, *S.P.* for *small potatoes*, and *g.t.d.h.d.* for *give the devil his due*. They had even more fun by representing the initials of playful misspellings, such as *K.G.* for *no go* (*know go*) or *k.y.* for *no use* (*know yuse*). Early in 1839, the Boston *Morning Post* originated one of these facetious abbreviations, turning *all correct*—or *oll korrect*—into *O.K.* It went from being an in-joke among newspapermen to a familiar expression during the presidential campaign of 1840, when Martin Van Buren—nicknamed "Old Kinderhook" from the place of his birth—adopted "O.K." as a kind of slogan. The Democratic O.K. Club helped to spread the abbreviation across America.[41]

The terse *OK* caught on in the age of the telegraph, when people paid to transmit text by the word, and soon it was widespread across America. Its popularity was no doubt owing to its flexibility, which Richard Lederer, a popular writer on the English language, describes this way: "*OK* is so protean that it can function as five parts of speech—noun: 'I give it my OK'; verb: 'I'll OK it'; adjective: 'He's an OK guy'; adverb: 'She sings OK'; and interjection: 'OK, let's party!'"[42] By 1866, *O.K.* or *okay* had crossed the Atlantic and started to show currency in British speech and writing. It's now in nearly universal use in the United States, Great Britain, Ireland, Australia, New Zealand, Canada, South Africa, and everywhere else English is spoken. And not only where English is spoken: Lighter calls it "probably the most widely recognized Americanism on earth." It has made its way into hundreds of languages, and billions of people—many of whom could not construct an English sentence—casually drop *okay* into conversations in languages Samuel Johnson and Noah Webster had never heard of.

CHAPTER 7

Words, Words, Words

JAMES MURRAY SURVEYS ANGLICITY

"WHAT DO YOU READ, MY LORD?" asked Polonius, as the morose prince stared into a book. Hamlet's comically literal response: "Words, words, words." But the language Hamlet is imagined to have spoken, Danish, couldn't compare to the language of his creator, Shakespeare, in words, words, words. English now has a larger vocabulary than any other language. An English Hamlet would have plenty of words to read.

This English vocabulary was large even when the language had only a few tens of thousands of illiterate speakers who attracted no international attention. Starting around the year 500, tribes from north-central Europe began to settle in the British Isles. These tribes, known as the Angles, the Saxons, and the Jutes, spoke their own closely related Teutonic or Germanic languages; once they displaced the existing Celtic population to the outer edges of the British Isles, their speech began both to achieve a kind of unity among themselves and to drift from its Continental cousins, eventually resulting in a distinct language. Today we name that language after one of the tribes: the speech of the *Angles* was then called *Ænglisc* or *Englisc*, and their country was *Engel land*.

Things changed sharply after 1066, when the French-speaking Duke of Normandy—Guglielmus Dux Normanniae, better known in France as Guillaume le Conquérant and in England as William the Conqueror—invaded the country of the Angles and Saxons and defeated the English king, Harold II. French—one of the Romance languages, derived from Latin—became the official language of statecraft and jurisprudence throughout England. Over the next few generations the French-speaking victors consolidated their power by putting Francophones in all the positions of power in the English government. English survived, but it was peasant-speak.

This wasn't the first time one culture invaded another, but the linguistic outcome was unusual. In most cases where speakers of one language invade a land that speaks another, one of the two languages wins: either the invaders force the natives to adopt their language, or they give up their own language and adopt that of the conquered population. The "losing" language generally leaves a few traces on the dominant language, but only a few. In England, though, the story was different. After 1066, the nobles were virtually all French speakers, while the peasants continued to speak their Germanic tongue, Old English. And over the course of the next few centuries the two tongues began to blend with one another, eventually emerging as a new language, Middle English.

It stands to reason that English speakers would borrow French words to describe new phenomena for which they had no native words: *majesty* (first used around 1300), *manciple* (around 1230), and *mayor* (around 1260) lacked obvious English equivalents, so English speakers were forced to borrow the French words. Even more interesting were the borrowings from French when there were already good English words. The English had long been using the words *swin* or *swyn* (first written down around 725), *cu* (before 800), and *scep* (around 825) to refer to common barnyard animals. The newly arrived French speakers, though, used their own terms: around the year 1300, they began referring to the same animals as *porc*, *boef*, and *motoun*. All six of these words, as it happens, have survived into modern English, but now they have different meanings: *swine*, *cow*, and *sheep* refer to the living animals—which would have been the English-speaking peasants' experience of them—and *pork*, *beef*, and *mutton* to the meat that they provide, the only way the French-speaking aristocrats would have dealt with them.

The phenomenon extends far beyond barnyard animals and meat; with very few exceptions, when we have two related words from these two language families, the Germanic word is the lower one, more blunt, more direct; the word from the Romance languages is more refined, more elevated. Pairs like *sweat* (Germanic) and *perspire* (French), *want* and *desire*, *buy* and *purchase*, and *friendly* and *amicable* make the case. It's no coincidence that many of the crudities in our language are one-syllable Germanic words, while the euphemisms we use to replace them in polite conversation—*copulate*, *defecate*, *flatulence*—come from Latin or French.

THIS COPIOUSNESS GIVES us many reasons to rejoice. For centuries, English speakers felt inadequate, and worried that their language didn't have the full expressive potential of Latin or French. Sheer numbers put that fear to rest—if something can be said, it can be said in English. But being relieved of one problem has led us into another: how to deal with all these words, these synonyms and near synonyms in their tens of thousands? Sorting through such a vast vocabulary is daunting.

An anonymous manuscript from the seventeenth century, "An Essay towards a New English Dictionary," was one of the earliest attempts to sort out words with similar meanings, but it never made it into print. More successful was John Trusler's *Difference, between Words, Esteemed Synonymous, in the English Language; and, the Proper Choice of Them Determined*, published in two volumes in 1766. A typical entry gives several related words— "*Grave, Serious, Staid*"—and explains the differences in application: "We are *staid*, through discretion and custom; *grave*, thro' humour and constitution; *serious*, thro' taste and affectation."[1]

An even more influential work followed a few decades later. In 1794, Hester Thrale Piozzi—a close friend of Samuel Johnson's, one of his earliest biographers, and one of the most learned women of her age—published two thick volumes titled *British Synonymy; or, An Attempt at Regulating the Choice of Words in Familiar Conversation*. There she offered advice for writers and speakers who wanted to use words more precisely. A typical entry is headed "DUCTILE, FLEXIBLE, SOFT, YIELDING, PLIABLE, MALLEABLE":

> The first of these is I know not why chiefly appropriated by books, and even used more when writing about things than persons. . . . I think the word very happy when applied to temper; however the hard as solid wise-ones of this world despise a FLEXIBLE disposition, and take advantage of a SOFT and YIELDING one. PLIABLE seems somehow referable more to body than to mind. . . . [2]

The examples keep coming, through many hundreds of seemingly interchangeable words.

After Piozzi, the flood—William Taylor published *English Synonyms Discriminated* in 1813; three years later, George Crabb released the first edition of his *English Synonyms Explained, in Alphabetical Order: With Copious Illustrations and Examples Drawn from the Best Writers*, often reprinted over the next half century. John Platts published *A Dictionary of English Synonyms* in 1825; Johann August Heinrich Tittmann et alia published a biblical study aid called *Remarks on the Synonyms of the New Testament* in 1833. Synonymies had become a publishing phenomenon.

As popular as these synonymies were in the early nineteenth century, though, they're entirely forgotten today, overshadowed by a much more influential and lasting work. The greatest English work on synonyms appeared in 1852, written by a man whose character is summed up well in the original *Dictionary of National Biography* of 1897: "Roget, Peter Mark (1779–1869), physician and savant."

WHEN ROGET WAS young, his family moved often; without regular schooling, the boy had to educate himself. As an eight-year-old he began his lifelong habit of writing lists—notebooks containing Latin words and their English translations, for instance. Before long the autodidact had become proficient in French, Italian, German, and Latin. His real interests, though, had little to do with words. At the age of fourteen, Roget began to study medicine at the University of Edinburgh, one of the world's finest medical schools. He distinguished himself, and in June 1798 completed his medical training with a thesis titled "De chemicae affinitatis legibus," or "On the Laws of Chemical Affinity." As a young doctor he enjoyed a reputation as a man of learning, corresponding with influential scientists and scholars including Erasmus Darwin (grandfather of Charles), Humphry Davy, Samuel Romilly, and Jeremy Bentham.

Roget adored grand schemes for public improvement: he investigated the causes of consumption; he worked with Bentham on improving London's sewage system; he even proposed a machine called a *frigidarium* to preserve food, an idea that would be realized decades later as the refrigerator. His experiments on the persistence of images on the retina paved the way for motion pictures. He was a pioneering computer scientist long before the first computer was built, working to design a calculating machine in correspondence with Charles Babbage. These plans were so far ahead of their time that they produced no practical results, but he also brought a number of useful inventions to fruition, including a new kind of slide rule and a sophisticated balance scale.

From 1804 to 1806 Roget served as private physician to William Petty, Lord Shelburne, 2nd Marquess of Lansdowne, who had once been Britain's prime minister. In 1808 he settled in London to begin a medical practice, and within a year was admitted to the Royal College of Physicians. His public lectures on animal physiology in Bloomsbury drew enthusiastic audiences. His book of 1833, *Animal and Vegetable Physiology Considered with Reference to Natural Theology*, offered a theory of the natural adaptation of organisms that anticipated Charles Darwin's *Origin of Species* by three decades. And in 1834 came his career-topping appointment to the Fuller professorship of physiology at the Royal Institution.

After a long career in medicine, Roget retired in 1840, at the age of sixty-one, and turned his attention back to a project that had intrigued him decades earlier. In 1805, when he was still in his twenties, he had begun jotting notes about words in his many notebooks, hoping to devise a method for classifying the riches of the English vocabulary. Over the years he "found this little collection, scanty and imperfect as it was, of much use to [him] in literary composition," and he resolved to make it equally useful to the rest of the world, so that "every one should acquire the power and habit of expressing his thoughts with perspicuity and correctness."[3] In his retirement, then, he devoted more and more time to this plan to classify all the words in the language, and he immersed himself in other schemes to classify vocabularies: Piozzi's *British Synonymy*, Joseph de Maimieux's *Pasigraphie*, and even the *Amarakosha*, or "immortal collection," of a fourth-century Sanskrit poet and grammarian.

From 1849 to 1852 he devoted all his time to his own word book, corresponding with his publisher, Longman, Brown, Green, and Longmans, the descendant of the Longman firm that in 1755 had copublished Johnson's *Dictionary*. It wasn't easy work: it "has given me incessant occupation," he recalled, "and has, indeed, imposed upon me an amount of labour very much greater than I had anticipated."[4] As it was nearing completion, Roget decided to use as his title a Greek word that meant *treasury*. The word had been used for reference books before, as when Henri Estienne (also known by his Latin name, Henricus Stephanus) published a huge four-volume dictionary, the *Thesaurus linguae graecae*, or "Treasury of the Greek Language," in 1572. Roget thought "treasury" was the perfect description of his new kind of reference book, and ever since then the word *thesaurus* has been used to refer to Roget's most famous invention.

On January 17, 1852, Longman published his *Thesaurus of English Words and Phrases, Classified and Arranged So as to Facilitate the Expression of Ideas and Assist in Literary Composition.* It cost fourteen shillings and initially had a modest press run of one thousand copies. But its success resulted in twenty-seven further printings before Roget's death in 1869; he left an enlarged edition for his son to publish a decade later; and then, through the first half of the twentieth century, even more editions were edited by his grandson. Roget's name joins those of Johnson and Webster as probably the only three lexicographers' names familiar to most English speakers.

ROGET'S LABORS SHOW an era coming to grips with the overwhelming extent of the English vocabulary. And his work could never be finished, because English was a moving target, constantly expanding—especially during Roget's century. The English language got bigger in the nineteenth century because the world got bigger in the nineteenth century. It was an age of social upheaval, giving us words like *Americanization* (1830) and *abortionist* (1872). It was an age of technological development, giving us *locomotive* (1829) and *anæsthetize* (1848). The *hydrocarbon* was first named by Michael Faraday in 1826; *gasolene* is attested from 1865; the *electron* received its name in 1891. A less abstruse application of technology was the *bicycle*, a word that first showed up in the *Daily News* in 1868, as a correspondent reported on the "Bysicles and trysicles which we saw in the Champs Elysées and Bois de Boulogne this summer."

The *ichthyosaurus* was identified in excavations in 1832, and scientific exploration on a different scale produced the new word *amoeba* in 1841. Most of the exploring, though, was being done not with the shovel or the microscope but with the sailing vessel. Britannia ruled the nineteenth-century waves, and as British explorers spanned the globe, they found new plants and animals that needed names. The botanist William Forsyth gave his name to the *forsythia* in 1846, and Charles Darwin was the first to import the Arabic and Spanish word *alfalfa* for "a kind of clover" he discovered in 1845 (he spelled it *alfarfa*). Darwin was also the first to coin the word *creationist* for those who found his theories hard to swallow. Explorers in India discovered a small mammal they called a *gerbil* in 1849. Travelers to Australia learned the word *kangaroo* late in the eighteenth century; in 1839 they learned to call the young of the species a *joey*. The study of these animals prompted the new words *herbivore* and *carnivore* in 1854, *insectivore* in 1863, and for the very hungry, *omnivore* in 1871.

As the British shifted their role from explorers to colonial administrators, they continued the business of importing words. The Raj gave them Hindi words like *pundit* (1816) and *thug* (1810), while British ventures in Africa produced *safari* (imported from Swahili in 1860). Some of these discoveries abroad were the result of beneficial cultural exchanges: in 1820, William Ward's *View of the History, Literature, and Religion of the Hindoos* introduced the West to *yoga*; Anglophones got their first tastes of *chutney* in 1813 and *korma* in 1832. Less peaceful encounters with the exotic East gave us *mujahidin* in 1887 and *kamikaze* in 1896 (seven years before the invention of the airplane). An already copious language was growing quickly.

THE VASTNESS OF the English vocabulary was on many minds in 1857, when Richard Chenevix Trench, an up-and-coming Irish clergyman and a dedicated logophile, addressed the Philological Society of London, a learned society devoted to the study of language. Like many others, he thought it was time to reduce the messy language to some semblance of order. Johnson and Webster had done a remarkable job in their pioneering dictionaries, but their books weren't comprehensive. They inevitably missed many thousands of words through inattention, and they couldn't include thousands of other words that had entered the language since their deaths. Their dictionaries, moreover, weren't compiled on historical principles—they didn't show when each word first entered the language, how root words ramified into different meanings, and how spellings shifted over time. Fixing these problems was the point of his address to the Philological Society.

Trench opened his lecture with a catalog of grievances about the state of English lexicography in the middle of the nineteenth century. "Our Dictionaries then appear to me," he declared, "deficient in the following points"—and followed up with seven numbered objections. The first: "I. Obsolete words are incompletely registered; some inserted, some not; with no reasonable rule adduced for the omission of these, the insertion of those other." Then came "II. Families or groups of words are often imperfect, some members of a family inserted, while others are omitted." Number III was that "Much earlier examples of the employment of words oftentimes exist than any which are cited; indicating that they were introduced at an earlier date into the language than these examples would imply."

Having criticized their failings as historical dictionaries, Trench moved on to their definitions, quotations, and word lists: "IV. Important meanings and uses of words are passed over; sometimes the later alone given, while the earlier, without which the history of words will be often maimed and incomplete, or even unintelligible, are unnoticed." The next may have been influenced by Roget's recently published work: "V. Comparatively little attention is paid to the distinguishing of synonymous words." He also had the illustrative quotations in mind: "VI. Many passages in our literature are passed by, which might be usefully adduced in illustrations." Finally came Number VII: "our Dictionaries err in redundancy as well as in defect, in the too much as well as the too little; all of them inserting some things, and some of them many things, which have properly no claim to find room in their pages." He therefore called for an inventory of the English language, and insisted that the editor's job was "to make his inventory complete."[5]

Producing that complete inventory would not be simple. The original plan called for a supplement to the dictionary of either Johnson or Webster, but the members of the committee soon realized that a supplement would be longer than the work it was supplementing. It was time for an entirely new work, and the Philological Society committee decided to go ahead with what they called *A New English Dictionary on Historical Principles*.

History has chosen a different title: once the publishing responsibilities were assumed by Oxford University Press, *A New English Dictionary* came to be known as *The Oxford English Dictionary*. It may be the world's most famous dictionary.

THE FIRST EDITOR of the new project was Herbert Coleridge, grandson of the famous poet, chosen for the job when he was still in his twenties. His *Glossarial Index to the Printed English Literature of the Thirteenth Century* promised great things, and he thought publication of the new dictionary could begin in as little as two years—"unless," he wrote, "any unforeseen accident should occur to paralyse our efforts." But the unforeseen accident did befall him, and he never had the chance to prove himself: almost before he could dip his pen in ink, Coleridge died of tuberculosis in 1861, just a few months past his thirtieth birthday.

Next up was Frederick Furnivall, an English lawyer who was one of the early and energetic members of the Philological Society, in which he served as secretary for more than half a century. Furnivall was passionate about societies, committees, and working groups of every sort: he founded the Early English Text Society, the Chaucer Society, the Ballad Society, the New Shakspere Society, the Browning Society, the Wyclif Society, and the Shelley Society. In these organizations he showed tremendous energy. Under his direction, the Early English Text Society issued around 250 editions of long-neglected works; without this scholarly legwork, the *OED* would have been impossible.

Despite his fondness for societies, though, Furnivall could be painfully antisocial. The bristly lawyer was a difficult colleague with a unique talent for making enemies. He found himself engaged in high-profile spats with members of his own organizations, as when he tried to blackball the common-law husband of Karl Marx's daughter from the Shelley Society. His work with the Early English Text Society, while copious and groundbreaking, could be sloppy; his passion for quantity meant that quality suffered. The same carelessness marked his work on the *OED*—he transcribed quotations inaccurately, failed to identify sources, and had a frustrating habit of losing paperwork. It's just as well that he never managed the project as a whole. He helped to design the layout of the dictionary, to settle many of its early policies, and to line up some of the original volunteers who did much of the work on what became the *OED*. Furnivall described the ongoing project as "a National Portrait Gallery, not only of the worthies, but of all the members, of the race of English words which is to form the dominant speech of the world."[6] But it would be someone else who painted the portraits.

THE NEW DICTIONARY, everyone realized, would require someone with Furnivall's energy and learning, but with far more organizational skill, attention to detail, and tact in dealing with contributors. Where to find such an editor? In 1876 Alexander Macmillan asked that question of friends and acquaintances, and one name came up several times. In April of that year he wrote a letter asking for the opportunity to discuss the project with a young Scottish schoolmaster, James A. H. Murray.

Murray was an impressive autodidact who, by the age of six, "had begun to hunt out strange words such as Latin and Greek in any books he could lay his hands on, and he copied them out on scraps of paper without knowing their meaning." Soon he added the Hebrew alphabet to his list of accomplishments. When, at the age of seven, he saw a Chinese translation of a passage from the Bible, he began trying to understand the logic of the characters. As his granddaughter later recorded, "He copied this many times in a scrawly hand until he had identified the characters for such words as beginning, God, word, light, life, witness, man and so on. . . . Years afterwards he could still write these characters from memory." As an adult he recollected his childish "mania for learning languages; every new language was a new delight, no matter what it was, Hebrew or Tongan, Russian or Caffre, I swallowed them all." He even boasted, "I at one time or another could read in a sort of way 25 or more languages."[7]

The amateur's passion needed to be channeled more constructively, and so he strove to be more disciplined in his approach to language. He began studying Old English and soon become entirely absorbed in Anglo-Saxon language, literature, and culture. Even his children were given Old English names. Harold and Hilda may not have thought their names too out of place in late Victorian England, but Elsie, Wilfrid, Oswyn, Ethelbert, Aelfric, Ethelwyn, and Rosfrith may have come to regret their father's Saxon enthusiasm.

Murray had heard about the plans for a new dictionary but hadn't become involved until Macmillan approached him. Negotiations went well; he met the delegates of Oxford University Press and on March 1, 1879, was offered the job. "I wanted to see an ideal Dictionary," he later recalled, "& to show what I meant by one."[8] We sometimes need reminders that the person behind the OED was still a young man: Murray is best known from a famous photograph of him in the Scriptorium, with a gloriously long, white Victorian beard worthy of Albus Dumbledore. But he was only forty-two when he took on the task, and he brought to it learning, patience, and almost superhuman energy. This was the man charged with surveying the entire extent of the English language.

JUST HOW BIG was Murray's task?—or, to put it another way, just how large is the English vocabulary? The president of the Global Language Monitor, Paul J. J. Payack, recently issued the following declaration:

> I now unequivocally state that as of 1:16 p.m. (Pacific) on the 20th day of January in the year 2008 AD . . . there were approximately 995,116 words in the English language, plus or minus a handful.

He added that the list "should have reached the 1,000,000th word mark by the time you read these words."[9] But the facetious precision of the claim is a giveaway. Linguist and lexicographer Jeremy Butterfield puts it well: "This is a question to which people unfailingly expect dictionary writers to know the answer—as if it is something that can be measured precisely, like the length of the Nile or the height of Mount Everest." In fact, he writes, "it's impossible to quantify English vocabulary with any precision."[10]

No one can plausibly estimate the number of English words because there's little agreement over the meaning of the word *word*. We might want to define a word as a string of letters, but words that happen to share a spelling aren't always considered the same word. *Bass* for a low note and *bass* for a fish, or *wind* the noun meaning breeze and *wind* the verb meaning twist, have completely separate histories; they share spellings only through historical accident and are therefore treated as different words in most dictionaries. Even when words have shared histories, they may get separate entries if they've branched off in different directions. Conversely, words with variant spellings are usually grouped together: *color* and *colour*, *chaperon* and *chaperone*, *realize* and *realise*. The inflected forms of a word—*book*, *books*; *happy*, *happier*, *happiest*; *shade*, *shades*, *shaded*, *shading*—are usually lumped together, though derived forms like *bookish*, *happiness*, and *shady* are usually treated as separate words. Still, these policies aren't universal, and different dictionaries take different approaches.

One characteristic feature of English makes it difficult to count all the words: anyone has the power to create new words simply by adding prefixes and suffixes. The suffix *-ness*, for instance, can turn almost any adjective into a noun, with words like *skinniness*, *tiredness*, and *redness*. Add *-er* or *-or* to most verbs and you have a new noun: *condemner, digger, aspirer*. You can virtually double the number of adjectives and adverbs by including *un-* or *non-* forms, just as you can turn many thousands of nouns into adjectives with suffixes like *-y*, *-ish*, or *-esque*. The combinatorial possibilities are vast, and many of the resulting words haven't made their way into dictionaries. It's easy to cobble together perfectly recognizable words that few dictionaries bother to include: *unchairlike, debutantish, carpetless, pseudoromantically, forgeryproof* (none of these five is recognized by my computer's spelling checker).

The meanings of most of these words are obvious to anyone

who knows the roots, and therefore don't usually need to be cataloged. When Samuel Johnson was at work on his *Dictionary* in the 1750s, he realized that there would be no end to such combinations, and wrote that, although he tried to include as many words as possible, "Words arbitrarily formed by a constant and settled analogy, like diminutive adjectives in *ish*, as *greenish*, *bluish*, adverbs in *ly*, as *dully*, *openly*, substantives in *ness*, as *vileness*, *faultiness*, were less diligently sought, and many sometimes have been omitted." That's probably the only reasonable policy to follow in most dictionaries, but it leaves open the question of just how many words there should be in a comprehensive inventory. Likewise with compound words, which also require judgment calls. "Compounded or double words I have seldom noted," Johnson wrote, "except when they obtain a signification different from that which the components have in their simple state." Words like *thieflike* and *coachdriver*, he said, didn't need definitions, "because the primitives contain the meaning of the compounds."[11] But even if you know the words *highway* and *man*, you won't be able to figure out *highwayman* without extra help.

What about foreign words? Everyone agrees that once-exotic words like the Greek *philosophia*, the French *ricochet*, the German *Kindergarten*, and the Yiddish *beygel* have now become naturalized English words, sometimes after undergoing minor spelling adjustments. Everyone also agrees that some words are unambiguously foreign, even if they may appear from time to time in English works: the French *lettre de cachet* and the German *Waldsterben*, for instance. But what about those in the middle ground? Is the Arabic *jihad* an English word yet? The German *Schadenfreude*? The Russian *glasnost*? What about foreign units of currency? Do we say yes to the British *pound*, the Swiss *franc*, and the Chinese *yuan*, but no to the Thai *baht*, the Ethiopian *birr*, and the Gambian *butut*? Different communities will be familiar with different foreign vocabularies: every New Yorker knows to call a corner grocery by its Spanish term *bodega*, though people in rural Idaho, Yorkshire, or New South Wales may never have heard the word.

Words can be limited not only in space but also in time: some

Before the invention of printing with movable type, each copy of a work had to be copied by hand. This leaf comes from an English Bible, translated by John Wycliffe, probably from the late fourteenth century.

Liber septimus

Capitulum 28

Han truwes were take for thre yere bytwene kyng richard & the soudan / & hubert bisshop of Salesbury yede to the sepulcre for hym self / and for the kyng and offred there an hooly oost / and cam thennes and sayled with the kynge to Cypres / Thennes the kynge sent forth to Sicile twey quenes / his wyf / and his suster neygh with al his meyne / and he myght not wel endure in the softe see / but he sayled with a strong wynde toward the countray of hystria with fewe men / and was dryuen til that he cam bytwene Aquila & Venyse / & ther he houed & blewnt hider and thyder / & hyd hym somwhat of tyme & men made grete pursueaunce of bytayles for hym / and so he was aspyed and? take of the dukes men of Austryche / whan that was knowen the kynge of fraunce made Iohan kyng Rychardes broder to torne lyghtly agaynst kyng rychard / and wryted? also themperour of almayn agaynst kyng rychard / than themperour made couenaunt with the duk of austryche for to haue the thyrdde part of the prouffyte & wynnyng that come of kyng rychard and? had? kyng rychard in to his owne warde / yet whyle kyng rychard bare the crosse and the sygne of our lord / And the emperour putte hym in a place that is called Trpuallis / there arystotle seith it were good a man to see his owne fader / but about palmsonday themperour brought forth kyng rychard to yeue his answer before many lordes of the emperours land / and he cam forth with so glad chere & answerd to alle thynge that was putte agaynst hym / that the Emperour was bowed not only to mercy / but also for to do hym grete reuerence & worship / than cam to the kyng that was so holden Wil liam bisshop of hely that was put oute of englond for his grete extorcions & outrages / he cam to the king for to espye what Wil the kyng had to hym ward? / & whanne he myght not begyle the king with gyle of blynde flateryng he had? euyl trust to hym self and torned agayne to fraunce with hoope of grace / But Hubert bisshop of Salesbury come oute of Sicile to the kynge and was sente in to englond? for gouernyng of the Royame and? also for to spede the kynges raunsone whan he was comen in to englond? he was chosen archebisshop by assent of the monkes of Caunter bury and? of the bisshops / and noo wonder / he toke the pal & and? was stalled? / and? toke anone the habyte of Chanon at

Around the year 1450 Johannes Gutenberg, a goldsmith, developed movable type, a technique that allowed the production of many copies of a work in just a fraction of the time required to copy a manuscript.

By the time Benjamin Franklin worked as a printer in the early eighteenth century, nearly three hundred years after Gutenberg's invention, literacy rates had increased sharply and a new world of "print culture" was emerging.

and all worldly Honour ; for ſo it will become us
to do, for the unmerited Favours conferred upon,
honoured Sir,

Your moſt dutiful Servant.

LETTER CXV.

*Another for Favours of not ſo high, yet of a
generous Nature.*

Worthy Sir,

I Should appear ungrateful, if I did not add this further Trouble to thoſe I have already given you, of
acknowledging your Goodneſs to me, in this laſt In-
ſtance of it. May God Almighty return to you, Sir,
an hundred-fold, the Benefit you have conferr'd
upon me, and give me Opportunity, by my future
Services, to ſhew my grateful Heart, and how much
I am, worthy Sir,

Your for ever obliged and dutiful Servant.

LETTER CXVI.

*An Excuſe to a Perſon who wants to borrow
Money.*

S I R,

I AM very ſorry, that your Requeſt comes to me
at a time when I am ſo preſs'd by my own Affairs,
that I cannot with any Conveniency comply with it.
I hope, Sir, you will therefore excuſe

Your moſt humble Servant.

L E T-

The printer and novelist Samuel Richardson offered advice to would-
be letter writers in *One Hundred and Seventy-Three Letters Written for
Particular Friends on the Most Important Occasions.*

JOHN DRYDEN.

John Dryden (top), the greatest poet of late-seventeenth-century England, was among the first to be self-conscious about proper English. Joseph Priestley, a chemist, educator, and radical politician, wrote one of the first English grammars for native English speakers.

Rev. Joseph Priestley,
LLD - F.R.S.

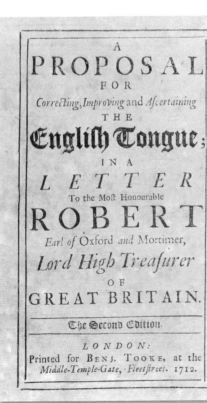

The satirist and poet Jonathan Swift was among the most vocal in calling for an academy to regulate English usage in *A Proposal for Correcting, Improving and Ascertaining the English Tongue* (1712).

The American Spelling Book.	Published,	1783	to	....
A Comprehensive Dictionary.	Published,	1806	to	1837
An American Dictionary.	Published,	1828	to	1846
An American Dictionary.	Published,	1847	to	1863
The same with Supplement.	Published,	1850	to	1863

NOAH WEB
Born 1758—Died
"The Schoolmaster of t

Noah Webster staked an American claim on the English language. His spellers, his readers, and especially his *American Dictionary*, read by tens of millions of students, earned him the title "Schoolmaster of the Republic."

An American Dictionary, (the well known "Unabridged")
—a complete revision. Published, 1864- . . . .
The same with Supplement and Biographical Dictionary.
Published, 1879- . . . .
The same with Gazetteer of the World. Published, 1884- . . . .
Webster's International Dictionary.—a complete revision.
Published, 189

Lindley Murray

{ SECOND EDITION,
  June 24, 1879.

AN APPEAL

TO THE

ENGLISH-SPEAKING AND ENGLISH-READING PUBLIC

TO READ BOOKS AND MAKE EXTRACTS FOR

THE PHILOLOGICAL SOCIETY'S

NEW ENGLISH DICTIONARY.

IN November 1857, a paper was read before the Philological Society by Archbishop Trench, then Dean of Westminster, on 'Some Deficiencies in our English Dictionaries,' which led to a resolution on the part of the Society to prepare a Supplement to the existing Dictionaries supplying these deficiencies. A very little work on this basis sufficed to show that to do anything effectual, not a mere Dictionary-Supplement, but a new Dictionary worthy of the English Language and of the present state of Philological Science, was the object to be aimed at. Accordingly, in January 1859, the Society issued their 'Proposal for the publication of a New English Dictionary,' in which the characteristics of the proposed work were explained, and an appeal made to the English and American public to assist in collecting the raw materials for the work, these materials consisting of quotations illustrating the use of English words by all writers of all ages and in all senses, each quotation being made on a uniform plan on a half-sheet of notepaper, that they might in due course be arranged and classified alphabetically and by meanings. This Appeal

The American grammarian Lindley Murray (top) wrote one of the most influential guides to English syntax at the end of the eighteenth century. Another Murray—Sir James—had an even greater influence in compiling the great *Oxford English Dictionary*.

DIRECTIONS TO READERS FOR THE DICTIONARY.

1. Write on a half-sheet of note-paper in accordance with the following models.

2. Give date of your book (if you can), author, title (short); give an *exact reference*, such as seems to you to be the best to enable any one to verify your quotation.

3. In *poetry*, as a rule, quote by *name* of piece, *Book, Canto*, and *Stanza*, or *line*; or in a play by *Act, Scene, line*. These references will serve for all editions.

4. In *prose* quote by *Vol., Book, Chap., Section*, and *page* (as far as the work is so divided—most books have *chapters*, and all have *pages*), and *name the edition* if not the first: thus
1849. J. S. MILL, *Logic*, Bk. III. ch. xiv. § 35. p. 17 (ed. 1856).

*5. Make a quotation for *every* word that strikes you as rare, obsolete, old-fashioned, new, peculiar, or used in a peculiar way.

6. Take special note of passages which show or imply that a word is either new and tentative, or needing explanation as obsolete or archaic, and which thus help to fix the date of its introduction or disuse.

*7. Make *as many* quotations *as convenient to you* for ordinary words, when these are used significantly, and help by the context to explain their own meaning, or show their use.

8. Carefully preserve the spelling, capitals, etc. of the original.

From Dr. Murray (4/1/81) Mill Hill, London. N.W.

Dear Madam, I shall be pleased to hear what progress you have made with the reading you kindly undertook for the Dictionary and by what early date I may rely upon receiving your valued contributions. This is the last year that we can devote to the General Reading and we are making an appeal to all Readers to help us to the utmost of their abilities during the remaining time. Kindly send what you have ready, and finish the remainder as soon as ever you can. Yours very truly, James A. H. Murray

Organizing hundreds of staff members and thousands of volunteer readers over the course of decades kept Murray busy, issuing directions and coordinating the reading project.

THE
DISTINCTION
BETWEEN
WORDS ESTEEMED SYNONYMOUS
IN THE
ENGLISH LANGUAGE,
POINTED OUT,
AND THE PROPER CHOICE OF THEM
DETERMINED.

Useful to all who would either write or speak with
Propriety and Elegance.

By the Rev. Dr. JOHN TRUSLER.

IN TWO VOLUMES.

THE THIRD EDITION,
WITH ADDITIONS AND AMENDMENTS.

VOL. I.

LONDON:
Printed for the AUTHOR;
And Sold by J. Parsons, Paternoster-Row, and
all Bookfellers.
M,DCC,XCIV.

BRITISH SYNONYMY;
OR,
AN ATTEMPT
AT
REGULATING THE CHOICE OF WORDS
IN
FAMILIAR CONVERSATION.

INSCRIBED,
With Sentiments of Gratitude and Refpect, to fuch of her
Foreign Friends as have made Englifh Literature
their peculiar Study,

BY

HESTER LYNCH PIOZZI.

IN TWO VOLUMES.
VOL. II.

LONDON:
PRINTED FOR G. G. AND J. ROBINSON, PATERNOSTER-ROW.
MDCCXCIV.

John Trusler and Hester Piozzi sorted through thousands of words of
similar meaning and produced two of the eighteenth century's most
important synonymies, predecessors to *Roget's Thesaurus*.

G Washington

A

DICTIONARY

OF THE

ENGLISH LANGUAGE:

IN WHICH

THE WORDS ARE DEDUCED FROM THEIR ORIGINALS;

AND

ILLUSTRATED IN THEIR DIFFERENT SIGNIFICATIONS,

BY

EXAMPLES FROM THE BEST WRITERS.

TO WHICH ARE PREFIXED,

A HISTORY OF THE LANGUAGE,

AND AN

ENGLISH GRAMMAR.

BY SAMUEL JOHNSON, L.L.D.

IN TWO VOLUMES.

VOL. I.

Cum tabulis animum cenforis fumet honefti :
Audebit quæcunque parùm fplendoris habebunt,
Et fine pondere erunt, et honore indigna ferentur,
Verba movere loco ; quamvis invita recedant,
Et verfentur adhuc intra penetralia Veftæ.
Obfcurata diu populo bonus eruet, atque
Proferet in lucem fpeciofa vocabula rerum,
Quæ prifcis memorata Catonibus atque Cethegis
Nunc fitus informis premit, et deferta vetuftas.   Hor.

LONDON:

PRINTED BY JOHN JARVIS, AND SOLD BY JOHN FIELDING, Nº. 23, PATERNOSTER-ROW.

MDCCLXXXVI.

Samuel Johnson's *Dictionary* was a monumental tribute both to English and to England, but even so devoted an American patriot as George Washington owned the eighteenth century's most important dictionary.

I. SELECTED LIST OF AMENDED SPELLINGS

ake	ache 1	harang	harangue 12
aile	aisle 2	hight	height 20
agast	aghast 3	indetted	indebted 16
alfabet	alphabet 4	iland	island 2
autograf	autograph 4	ile	isle 2
autum	autumn 5	lam	lamb 15
bedsted	bedstead 6	leag	league 12
bibliografy	bibliography 4	lim	limb 15
biografy	biography 4	num	numb 15
boro	borough 7	pamflet	pamphlet 4
bild	build 8	paragraf	paragraph 4
bilding	building 8	fonetic	phonetic 4
campain	campaign 9	fonograf	phonograph 4
camfor	camphor 4	fotograf	photograph 4
quire	choir 10	tisic	phthisic 21
cifer	cipher 4	tisis	phthisis 21
coco	cocoa 11	procede	proceed 18
colleag	colleague 12	redout	redoubt 16
colum	column 5	redoutable	redoubtable 16
condit	conduit 8	redouted	redoubted 16
counterfit	counterfeit 13	sent	scent 22
curteous	courteous 14	sion	scion 22
curtesy	courtesy 14	sissors	scissors 22
crum	crumb 15	sithe	scythe 22
det	debt 16	siv	sieve 23
dettor	debtor 16	slight	sleight 20
diafram	diaphragm 4, 9	solem	solemn 5
dout	doubt 16	soveren	sovereign 9
dum	dumb 15	succede	succeed 18
eg	egg 17	surfit	surfeit 13
excede	exceed 18	telegraf	telegraph 4
foren	foreign 9	telefone	telephone 4
forfit	forfeit 13	thum	thumb 15
furlo	furlough 7	tung	tongue 12
gastly	ghastly 3	wier	weir 24
gost	ghost 3	wierd	weird 24
gard	guard 19	yoman	yeoman 25
gardian	guardian 19		

Charles Payson Gurley Scott's *Simplification of English Spelling*, published by the Simplified Spelling Board in 1908, was one of dozens of proposals for rationalizing English orthography.

George Bernard Shaw campaigned for a more logical spelling system, with frustratingly little success. The arrival of electronic computers, signaled by ENIAC, has probably done more to alter spelling habits than the efforts of hundreds of educators.

Stand-up comic George Carlin became famous, and infamous, on the strength of his raucous catalog of words you can't say on television—a list that was then adopted by the Federal Communications Commission.

English words have been used continuously for fifteen hundred years, but many blossom, flourish for a few decades or centuries, and then fade away, no longer deserving a place in a general English dictionary. The word *book* was first used around the year A.D. 900, making it eleven hundred years old—but it's still in everyday use, even in the Internet age, and will likely be with us for centuries more, even if printed paper will someday be found only in antique shops. But around the same time that *book* appeared in English, the verb *forlet* was also introduced, meaning "To allow; to abandon; to leave someone helpless; to leave land uncultivated; to leave off or renounce." It was used for seven centuries, but eventually petered out around 1600. Few would consider it an English word today, even though it had that distinction for seven hundred years.

How obsolete does a word have to be before it's dropped from the language? Few people say *thou* or *dost* today in casual conversation, but the words appear in prayers and hymns; even though they're obsolete, they're still useful enough to be considered part of the language. Other archaisms—*alack*, *betwixt*, *forsooth*, *mayhap*, *quoth*, *thither*—might still be used in poetry or historical fiction, and certainly show up in older works that moderns read. But what about really obsolete and obscure words like *baccated*, *minchen*, or *zyxt*? And it's not only old words that present problems. Slang is notoriously difficult to catalog—new words and expressions can come and go in a few years, even a few months. Most lexicographers are hesitant to include new examples of slang for fear they'll be forgotten by the time their dictionaries go to press.

Another huge class is routinely excluded from tallies of English words. Most general English dictionaries omit proper nouns—if we had to count the name of every person and place in the world, the word list would expand into the tens of billions. But while it's impossible to include every name, it would be foolish to omit all of them, since many function like any other word. *Casanova* was a real person, but his name has become a common noun for a lover. Another legendary lover was only a character in a play—*Lothario* was the seducer in Nicholas Rowe's play *The Fair Penitent*—but he has also lent his name to real-world amorists. And then the familiar adjectives derived from proper names—*Marxist*, *Darwinian*, *Kafkaesque*—usually need to be included, but there's no agreement on how large this list should be. *Freudian* is common enough that it deserves a place, but what about words derived from less ubiquitous figures—*Shavian* (from George Bernard Shaw), or *Bismarckian* (from Prince Otto Eduard Leopold von Bismarck), or *Bunyanesque* (from John Bunyan)? We could easily add thousands of new words based on people: a novelist might have an *Updikean* style, a dancer might move with *Baryshnikovian* grace, a politician might have *Clintonian* tendencies, a rock singer might show *Springsteenesque* energy. Are these English words?

Finally, English bristles with nonce words—words invented on the spur of the moment, meant to be used only once. Horace Walpole—the author of the first Gothic novel, and one of the eighteenth century's most dedicated letter-writers—was fond of coining new words when the mood struck him. He didn't invent the insult *nincompoop*, but he does get credit for the derived form *nincompoophood*, a word that could stand to be reintroduced. When he wanted to refer to "greenness" and "blueness," he made up *greenth* and *blueth*. When he wanted a word meaning "intermediateness," he coined *betweenity*. And while most of these disappeared as quickly as they were invented, a few of his coinages have stuck: Walpole was fond of a fairy tale about three princes from Sri Lanka, once known as Serendip, who made a series of unexpected discoveries, so he made up a word to describe the phenomenon. More than two centuries later we still use *serendipity* for lucky chances.[12]

Another frustration for would-be word counters is what linguists call *word-class conversion*, words that change their parts of speech. New technologies often produce them: nouns like *mouse* and *text* have found new life as verbs in the age of desktop computers and mobile phones. Many people object to these word-class conversions, and sometimes with good reason; the habit prompted Bill Watterson, creator of the comic strip *Calvin and Hobbes*, to observe, "Verbing weirds language." Word-class conversion, though, isn't a uniquely modern barbarism. It's been happening for many centuries. *Block* was once only a noun, but it didn't take long for it to become a verb, and no one today objects to something being *blocked*. *Move* went in the other direction, beginning as a verb, but it's now an uncontroversial noun in phrases like *checkmate in four moves* and *we hired a van for our last move*.

Another huge class of words is universally acknowledged as legitimate but remains excluded from most general dictionaries: scientific and technical terms. This may seem an unfortunate and unwise exclusion, but the technical vocabulary is vast, and including such words in a dictionary would threaten to dwarf the rest of the language. Two of the laboratory sciences, biology and chemistry, make the point well. No one has an accurate count of all the species on earth—plants, animals, fungi, protists, monera—but some guess that twenty million may be within an order of magnitude of the real number. Should the name of every one of these species earn a place in a dictionary? And things are even more baffling in chemistry, where every compound has a name. There are even names waiting for compounds that haven't yet been shown to exist. Almost any theoretically possible combination of molecules has a name, but if a dictionary included them all, no one would be able to find the familiar English words amid the oxides, sulfates, and dimethyl phthalates.[13]

But if including everything scientific is impossible, so is excluding everything scientific. Everyone recognizes the need to include some scientific words like *fruit fly*, *koala*, *carbon*, and *salt*. But why should a lexicographer include *daffodil* and *atom* but omit *brasolaeliocattleya* (a kind of orchid) and *graviscalar bosons* (theoretical subatomic particles)? There's no difference in the character of the words, only in the familiarity of the things they identify. If some future technological breakthrough makes us all familiar with graviscalar bosons, they'll eventually show up in the major general dictionaries. Until then, they have to remain in the language's antechamber.

The hard sciences are an obvious source for arcane words, but every field of knowledge has its specialized vocabulary, indispensable among initiates but unrecognized by most outsiders: carpentry (*astragal*, *furdown*, *plancier*), dentistry (*bruxism*, *frenum*, *occlusal*), wine making (*chaptalization*, *maderize*, *remuage*), metallurgy (*hypoeutectoid*, *nitriding*, *spheroidizing*), and so on.[14] Few of these terms of art have made it into even unabridged dictionaries. David Crystal recently surveyed the amount of linguistic terminology that's recognized in a dictionary as expansive as the *Oxford English Dictionary*. He read an important but very technical article on linguistics and cataloged seventy-four phonological terms used to describe the tone of voice. Only four of them appeared in the *OED*, and none at all in *Webster's Third New International*.[15] If this is anything like a representative sample, we can assume that just a tiny fraction of the world's technical vocabularies make it into general dictionaries. There's no such thing as an unabridged dictionary.

THESE EXAMPLES SHOW why it's impossible to give a good answer to the number of words in the English language—guesses range from a few tens of thousands up to the hundreds of millions, depending on how widely we choose to cast our nets. It's easy to multiply difficulties indefinitely. When we have the luxury of looking on from the sidelines, we can afford to say "the size of the vocabulary is indeterminate."

Murray, though, couldn't dodge the question. His job was to produce a comprehensive inventory of the English language, and that meant making tens of thousands of judgment calls over whether a word is really English. He stated the problem clearly in his preface to the *OED*: the size of the vocabulary is not "a fixed quantity circumscribed by definite limits"; it consists instead of a "vast aggregate of words and phrases." He likened this mass to "those nebulous masses familiar to the astronomer, in which a clear and unmistakable nucleus shades off on all sides, through zones of decreasing brightness, to a dim marginal film that seems to end nowhere." Or, to switch from an astronomical metaphor to a biological one, "it may be compared to one of those natural

groups of the zoologist or botanist, wherein typical species forming the characteristic nucleus of the order, are linked on every side
to other species, . . . till it fades away in an outer fringe of aberrant
forms."[16]

This is the problem that led Murray to coin the word *Anglicity*—
a word that appeared in the first published part of the *OED*, *A–
Ant*, with the notation "rare⁻°," a symbol glossed as "indicates a
word or sense for which no contextual examples from printed
sources were available to the editors." He almost never made up
words to insert in his dictionary, but he needed one that meant
"Englishness," and *Anglicity* did the trick. It allowed him to speak
of the English language as a set of circles, some concentric, some
overlapping. But these were no ordinary circles. "The English language," he explained to the Philological Society in 1880,

> is not a square with definite sides containing its area; it is
> a circle, but a circle such as Euclid never contemplated,
> having as its centre a point which hath many parts, and
> nowhere bounded by any line called a circumference. It is
> a spot of colour on a damp surface, which shades away
> imperceptibly into the surrounding colourlessness; it is an
> illuminated area in a midnight landscape, whose beams
> practically end somewhere, though no eye hath beheld the
> vanishing line.[17]

At the center, he explained in the preface, is "a nucleus or central mass of many thousand words whose 'Anglicity' is unques-
tioned."[18] The "*Common Words* of the language" include both
formal and informal words, but all of them are universally recognized as essential parts of the language. It's hard to say exactly
how large this "central mass" is. By some estimates, just ten words
account for a quarter of modern written English: one of every
four written words is *the, be, to, and, of, a, in, that, have*, or *I*, in
their various forms (*have, has, having*). Expand the list to the hundred most common words in English—including *it* (number 11),

not (14), *you* (19), *by* (25), *she* (31), *what* (41), *when* (51), *time* (58), *year* (64), *think* (72), *also* (82), *work* (88), *how* (91), and *give* (100)—and fully one half of all written English is accounted for.

But while it's possible to count the most popular words in English, there's no way to reckon the least popular words, and as you go further from the "nucleus," their Anglicity becomes less obvious: "there is absolutely no defining line in any direction," Murray explained; "the circle of the English language has a well-defined centre but no discernible circumference." Still he knew that the theoretical question would require a pragmatic answer, and that "the lexicographer must . . . 'draw the line somewhere.'" And so he laid out his policies. The lexicographer "must include all the 'Common Words' of literature and conversation, and such of the scientific, technical, slang, dialectal, and foreign words as are passing into common use, and approach the position or standing of 'common words.'"

The policies he spelled out allowed, even forced, him to draw lines. The first question was chronology: would it be possible to include words from the entire history of the language, from the fifth century to the nineteenth? He ultimately decided to exclude those that had disappeared in the Old English period: he drew a line around 1150, a date that seemed to him "the only natural halting-place, short of going back to the beginning." The decision was entirely a practical one. The character of the language had changed too much since the twelfth century; a dictionary of Old English would require fundamentally different editorial policies from a dictionary of Middle and Modern English, and so he resolved to omit the words that hadn't been used in at least seven hundred years.[19]

But any word that had been used since 1200—even if it first entered the language in the Old English period—was, at least in theory, fair game for inclusion. He sought to include "all the common words of speech and literature," of course. He was willing to be a little more permissive "in the domain of science and philosophy . . . than in that of slang or cant"; scientific language may be obscure, but it tends to be lasting, whereas ephemeral slang can come and go in the space of years, even months. But just how far should he travel in "the domain of science"? And what should he do about all those complicated technical vocabularies? There he was forced to depend on a rule of thumb. "The aim," he wrote, "has been to include *all words English in form*, except those of which an explanation would be unintelligible to any but the specialist; and such words, not English in form, as either are in general use, like *Hippopotamus, Geranium, Aluminium, Focus, Stratum, Bronchitis*, or belong to the more familiar language of science, as *Mammalia, Lepidoptera, Invertebrata*."[20]

One final principle guided his choice of words: Murray was a dedicated descriptivist, not a prescriptivist, and that meant his selection should have nothing to do with whether or not he liked the words. Trench had made the case in 1857: "A Dictionary," he wrote, "according to that idea of it which seems to me alone capable of being logically maintained, is an inventory of the language: much more indeed, but this primarily, and with this only at present we will deal. It is no task of the maker of it to select the *good* words of a language. If he fancies that it is so, and begins to pick and choose, to leave this and to take that, he will at once go astray."[21] The man charged with fulfilling Trench's vision agreed with him firmly on this point.

A NEW ENGLISH Dictionary was supposed to take ten years, and it was going to occupy two thousand pages spread out over four volumes. Those early estimates ended up being comically inaccurate. Even the first part of the letter *A*—the dictionary originally came out in unbound fascicles of a few hundred pages each—didn't appear until February 1, 1884, almost thirty years after work began, and the first volume containing all of *A* wasn't published until 1888. Because of the glacial pace, which frustrated the Oxford delegates to no end, Murray didn't live to see the completion of his life's work: he died in 1915, when the *OED* had reached only volume 8, containing the letter *Q*. But his assistant, Henry Bradley, took it over on Murray's death, and William Craigie and C. T. Onions supervised the last few volumes. (It was in this phase that a young Oxford graduate, recently evacuated from the trenches of the First World War because of illness, joined the project—J. R. R. Tolkien, who contributed etymologies for many words between *waggle* and *warlock*.) The final volume appeared in 1928, seventy-one years after Trench's lecture, and one week short of fifty years after Murray received his invitation to come to Oxford. Four volumes had become twelve, and 2,000 pages had turned into 15,487. And the number of words? 414,825.

The *OED*'s story doesn't end in 1928. No sooner had the last fascicle, *wise–zyxt*, appeared—on April 19, 1928—than the editors realized the half-century labor had to be updated. The volume for *A* had appeared forty years ago, and much of the work was done ten years before that. Too much had changed. The editors also discovered the omissions and errors that are inevitable in any big undertaking like this. A thirteenth volume, supplementing the first twelve, appeared in 1933 as the whole set was reissued.

But even that didn't settle the matter. Beginning in the 1950s, Oxford realized that a rapidly changing language once again needed updating. In 1957, exactly a century after Trench's lecture to the Philological Society, Oxford University Press hired a full-time lexicographer who would take over Murray's job for the twentieth century. Robert Burchfield, a New Zealand–born linguist charged with bringing the great dictionary up to date with four volumes of *Supplements* in the second half of the twentieth century, marveled at the predecessor he had never met, but whose influence he felt daily. "Sir James Murray and his colleagues," wrote Burchfield, "established a model for all time. Whenever I have cause to examine the competing models, the great historical dictionaries of Germany, Sweden, Holland, and France, . . . the superiority of Murray's techniques and of the layout of his page is clear. By one practical test or another the *OED* emerges as the most ambitious and the most successful treatment of a national language ever undertaken."[22]

Burchfield's *Supplements* were, in their own way, nearly as remarkable an achievement as Murray's original dictionary. Murray's work took decades longer than expected; Burchfield followed his mentor in this respect. The original plan was for seven to ten years of work, but supplements didn't begin appearing until 1972, and the fourth volume took until 1986, twenty-nine years after Burchfield signed on as editor.[23]

Still there were frustrations. The arrangement of the whole set was inconvenient: to be sure you had all the information about a word, you had to look in the main body of the twelve-volume dictionary, in the one-volume supplement of 1933, and in the four-volume supplement of 1972–86. In 1983, therefore, Oxford University Press began a project to transcribe all the information into computer-readable form, and in 1989 it integrated all the volumes together. Even the typing work was done on a colossal scale: a total of 350 million characters had to be typed by more than a hundred employees of International Computaprint Corporation, and the work was checked by a team of fifty-five proofreaders. To help with the editing, Oxford University Press designed a custom software package known as Oedipus Lex.

Along the way, the supplements were integrated into the alphabetical series of the original volumes, some errors were corrected, the typography was cleaned up, and a new system of representing pronunciation was introduced. Around five thousand words were added, and they often show their origins in the 1980s—some timely (*glasnost*), some amusing (*Pythonesque*), some grim (*AIDS*). The result was the second edition of Murray's great dictionary, published on March 30, 1989, now called *OED2*. Its twenty volumes were offered for sale at £1,500, or $2,500.[24]

The reviews were almost uniformly good. The *Christian Science Monitor* declared it THE DEFINITIVE WORD ON ENGLISH. *Newsweek* reviewed it under the headline A CELEBRATION OF LANGUAGE. Canada's *Globe and Mail* proclaimed MOTHER LODE OF THE LANGUAGE HAS SOMETHING FOR EVERYONE. Even the *Sydney Morning Herald*, which announced it under the quirky headline OED2: AWESOME, STRANGE, SLIGHTLY DOTTY, approvingly quoted the novelist Anthony Burgess, who called it the greatest publishing event of the twentieth century.

But there was no time for resting on laurels in the Oxford editorial offices. No sooner had *OED2* appeared than they realized that, once again, the letter *A* was decades out of date. A bigger problem was that much of the information that Murray and his colleagues had collected in the 1870s through the 1920s had been superseded by new research into the language. Burchfield worked to fill in the gaps Murray left in his dictionary, but he rarely corrected Murray's errors and almost never revised the old definitions for clarity. The second edition was mostly a consolidation of the old research and the new, but no one had revisited the old research in nearly a century. It's telling that the review of *OED2* in the *Times* of London ended with a one-sentence paragraph: "A third edition is planned for the twenty-first century."[25]

That third edition is still under way, though in a medium Murray would not have recognized, as metal filing cabinets have given way to digital file folders. In the 1990s, Oxford University Press geared up for its biggest lexicographical project since the 1870s: a third edition of *The Oxford English Dictionary*. This would be more than the old *OED* with new entries; it was to be a wholly new work, built on Murray's plans but with new materials, and from the ground up. The ongoing *OED3* uses the information in the original *OED* when it is right, but corrects it when it is wrong, clarifies it when it is awkward, and uses high-tech search tools to track down obscure words in unexpected places.

It's fitting that the dictionary that wrestled more than any other with the size of the English language should be of ever-expanding size itself. The Victorian lexicographers who first proposed *A New English Dictionary on Historical Principles* gave every impression of seeing that project as "definitive." But a century and a half of experience has convinced their successors that no dictionary can ever hope to be complete; Trench's dream of a comprehensive inventory of the language can never become a reality. It would be impossible to capture the whole of the language in a dictionary even if the *OED* were expanded from twenty heavy folio volumes to a hundred. The language is, by its very nature, a work in progress; the only way a dictionary can hope to do it justice is to be a work in progress too.

CHAPTER 8

The Taste and Fancy of the Speller

GEORGE BERNARD SHAW
REWRITES THE ABCS

PITY THE POOR LEARNER OF ENGLISH.

In some respects our language is a cinch to learn. Our words take just a few forms: nouns can appear bare, with *-s*, with *-'s*, or with *-s'*—that covers the noun. Most verbs take *-s* or *-es* in the third-person singular (*shows, washes*), the "zero form" (the unmodified root) in the other present-tense forms (*show, wash*), *-ing* in the participle or gerund (*showing, washing*), and *-ed* in the past tense (*showed, washed*). The handful of very irregular verbs (*be, go, take*) is small. Our syntax is also comparatively simple: adjectives go before nouns; adverbs can go nearly anywhere; most of our declarative sentences follow the order subject–verb–object; in questions we often reverse the subject and the verb (changing the declaration *the weather is bad* into the question *is the weather bad?*). This overstates the simplicity of English but, after you've studied a language like Latin or German, English grammar is a piece of cake.

The relationship between the written and the spoken forms of the language, on the other hand, is enough to drive people to distraction. Our spelling is a mess.

In languages without alphabets—Chinese, for instance, with its huge catalog of symbols (often called *ideograms*, though linguists prefer *logograms*)—there's no pretense of a sound-for-sound connection between the written and spoken forms of the language. Given the same symbol, a speaker of Mandarin will pronounce it *yī*, a speaker of Cantonese will pronounce it *yat*, and a speaker of Hokkienese will pronounce it *tsit*. The logogram stands for an idea, not for a set of sounds. (Linguists don't even agree on whether to call the varieties of Chinese different dialects, different languages, or something else altogether.)

Alphabetic languages, on the other hand, ostensibly use their letters to represent individual sounds. Want to pronounce Spanish? Spend twenty minutes learning the sounds of the letters and you're ready to go. German and Italian are almost as easy. French—where *eaux* can spell *o*—has a more complicated relation between writing and pronunciation than Spanish or Italian, but once you learn the rules, it's rarely difficult to puzzle out a pronunciation. There are exceptions to the rules, but they're few.

English, on the other hand, sometimes seems to have more exceptions than rules. A common combination like *ough* is notorious: *The American Heritage Dictionary* lists 328 English words containing that string of letters, but it can be impossible to guess which of their many sounds they might take in those words. A newcomer to the Victorian poet Arthur Hugh Clough, someone encountering a noun like a *brougham* for the first time, or a Harvard freshman stopping by the Houghton Library can only guess and hope to get lucky.[1] The title of Dr. Seuss's book *The Tough Coughs as He Ploughs the Dough* points out four very different sounds represented by that strange combination of letters.

"The words with *ough* are perhaps an extreme case," wrote spelling reformer Walter Ripman in 1948, "but there are many others just as bad." He went on to offer examples: "*Deceit* and *receipt*, *water* and *daughter*, *six* and *sticks*, *time* and *rhyme*, end in the same sounds, but how they differ in spelling. *No* and *know*, *nose* and *knows* have identical sounds, but their spelling is anything but identical."[2] David Wolman, in an entertaining look at English spelling, notes that "the sound commonly represented by the letters *sh*, as in *shine*, is the same sound in *sugar*, *emotion*, *omniscience*, *charade*, *social*, and *fissure*."[3] We might add the pronunciation of *laughter*, and then observe what happens to both the vowels and the consonants when we add a single letter and make it *slaughter*.

Now imagine an English learner asking for the logic behind our spelling system. Even calling it a "system" seems wrong, since so little is systematic: it seems to have been cobbled together out of mere caprice and whimsy. We're left with a bizarre roster of homophones, homographs, silent letters, and mysterious combinations. It seems a cruel joke that even the word *orthography*—from the Greek for "correct writing"—involves two sounds for the letter *o*, an *a* pronounced as *uh*, a *th* that doesn't sound like a *t* or an *h*, a *ph* when an *f* would do just as well, and a *y* used as a vowel.

There are rules about English spelling and pronunciation, but they're not very helpful. "*I* before *E*, except after *C*, or when sounded as 'ay,' as in 'neighbor' or 'weigh' "—since the 1860s, this little mnemonic has served students struggling with the eccentricities of English orthography. But what about *caffeine*? What about *protein*, or *seize*, or *weird*? All have *E* before *I*, and not one is sounded as "ay." *Either* can be pronounced *eether* or *eyether*, but at least in American English it's never "sounded as 'ay.' " And there are plenty of *I*'s before *E*'s even after *C*'s: think of *efficient* or *glacier* or *science* or *species*. Another rule is that, in American English, words like *agonize*, *authorize*, *categorize*, *centralize*, and *digitize* always end in *-ize*, not *-ise*—but then how to account for *advertise*, *advise*, *chastise*, *circumcise*, *comprise*, *compromise*, *demise*, *despise*, *devise*, *disfranchise*, *enfranchise*, *enterprise*, *excise*, *exercise*, *improvise*, *incise*, *revise*, *supervise*, *surmise*, *surprise*, and *televise*?

WHY IS ENGLISH spelling such a mess? Or to put it the way Wolman does, "Why does English have such a screwy spelling system, and who can be blamed?"[4] Historical linguists have trouble with *why* questions, usually answering them with the nonanswer "historical reasons"—which is an academic's way of saying "It just *is*, that's all." But if we can't really know *why* things got this way, we can at least trace *how*.

The first problem is that we're using an alphabet that was designed for a different language. We use a modified version of the Latin alphabet, first developed around 700 B.C. It's a poor match for the English language because it doesn't have enough letters for our sounds. The classical Latin alphabet had only twenty-three letters, and our slightly expanded version twenty-six (we've added *j*, *v*, and *w*, not used by the Romans). What's more, several of our letters are, strictly speaking, unnecessary: *x* is simply *ks*; *q* is nothing but the *k* sound; and *c* on its own can take the sounds represented by either *k* or *s*. This means that there are really twenty-three sound-symbols available in our alphabet, but the Modern English language has more than forty phonemes—significant sounds—and mapping forty-some sounds onto twenty-some letters is bound to be a losing game.

Our current alphabet isn't the only one that's been used to record the English language. A "runic" alphabet, used in north-central Europe and Scandinavia, contained as many as thirty-three letters. Sometime around the seventh century, though, Irish missionaries and scribes reintroduced the Latin alphabet to England, and by the eleventh century the old runic alphabet had died out completely. Because the twenty-three Latin letters weren't enough to cover all the sounds of the English language, English scribes borrowed a few runes to supplement their alphabet. Two of these letters, used through the Old and Middle English periods, stood for the two *th* sounds in Modern English: the "thorn," written as þ, was usually the unvoiced *th* of words like *thin* and *with*, whereas the "eth," written as ð, was usually the voiced *th* of *that* and *then*. Another Old English letter, the "ash," written as æ, was the "flat" *a* sound of words like *ash* and *have*; this left the letter *a* for the "broad" *a* sound of words like *father*. The strangest of the obsolete letters was the "yogh," written in the Middle English period as 3, which was a back-of-the-throat gurgle, similar to the *ch* in the Scottish *loch* or the German *acht*. But even with these supplementary letters, there still weren't enough symbols to cover all the sounds that appeared in English words. Scribes were obliged to cobble together combinations of letters to represent the sounds in our language. Classical Latin, for instance, had no *sh* sound. English does: how to represent it? Today we use two letters from the Latin alphabet, *s* and *h*, even though the sound doesn't correspond to either of those letters. We do the same with *th*, *ch*, and other combinations.

Within the limits of these problems with the alphabet, though, English spelling was once fairly rational—nearly as phonetic as Italian or German today. In the Middle English period, every letter had a sound, every sound had a letter or a combination of letters, with not many exceptions. In Chaucer's day, for instance, the late fourteenth century, nearly every letter was sounded. The opening of the General Prologue to *The Canterbury Tales* goes like this:

> Whan that Aprille, with his shoures sote
> The Droghte of March hath perced to the rote . . .

In the 1380s and '90s, when the poem was new, it would have been pronounced something like, "Hwahn thaht Ah-prill-uh, with his shoo-ruhs soh-tuh, the drookht of March hahth pair-sed toh the roh-tuh." Silent *e*'s weren't silent; *gh* sounded like *g* and *h*. The modern dispensation, with silent letters, doubled consonants, and strange vowel combinations, was unknown in the fourteenth century.

In the decades after Chaucer, though, the language was undergoing some significant changes, as Middle English gave way to Early Modern English. And it was in this era that spelling got really complicated.

A NEW TECHNOLOGY had a powerful influence on English spelling: printing reached England in the 1470s. When William Caxton set up his press, he had to buy his materials from the Continent. Caxton began his career as a cloth merchant and importer-exporter. He settled first in Bruges, then in Cologne, Germany, where he began dealing in printed books. All the while he was working on his own translation of Raoul Lefèvre's *Recueil des histoires de Troie.* Eventually he bought a printing press and took it back to Bruges, where he set up his own printing house. The first book to come off his press, late in 1473 or early the next year, was his translation of Lefèvre, making it the very first book in the English language to take advantage of the new technology.

Title pages as we know them were not used in the fifteenth century; instead books just opened with a formula like "Here beginneth," followed by all the relevant details. Here's how Caxton opened his *History*:

> hEre begynneth the volume intituled and named the re-
> cuyell of the historyes of Troye / composed and drawen
> out of dyuerce bookes of latyn in to frensshe by the ryght
> venerable persone and worshipfull man. Raoul le ffeure.
> preest and chapelayn vnto the ryght noble gloryous and
> myghty prynce in his tyme Phelip duc of Bourgoyne of
> Braband &c in the yere of the incarnacion of our lord god
> a thousand foure honderd sixty and foure / And translated
> and drawen out of frenshe in to englisshe by Willyam Cax-
> ton mercer of ye cyte of London / at the comaûdemêt of
> the right hye myghty and vertuouse pryncesse hys redoub-
> tyd lady. Margarete by the grace of god. Duchesse of Bour-
> goyne of Lotryk of Braband &c. / whiche sayd translacion
> and werke was begonne in Brugis in the Countre of Flaun-
> dres the fyrst day of marche the yere of the Incarnacion of
> our saide Lorde gode a thousand foure honderd sixty and
> eyghe / And ended and fynysshid in the holy cyte of Colen
> the .xix. day of septembre the yere of our sayd lord god a
> thousand foure honderd sixty and enleuen &c.

Not the pithiest of titles, perhaps, and it's hard to imagine modern publishers favoring it. But it holds its place in history as the first thing ever printed in English. Modern scholars call it *The History of Troy.*

After spending a few years printing books and shipping them back to England for sale, in 1475 or '76 Caxton returned to his homeland and set up his press in Westminster, still using the Continental typefaces he had used in Bruges. The first book he printed there was Geoffrey Chaucer's *Canterbury Tales*, and he followed it up with more than a hundred new works over the course of his nineteen-year career. On his death in 1492, the business was continued by his foreman, Wynkyn de Worde, who expanded the business even further. And Caxton, de Worde, and their successors, though they lived half a millennium ago, did much to shape the way we spell today.

How DID THE printing press change English orthography? Manuscript spellings are usually more variable than print spellings: because every copy of a book might be prepared by a different scribe, it was difficult to enforce a standard. The result was tremendous variation. *The Oxford English Dictionary* records all the following as legitimate historical spellings of the word *through* in the manuscript era, not counting any of the forms it labels "scribal errors":

> dorow, dorth, drogh, thorgh, thorght, thoro, thoro',
> thorogh, thorou, thorough, thoroughe, thorow, thorowe,
> thorowgh, thorowh, thorro, thorrow, thoru, thorugh,
> thorughe, thoruh, thoruʒ, thorw, thorʒ, thour, thourch,
> thourgh, thourth, threu, threw, thro, thro', throch,
> throche, throcht, throgh, throght, throu, throuch,
> throucht, throughe, throuw, throw, throwch, throwe,
> throwgh, throwghe, throwʒe, thru, thruch, thrucht,
> thruff, thrugh, thrughe, thruht, thruʒ, thrw, thrwch,
> thurf, thurgh, thurghe, thurght, thurow, thurrou, thur-
> rowe, thurʒ, trogh, troght, þerh, þorch, þorgh, þorghe,
> þorh, þorogh, þorou, þorouʒ, þorow, þorowe, þoroʒ,
> þoru, þoruh, þoruhe, þoruth, þoruʒ, þorw, þorwe, þorþ,
> þorʒ, þour, þourgh, þourh, þourw, þourʒ, þourʒe, þro,
> þroughe, þrouʒ, þruh, þurch, þuregh, þureh, þurf, þurgh,
> þurght, þurh, þurrh, þurth, þuru, þuruh, þurw, þurþ,
> þurʒ, þurʒe, þurʒth.

All this variation offered some advantages. For most of the early modern era—from the beginnings of Modern English to the middle of the eighteenth century, and perhaps a bit beyond—English spelling could be flexible.

Flexibility is good, but it also poses a problem. David Crystal sums it up:

> The problem was for the reader, not for the writer. As an author I can write the word *poor* as *poor, poore, powr, power, puer, pur, puur, pure,* and in many other ways. Because I am the writer, I know what I mean. But you, as the reader, you have to work it out for yourself. If you read *The kinge has a puer companion,* what is it supposed to mean? Is it *poor* or *pure*—or even *power(ful)?* . . . Context will often help you work out what is going on, but not always.[5]

Standardized spelling makes life easier for the reader. That's why, when print made it possible to ensure that the spelling was consistent from copy to copy, there was also a drive to make spelling consistent from work to work. Eventually one spelling would be right, and the rest wrong.

That's not to say that printing fixed the language all at once. For centuries there was room for variation, and printers were often glad for the freedom it offered. Typesetters, for instance, could take advantage of the accepted spelling variation to make their job easier. Justifying type—setting it so that the left and right margins are both flush—is as easy as can be in the age of the word processor, when a single mouse click gets the job done. In the days when typesetting involved placing lead slugs in a metal rack, getting the margins to line up was more challenging. This is where flexible spelling offers clear advantages. Is a line a little too short? Spell *only* as *onely* or *onelie,* and you've stretched the line out a little longer. Is a line a little too long? Turn *stopped* into *stop'd* or *stopt;* you save a few millimeters.

But things were changing. The phrase "bad speller" rarely

appears in English-language books before the 1770s—English readers before that date never imagined that there was only one way to spell a word. Many dictionaries of quotations attribute a quip to Andrew Jackson, president of the United States in the 1830s and a notoriously poor speller: "It is a damn poor mind indeed," Jackson supposedly said, "which can't think of at least two ways to spell any word." The line is funny only because by the 1830s there usually *was* only one way to spell a word. The joke would have made no sense in 1630 or 1730, when virtually everyone found multiple ways to spell words. Charles Dickens, also writing in the 1830s, got a laugh by showing the collision of the two worlds, one in which spelling was variable, one in which it was fixed. In *The Pickwick Papers*, a judge asks a character for his name, and gets the answer, "Sam Weller, my Lord." "Do you spell it with a 'V' or a 'W'?" asks the judge. "That depends," answers Sam, "upon the taste and fancy of the speller. . . . I never had occasion to spell it more than once or twice in my life, but I spells it with a 'V.'" His father cheers him on from the gallery: "Quite right too, Samivel; quite right. Put it down a we, my Lord, put it down a we."[6]

IN ONE SENSE Caxton picked a good time to get into the publishing business. The fifteenth century was a period of intellectual excitement and increasing literacy. Someone who owned the means of literary production stood to make a lot of money, and printing did indeed make Caxton a rich man. In another sense, though, it was a lousy time to bring printing to England because, just as English spelling began to settle down, English pronunciation was going through major changes. Caxton lived in the middle of what linguists call the "Great Vowel Shift," one of the biggest and most mysterious systemic changes in the history of our language.

The vowels in Old and Middle English weren't quite identical to those in the other European languages, like Spanish, Italian, and German, but they were much closer than they are today. The English *a* was usually sounded like the *a* in *father*, which is the same as the Spanish or Italian *padre* and the German *Vater*. The English *e* was usually sounded like *ay*, which is the same as the Spanish, Italian, or German *e*. The English *i* was usually an *ee* sound, again as in Spanish and Italian. The English *o* was usually the *o* of *show*, not the *o* of *hot* or *bother*. And the English *u* was always *u* as in *blue*, never the *uh* sound of *bug* or *under*. There were a few departures from these rules, but nothing compared to the modern mess of vowel sounds that we've learned to live with.

But sometime in the fifteenth century—for reasons that remain unknown—the vowel sounds began shifting, literally moving around in the mouth. Phonologists say that many of the long vowels moved higher and that some of the vowels that were already high were diphthongized (turned into two sounds). The sound represented by long *e*, for instance, which once sounded like "ay," moved to become "ee"—a sound pronounced closer to the front of the mouth. The sound represented by *i*, which once sounded like "ee," moved to become the so-called long *i* of *ice* or *high*, which is actually two vowel sounds—"ah" and "ee" run together. Over the course of decades, a new system of pronunciation came into being, just as the older system of pronunciation was being fixed as the basis of our spelling. Printers' spellings arrested English orthography at a time when English phonology was changing rapidly. The result was to introduce distance between the written and the spoken forms of the language.

MORE PROBLEMS CONSPIRED to make life difficult for Caxton and other early English printers. English scribes, writing by hand, had little difficulty supplementing the Latin alphabet with peculiarly English letters like þ and ð; English printers, however, had to make do with the letter forms created on the Continent. The types themselves—the slugs of lead bearing the inverted forms of the letters on their faces—had been designed in Germany, and they were well suited for the German and Latin languages. But no one in Germany had bothered to create types for the letters unique to English. Caxton, therefore, had to print English works without the thorn, eth, or yogh.

It's not difficult to imagine the challenges facing an early English typesetter. The manuscript copy before him contains the word *þrou3*, but the case of type doesn't have two of those letters—what is he to do? Without the thorn or eth, print shops had to substitute *th*; without the yogh, printers could only substitute *gh* as the nearest equivalent. And the result is that some sounds that have disappeared altogether have left fossil traces in our spelling.

It's tempting to speculate about what might have happened if the first printers had set up shop in England a few decades later than they did. By the middle of the sixteenth century the Great Vowel Shift was virtually complete; the obsolete thorn, eth, and yogh were largely forgotten. Had we arrested our spellings then, it's likely that many of the most grotesque irregularities would never have appeared in our orthography. It might also have meant that later changes in pronunciation would have been reflected in spelling. Not long after English began to be printed, many of its spellings appeared purely arbitrary; English speakers have never had a systematic expectation that they should always faithfully represent sounds. Had our early printed books captured our pronunciations more accurately from the beginning, it's possible that we would have been less tolerant of later inconsistencies, and would have changed our spellings to keep up with our changing pronunciations.

CAXTON'S INFLUENCE OVER English spelling was the result of conscious effort, but he didn't often set out to *change* spellings, only to *choose* one form as the preferred one. Some of his successors, though, worked with missionary zeal, hoping to manipulate the spelling system. Though they had the best of intentions, the effect of their work was to make spelling even more irrational.

In the Middle English era, *debt* and *doubt* were usually spelled *dette* and *doute*—as they appeared in Old French, their source. In the Renaissance, though, scholars wanted to draw attention to the relationship between these words and their Latin originals, and so the Latin *debitum* and *dubitare* lent their *b*'s to the otherwise phonetically spelled English words. The same thing happened with *subtle*: the earliest spellings took forms like *sotill*, *sotel*, and *soutil*, from Old French *soutil*, until scholars pointed out that it came from Latin *subtilis*—and so a silent *b* was stuffed into the word. And *b* wasn't alone. The fourteenth-century *receyt* or *receite* picked up a *p* because it could be traced back to Latin *recepta*, the early *samoun* or *samon* got an *l* from Latin *salmonem*, and the fourteenth-century *vitaile* became *victual* when etymologists remembered it was de-rived from Latin *victus* 'food', even though the pronunciation re-mained *vittle*.[7]

These etymological spellings, as they were called, were prone to a few problems. The first is that they were applied inconsistently. *Receipt* got its etymological *p*, but *deceit* and *conceit*—from the same Latin root—went without (though the *p* survives in the de-rived words *deception* and *conceptual*). Even more bothersome is that the scholars' etymologies were often wrong. The spellings *delit* and *delite* were common in the thirteenth and fourteenth cen-turies, and that makes sense: the word comes from French *delitier* or *deliter*. But some spelling reformers incorrectly thought it was related to English *light* and put the *gh* where it didn't belong. The same thing happened to the word *island*, apparently through con-fusion with the word *isle*. That shorter form is a thirteenth-century import from the French *ile* and can be traced back to the Latin *in-sula*, which is where the *s* comes from. But the longer word *island* doesn't come from Latin at all; it's a Germanic word, and the early forms are *iland* or *yland*. The *s*, in other words, can be defended in *isle*, but it doesn't belong in *island*. And two words that began with *h*, *hol* and *hore*, became *whole* and *whore* when etymologists mis-takenly traced them back to the wrong root words.

There were still more sources of confusion as English continued to import new words from foreign languages. While the pronunci-ations were often changed to suit English habits, the spellings were usually left intact—even though the relationship between sound and spelling in other languages was different. Consider a term like *hors d'oeuvre*, which started showing up in English in the early eighteenth century. This is a tricky word for many English speak-ers, because we don't have the French *œu* sound in our language,

and our native words never call for the half-pronounced *r* sound after the *v*. Rather than trying to approximate the original French
pronunciation, therefore, we've simply anglicized it, producing "or-
durv." But even as the pronunciation was anglicized, the French
spelling remained intact—with the result that about half the letters
aren't pronounced the way they would normally be in English.

MANY PEOPLE FIND this state of affairs amusing. To those who
would fix English spelling, though, the problems caused by irregular and irrational orthography are no laughing matter, and their
tone can be downright messianic. If our spelling were rational,
they argue, we'd have time to devote to more productive things—
but no; we're forced to spend years of our lives memorizing arbitrary combinations of letters. "In our spelling," wrote Walter
Ripman of the Spelling Society, an international group based in
England,

> there is such a wide divergence between the spoken and the
> written or printed language that excessive energy has to be
> concentrated on acquiring the latter. . . . The spelling is so
> irregular that to learn it means, not the use of the reason-
> ing powers, but sheer memorising. . . . There is no excuse
> for the appalling waste of time involved in acquiring our
> spelling, nothing to make up for the irritation it so often
> causes.[8]

And to people who make complaints like this, the answer is simple:
it's time to reform English spelling.

People began objecting to the irrationality of English spelling
in the sixteenth century. In 1569, for instance, John Hart found
"such confusion and disorder, as it may be accounted rather a kinde
of ciphring"—English spelling was little better than a code. The
problem, he explained, is that English spelling "is vnfit and wrong
shapen for the proportion of the voice."[9] And the calls for change
kept coming in the seventeenth and eighteenth centuries. In 1665,

the diarist John Evelyn hoped that someone would introduce "a more certaine Orthography, . . . as by leaving out superfluous letters, &c.: such as *o* in woomen, people; *u* in honour; *a* in reproach, *ugh* in though, &c." He called for new techniques to bring the spoken and the written languages closer to one another.[10] In 1704, the author of an anonymous book, *Right Spelling Very Much Improved*, found it "very strange in this Learned Age, wherein so *many* affect to *Speak fine*," that "so *few* should endeavour to *Write English* tolerably *true*." (He had clear ideas, too, about who was most to blame: " 'tis pity these gross Mistakes should lie most at the Door of the *fairer Sex*.")[11]

Later in the eighteenth century, Benjamin Franklin offered a new alphabet that would do away with the most obvious inconsistencies in English spelling. "In this Alphabet," for instance, "*c* is *omitted* as unnecessary; *k* supplying its hard Sound, and *s* the soft"; furthermore, "the *g* has no longer *two different* Sounds, which occasioned Confusion; but is, as every Letter ought to be, confined to one;—The same is to be observed in *all* the Letters, Vowels, and Consonants." He also thought it a wise policy "that there be *no superfluous* Letters used in spelling," and proposed six new letters to let the written language match the spoken.[12] Franklin never pursued this scheme seriously, but one of his disciples, Noah Webster, did, in the first three decades of the nineteenth century.

THE HEYDAY OF spelling reform efforts was the late nineteenth century, when it seemed impossible to open a newspaper or a magazine without coming across another scheme to tidy up our messy language. It was an era of grand projects for the public good. If streetlights could be installed throughout the metropolis, if police forces could ensure the public safety, if health could be managed to eliminate cholera—surely, then, English spelling could be rationalized. Compared with being mugged in dark city streets or infected by deadly diseases, the pain of learning arbitrary spellings may be minor. But pain was pain, and if the problem could be solved, then earnest Victorians thought something should be done.

The periodical press was filled with proposals for spelling reform. Some were serious, some were questionable, some were
downright screwball. Some of the commentary could be funny: one
Victorian (not, as often reported, G. B. Shaw) suggested *fish* might
be spelled as *ghoti*, using the *gh* from *laugh*, the *o* from *women*, and
the *ti* from *motion*. It's not a fair challenge, of course; English
speakers know that *gh* never sounds like *f* at the beginning of a
word, and *ti* never sounds like *sh* at the end. By the same logic, *ghoti*
might just as well go unpronounced altogether, with the *gh* from
through, the *o* from *people*, the *t* from *listen*, and the *i* from
friend—but we all know that no word is made up entirely of silent
letters. English spelling can be irrational, but it does have its limits.

There were also wags on the other side, eager to ridicule the
earnestness with which the reformers went about their business.
Perhaps the most famous example is a sly piece by one M. J. Shields.
Shields began quite modestly, proposing a series of incremental
changes to English spelling, year by year:

> In Year 1 that useless letter "c" would be dropped to be
> replased either by "k" or "s," and likewise "x" would no
> longer be part of the alphabet.

So far, so good. But as he went on, his suggestions became
stranger by degrees:

> Year 3 might well abolish "y" replasing it with "i" and
> Iear 4 might fiks the "g/j" anomali wonse and for all. Jen-
> erally, then, the improvement would kontinue iear bai
> iear with Iear 5 doing awai with useless double konso-
> nants.

After fifteen years or so,

> it wud fainali bi posibl tu meik ius ov thi ridandant letez
> "c," "y" and "x"—bai now jast a memori in the maindz ov
> ould doderez—tu riplais "ch," "sh," and "th" rispektivli.

The result? "Aafte sam 20 iers ov orxogrefkl riform," Shields predicted, "wi wud hev a lojikl, kohirnt speling in ius xrewawt xe
Ingliy-spiking werld." The parody of the more sincere reformers is
uncannily accurate; only the incomprehensible babble at the end
of the process serves to remind readers that he wasn't making his
proposals in good faith.[13]

THE EARLY TWENTIETH century's most ardent champion for a new
alphabet was George Bernard Shaw. As a playwright—a recorder
of the spoken word—he had reason to care: "The fact that English
is spelt conventionally and not phonetically," he complained in
1900, "makes the art of recording speech almost impossible. What
is more, it places the modern dramatist, who writes for America as
well as England, in a most trying position." But the problem
wasn't limited to playwrights: everyone, he insisted, suffered from
arbitrary spellings. "An intelligent child," he explained, "who is
bidden to spell *debt*, and very properly spells it *d-e-t*, is caned for
not spelling it with a *b* because Julius Caesar spelled it with a *b*."[14]

He therefore proposed a radical scheme. No half measures for
Shaw: in an essay called "Spelling Reform v. Phonetic Spelling: A
Plea for Speech Nationalisation," published in London's *Morning
Leader* in 1901, he attacked two writers who proposed modest
changes but were unwilling to go so far as a fully phonetic system.
"You must either let our spelling alone or else reform it phonetically," he argued. The English alphabet, after all, "is a phonetic one
as far as it goes; and our established spelling is phonetic spelling,
partly out of date, and partly corrupted by an ignorant academic
attempt to make it more etymological."[15]

Some of his problems were those of the aesthete: "The apostro-
phies [*sic*] in ain't, don't, haven't, etc., look so ugly that the most
careful printing cannot make a page of colloquial dialogue as
handsome as a page of classical dialogue." What are those apostrophes doing in there? They signal "omitted letters," but without any
consistency. "Besides," he observes ironically, "shan't should be

sha' 'n't, if the wretched pedantry of indicating the elision is to be carried out"—if we omit two letters, we should indicate the omissions with two apostrophes. Shaw himself abandoned the ugly apostrophes without consequences, and he recommended that the world should follow him: "I have written aint, dont, havnt, shant, shouldnt and wont for twenty years with perfect impunity, using the apostrophe only where its omission would suggest another word: for example, hell for he'll. There is not the faintest reason for persisting in the ugly and silly trick of peppering pages with these uncouth bacilli." (That eccentric aestheticism extends to other aspects of typography. He found the use of italics "deplorable. To the good printer the occurrence of two different founts on the same page is at best an unavoidable evil." Do away with them for titles, Shaw recommended—do away, even, with quotation marks. "Let me give a specimen," he offered. "1. I was reading The Merchant of Venice. 2. I was reading 'The Merchant of Venice.' 3. I was reading *The Merchant of Venice*. The man who cannot see that No. 1 is the best looking as well as the sufficient and sensible form, should print or write nothing but advertisements of lost dogs or ironmongers' catalogues: literature is not for him to meddle with."[16])

Shaw was a dedicated reformer to the end—and beyond the end. He willed most of his estate to efforts to reform English spelling, hoping that a substantial cash prize for the developer of a new system would motivate people to come up with one. The problem, though, hasn't been a lack of people willing to create new systems; it's the lack of willingness of the masses to follow the abundant new systems. Even the royalties from *My Fair Lady*, which made Shaw's estate exceedingly rich, haven't yet succeeded in making English spelling any more phonetic.

WHY, WITH SO many smart and dedicated people working so long and so hard to make English spelling more logical, do we still have to put up with forms like *knight*, *oenophile*, *phlegm*, *rhythm*, and *trough*? And that's not to mention other commonly misspelled words like *accommodate*, *broccoli*, *calendar*, *dispensable*, *gauge*, *minuscule*, and *misspell*, all of which trip up even accomplished writers.

At least seven obstacles stand in the way of any attempt at spelling reform. The first, mentioned above, is the most basic: our alphabet has twenty-six letters, but there are forty-some significant sounds in standard English. A reformer then has to decide whether to make up as many as twenty new letters or symbols, or simply to rationalize the worst eccentricities in the current spelling system, keeping things like silent *e*'s and combinations like *ch*, *sh*, and *th*. The problem is that the more thorough the reform, the more difficult it will be to get the world to accept it.

One minimally intrusive possibility is to remove the more obvious irregularities without reforming the alphabet itself. We might abandon *of*, for instance, for *uv*, and replace *neighbor* with *nabor*. We could get rid of the apparently randomly doubled letters— change *spell* to *spel*—and replace two-letter combinations with one letter when a single letter will do, as in *alfabet*. And while some silent *e*'s serve a purpose, distinguishing *can* from *cane* and *bit* from *bite*, others do nothing at all—*bizarre*, *cigarette*, *giraffe*, and *have* could just as easily be *bizar*, *cigaret*, *giraf*, *hav*. Other silent letters could also go, giving us spellings like *dam*, *anser*, and *onest*. This would probably be the easiest kind of spelling reform to put into effect, because the newly spelled words are immediately recognizable by those even without special training—it's as close to intuitive as spelling reform can be.

This solution is, however, far from perfect. It still represents some single sounds, for instance, as combinations of letters, when one letter for each sound would make more sense. The letters *th* usually make the single sound of the *th* in *thin* or *that*, but sometimes *th* actually sounds like a *t* followed by an *h*, as in *hothouse*, *shorthand*, and *sweetheart*; likewise, the two-letter combination *sh* usually represents the single sound of *shop* and *fish*, but sometimes, as in *crosshatch*, *grasshopper*, and *hogshead*, it's two separate sounds, *s* and *h*. Without some extra symbols in the alphabet, we can't show the full range of sounds in a one-symbol-for-one-sound relationship.

The question, then, is where to get the extra letters, and how many there should be. Some have proposed using the "wasted" letters in English for these purposes. For instance, the letter *x* is almost always just *k* and *s* (or *k* and *z*) put together: it would be easy to replace *extra* with *ekstra* and *examine* with *ekzamin*. That would then free up the letter *x* for some other use—perhaps it could take the place of *th*. Likewise, *c* can almost always be replaced with a *k* or an *s*: *cap* could be *kap*, and *nice* could be *nise*. That would then let us use the letter *c* for another sound, say, the *ch* in *chop*.

Another possibility is not merely to shuffle the current symbols around, but also to supplement them with new variants. We might add marks to the current twenty-six letters—a slash through a *c* might indicate it has the "hard" sound of *k*, for instance, or a mark over the *s* might indicate it's pronounced *sh* (*šip* for *ship*). Noah Webster did exactly this in his *American Dictionary* in 1828, printing the "hard" *c* (as in *cat*) with a line through it and the "soft" *g* (as in *general*) with a dot over it. It never caught on, but it's not necessarily an absurd idea. The French do something like it already—when *c* comes before an *a* it's usually pronounced as a *k*, but when it's marked with a cedilla (a little comma under the letter, *ç*), it takes an *s* sound, as in *façade*.

Another step up in complexity is to introduce wholly new characters into the alphabet, presumably in order to give it as many letters as it has sounds. That *sh* sound might be marked as *ʃ*, for example, and we might use Greek *θ* or Old English *þ* for *th*. This is more or less what happened in the International Phonetic Alphabet, or IPA, developed by an international team of linguists in the 1880s and updated from time to time ever since. In this scheme each significant sound is assigned its own symbol; there are no exceptions and very few ambiguities. It also includes sounds that don't appear in standard English: the trilled *r*, the back-of-the-throat *ch* of *loch*, even the *click* sounds of the Xhosa language. The International Phonetic Alphabet has the great advantage that it lets print come as close as possible to sound recording; ði Intərnæʃənəl fənɛtɪk ælfəbɛt has the even greater disadvantage, though, that it looks like indecipherable gibberish to those who've not been trained in its intricacies.

The second problem is that there's no widespread agreement on *whose* pronunciation should provide the basis for the spelling. The variety of pronunciations across the English-speaking world is staggering. British and American speakers now use the same spelling, *leisure*, for a word they pronounce differently. Should the British *leh-zhuh* and the American *lee-zher* be spelled differently? Should different regions of the world, even different regions of the country, have different systems of spelling? The more you think about it, the messier it gets: should rich and poor people have different spellings? Northerners and Southerners? Blacks and whites? Or should someone settle on a single preferred pronunciation? And who would be bold enough to tell the rest of the world that their pronunciation is inferior? In countries with official language academies, the answer is straightforward, but English has no central authority.

A third problem sounds odd, but it's true: many people aren't aware of how they pronounce words. When asked how to make the words *cat*, *dog*, and *horse* plural, most people say you simply add an *s*. In spelling, that's right: *cats*, *dogs*, *horses*. In speech, though, we actually add three different sounds. We pronounce *cats* as *cats*, but *dogs* is actually pronounced *dogz*—because the g is a voiced consonant, we add what's called a voiced sibilant when we make it plural—and the sound of *horses* is made up of *horse* plus another entire syllable, *iz*. Asking people to spell exactly the same way as they write is to demand of them a degree of self-consciousness that few can muster.

A fourth problem—probably minor, though there have been passionate arguments about it over the centuries—is that changing spelling to match pronunciation threatens to obscure much information about word origins. English spellings preserve information about word origins that aren't obvious from English pronunciations—showing, for instance, the close connection

between *receipt* and *reception*, despite their very different pronunciations. A "rational" phonetic spelling system might render *photograph* and *photography* as *FOH-tuh-graf* and *fuh-TAH-gruh-fee*,
but then the shared origin of the words—from the Greek *photos*
'light' and *graphein* 'to write'—would be obscured.

The fifth problem is change itself. The great merit of spelling
reform is that it would no longer require generations of students
to spend years learning how to spell. The main obstacle, though, is
that one generation would have to learn an entirely new system,
which would require tremendous effort. To see how much luck such
grand, sweeping changes typically have in the English-speaking
world, consider the fate of the metric system. On December 23,
1975, President Gerald Ford signed into law 15 U.S.C. Chapter 6
§(204) 205a–205l, better known as the Metric Conversion Act. The
new law announced that the "declared policy of the United States"
was "to designate the metric system of measurement as the preferred
system of weights and measures for United States trade and commerce." After more than three decades of effort, only two-liter bottles
are familiar to most Americans; those outside technical fields have
little idea what centimeters, kilograms, and hectares are. Britain,
Canada, Ireland, Australia, and New Zealand have made bigger
strides toward the metric system, but pints, pounds, and miles are
still common wherever English is spoken.

Spelling reform would be more complicated still. Suppose a
new system of English spelling is adopted—within a generation or
so, centuries' worth of English literature would be unreadable.
Would we have to wait for someone to "translate" the works of
Jane Austen or Charles Dickens into the new spelling? Would the
billions of English pages now on the World Wide Web become effectively unsearchable? The inconvenience of change was one of
the reasons Samuel Johnson had little patience for spelling reformers in 1755. Some, he said, "have endeavoured to accommodate orthography better to the pronunciation, without considering that
this is to measure by a shadow, to take that for a model or standard
which is changing while they apply it." Johnson saw little prospect
of success: "who," he asked, "can hope to prevail on nations to

change their practice, and make all their old books useless? or what advantage would a new orthography procure equivalent to the confusion and perplexity of such an alteration?"[17] He reminded his readers that "for the law to be *known*, is of more importance than to be *right*." Change, he said, "is not made without inconvenience, even from worse to better. There is in constancy and stability a general and lasting advantage, which will always overbalance the slow improvements of gradual correction."[18]

This leads us to a sixth problem: it's reasonable to assume that pronunciations will keep changing, as they always have. Should we keep changing spellings to reflect the changing pronunciations?— or would it make sense to declare a permanent standard? Johnson saw this problem too: he argued that "our written language" shouldn't "comply with the corruptions of oral utterance, or copy that which every variation of time or place makes different from itself, and imitate those changes, which will again be changed, while imitation is employed in observing them."[19]

The seventh and final problem is that, despite the passion of the reformers, the large majority of English speakers and readers simply don't see the need for sweeping change—however much they may resent devoting their youth to memorization. Once again, Johnson was skeptical: he denied "that particular combinations of letters have much influence on human happiness," and knew that it was possible to teach the truth "by modes of spelling fanciful and erroneous: I am not yet so lost in lexicography," he reminded readers, "as to forget that *words are the daughters of earth, and that things are the sons of heaven*."[20]

NONE OF THIS is to say that exchanging irrational for rational spellings is impossible, or that it never happens. Spellings are always changing, and sometimes they get more logical. In the eighteenth century, a doctor who helped patients by working with his hands instead of simply prescribing medicines was called a *chirurgeon*, from a pair of Greek roots: *chir-* 'hand' is the root of *chiropractor*, literally "one who practices with his hands"; *-urg-* 'work' shows up in like *metallurgy*, *liturgy*, and *dramaturge* (one who works with the stage). A *chirurgeon*, therefore, was a "hand worker." But in 1755 Johnson noted in his *Dictionary*, "It is now generally pronounced, and by many written, *surgeon*," and it's *surgeon* that has survived. Spellings like *shew* and *hiccough*, common a century ago, have almost completely disappeared, giving way to the more rational *show* and *hiccup*.

Still, inconsistencies remain, and groups advocating a reformed English spelling haven't disappeared. An Internet search for the phrase "spelling reform" turns up 4.5 million Web pages devoted to the subject, including the home pages of groups like the Simplified Spelling Society and the American Literacy Council. Countless people have devoted countless hours to rendering our orthography rational. But all the systems are incompatible with one another, and none seems to have attracted the attention of a government, a major newspaper, or a major publishing firm. And in the end, despite all the good reasons proposed by the dedicated reformers, it seems most people simply don't find English spelling sufficiently bothersome to go to the trouble of changing it.

They may be right. There's no empirical evidence that a logical spelling system makes for happier people. The very regular system of Spanish, the inconsistent alphabetic system of English, the entirely arbitrary system of Chinese logograms—they would seem to result in different levels of happiness, with rational Spain at the top and arbitrary China at the bottom. But since no systematic survey has ever shown that memorizing characters makes a people less content, less productive, or less sane, it's hard to convince English speakers that a simple spelling would make them happier, more productive, or more emotionally balanced. Maybe someone will yet succeed where so many others have failed. Those who've paid attention to the history of attempts to reform spelling, though, don't hold out much hope.

CHAPTER 9

Direct, Simple,
Brief, Vigorous, and Lucid

HENRY WATSON FOWLER SHOWS THE WAY

EIGHTEENTH-CENTURY ENGLAND'S two most original grammarians, Robert Lowth and Joseph Priestley, were very smart men—smarter, in fact, than many of their detractors—and, more important, they were reasonable. Their reputations have suffered unfairly.[1]

Their successors, on the other hand, gave prescriptivism a bad name. Lindley Murray was more prescriptive and less reflective than his predecessors, and as the eighteenth century turned into the nineteenth, prescriptivism became ever more prevalent and ever less tolerant of variation. The new mode differed from that of the eighteenth-century grammars: no longer systematic overviews that issued a few pronouncements by the way, the new books were lists of interdictions—to speak proper English was to obey a series of prohibitions. This new *thou-shalt-not* style of many of the nineteenth century's so-called grammars is summed up on the title page of Oliver Bell Bunce's 1883 guide, *Don't*, published under the pseudonym "Censor." "Most of the rules of society," Bunce wrote in his preface, "are prohibitory in character." He was happy to oblige with a list of his own prohibitions:

Don't speak ungrammatically. Study books of grammar, and the writings of the best authors.

Don't pronounce incorrectly. Listen carefully to the conversation of cultivated people, and consult the dictionaries.

Don't mangle your words, nor smother them, nor swallow them. . . .

Don't use slang. . . .

Don't use meaningless exclamations, such as "Oh, my!" "Oh, crackey!" etc. . . .

Don't say *ketch* for *catch*, nor *ken* for *can*. Don't say *feller* for *fellow*, or *winder* for *window*.[2]

The state that prescriptive grammar reached is evident in the works of one of the leading Victorian writers on English, Richard Grant White. Born in New York in 1822, he devoted much of his early career to Shakespeare studies, but his most popular books were *Words and Their Uses* (1870) and *Every-Day English* (1880). The first promised a "consideration of the right use and the abuse of words and idioms, with an occasional examination of their origin and their history. It is occupied almost exclusively with the correctness and fitness of verbal expression."[3] It's a fine example of Victorian prescriptivism, and is, in H. L. Mencken's memorable formulation, "a mine of more or less authentic erudition."[4]

White opened *Words and Their Uses* with a clear and forceful expression of the *norma loquendi* principle: "Usage in the end makes language; determining not only the meaning of words, but their suggestiveness, and also their influence." But no sooner did he advance that argument than he backed off. "When a language is subjected to the constant action of such degrading influences as those which threaten ours," he asserted, "it may be well to introduce into its development a little consciousness"—that is to say, when usage leads in the wrong direction, then it's time to resist. He even went on to say that "it would be very weak reasoning that would draw from the fact that language is formed, on the whole, by consent and custom"—this, he found, was "an argument in favor of indifference as to right or wrong of usage."[5] *Norma loquendi* was left in the cold.

Indifference as to right or wrong usage was not among White's vices, and so he tried to offer an alternative account of what made for correctness in English. He granted that "usage may be compulsory in its behests," but still maintained that, "as in all other human affairs, that which is may be wrong"—just twenty pages after declaring usage the supreme law, he was arguing the opposite. Some things, he argued, are simply and unambiguously wrong, no matter how many people say them: "There is a misuse of words which can be justified by no authority, however great, by no usage, however general."[6] It was the responsibility of grammarians like him to protect the language from breaking down.

ONCE WE ABANDON usage—the prevailing practice of the entire English-speaking world—as a standard, there remain at least five grounds on which to object to a word, a phrase, or a usage:

- Taste—good English is what I like.
- Authority—proper usage is established by the great writers.
- Etymology—the true meaning of a word comes from the meaning of its root, usually the Germanic, Latin, or Greek word from which it was derived.
- Analogy with classical grammar—Latin and Greek provide the best model of grammar, and the rules that govern those languages should also govern English.
- Logic—we should have no concerns at all with arbitrary rules, but let simple logic dictate what's correct and what's incorrect.

Taste is the first category and, while White often proclaimed that taste shouldn't concern a grammarian, he wasn't shy about expressing his opinions. Although *experience* had been a verb for three hundred years when he wrote *Every-Day English*, he still snarled that he couldn't abide it—and yet he also admitted that his objection "has no better ground than that of taste or individual preference, which should be excluded from discussions like the present." That is to say, taste *shouldn't* enter judgments about language. "Yet," White continued, "I am inclined to make that objection very strongly."[7] And so he made it: White didn't like the verb *experience*, so you shouldn't use it. Other summary judgments are likewise grounded on nothing more than taste:

> DONATE.—I need hardly say, that this word is utterly abominable—one that any lover of simple honest English cannot hear with patience and without offence.

> INAUGURATE is a word which had better be eschewed by all those who do not wish to talk high-flying nonsense, else they will find themselves led by bad examples into using it in the sense of begin, open, set up, establish.

> REAL ESTATE is a compound that has no proper place in the language of every-day life.[8]

There's not much that can be said about using taste as a criterion for the language, other than *de gustibus non est disputandum*—there's no accounting for taste. One reader may find bureaucratic English, newfangled coinages, freshly verbed nouns, and clumsy constructions as irritating as nails on a blackboard. But another may find exactly the same things useful, charming, even graceful—and who's to say whose taste is better?

"BECAUSE I LIKE it" is rarely considered a good reason for accepting a word. "Because great writers like it," on the other hand—that's a whole 'nother story. And 'nother, this argument from authority goes, *must* be acceptable, because it appears in the *Rule of St. Francis*, the *Paston Letters*, John Skelton's poems, the Geneva Bible, and the writings of Queen Elizabeth I, Charlotte

Smith, and Zora Neale Hurston: they used it, so we're allowed to use it.

The fact that there's never been an English academy hasn't stopped people from demanding regulations, and even without an official institution it was still possible to draw on authority. This time, though, it was not the authority of a government or a roster of distinguished academics, but the authority of the great writers of the past, who were posthumously recruited into a ghostly academy. The logic here is that if Shakespeare did it, it must be okay; if he didn't—and if Pope, Johnson, Dickens, Emerson, and Thoreau didn't—then there must be something wrong with it. The job of the prescriptive grammarian is to encourage writers to model their usage on the great writers of the past.

There's nothing odd about modeling a style on some earlier master; schoolchildren have long been taught to write by imitating great writers, just as many painters learn their craft by copying acknowledged masterpieces. In his autobiography, Benjamin Franklin described how he tried to improve his style by imitating the eighteenth-century essayist Joseph Addison. Franklin took some of Addison's *Spectator* essays, "& making short Hints of the Sentiments in each Sentence, laid them by a few Days, and then, without looking at the Book, tried to compleat the Papers again." When he had finished with an essay, he compared his attempt with Addison's original, discovered his faults, and corrected them.[9]

The most extreme example of this habit took place not in English but in Latin during the Renaissance. That's when a group of Italian scholars self-consciously called for a "rebirth" of the culture and values of the ancient Greeks and Romans. They wrote in Latin, and not what they considered the corrupt, degraded *modern* Latin of the church and law courts, but *real* Latin—Latin as it was written a thousand years earlier, and especially the Latin of Marcus Tullius Cicero, the great legal orator and philosopher. This led to a sixteenth-century movement called "Ciceronianism," in which the ideal style of modern Latin was as close as possible to Cicero's style. Some were content to follow his characteristic flourishes or his usual modes of constructing arguments, but a few vowed that even Cicero's vocabulary had to be followed closely. Writers like Pietro Bembo took pride in never using a word unless it appeared somewhere in Cicero's works. If a writer needed to refer to something invented since Cicero's death, or something that Cicero simply neglected to mention, he or she was out of luck. And a few exceptionally zealous Ciceronians went even further. The Belgian humanist Christophe de Longueil was notorious for refusing to use a word unless the *inflected form* appeared in Cicero's works. An English analogy might be using only the words Shakespeare used—and while Shakespeare used *salute*, *saluted*, *salutes*, and *saluteth* in his works, he never used *saluting*, so neither can you. To borrow a Shakespearean phrase, that way madness lies. Regulating modern style by ancient principle can be disabling—it would paralyze anyone into incoherence, since there's no way to escape crippling self-consciousness.

White sometimes leaned on the authority of great writers. "Since the time when King Lear was written and our revised translation of the Bible made," he wrote, "the English language has suffered little change": the time of James I was the language's golden age. The age of Queen Anne also had much going for it, since "the highest reputation for purity of style in the writing of English prose has been Addison's." Authority was sometimes enough to make him reconsider his own prejudices. We saw already that he objected to *experience* as a verb; evidence of an authority on the other side led him to rethink it: "I have been able to find, by diligent search, only one example of any authority— the following, quoted by [the novelist Samuel] Richardson."[10] (But the Richardson example still wasn't enough to change his mind: White decided to stick to his guns.)

Like arguments based on taste, appeals to authority aren't all bad. Cicero and Shakespeare were great writers, and there's nothing wrong with modeling a style on them. But there are limits beyond which appeals to authority are useless, and slavish imitation is always foolish. The best answer to assertions like "Charles Dickens often ended sentences with prepositions" or "Mark Twain never split an infinitive" is "So what?" Cicero and Shakespeare, Dickens and Twain were great writers, but they've been dead for a long time. They have no jurisdiction over us.

WHITE, THOUGH, WASN'T willing to grant jurisdiction over the language to anyone who came before him. And when authority is lacking—or when authorities offer competing points of view—it's possible to turn to etymology. The word *etymology* comes from the Greek *etymon* 'root meaning of a word'. For some, "root meaning" and "true meaning" were interchangeable.

The word *decimate* offers an example of etymological reasoning. It comes from the Latin *decimare* 'to take one tenth'; its root is *decem* 'ten'—the same as in *decimal* (a base-ten system) and *dime* (Latin *decimus* evolved into Old French *disme*, and then to English *dime*). The Latin word referred to a gruesome Roman punishment of rebellious troops, described by the ancient biographer Plutarch: "*Antony* finding that his Men had in a great Consternation deserted the Defence of the Mount, . . . resolved to proceed against them by Decimation, which is done by dividing the Legions by Tens, and out of every Ten, to put one to Death, as it happens by Lot."[11] So *decimate* means—or meant—to execute every tenth man. But can it be used more loosely? Can a plague decimate a population? Can something more abstract, like a program, be decimated? Can a bad economic policy decimate the middle class? Can something be "totally decimated"? White thought not: "to use decimation as a general phrase for great slaughter is simply ridiculous."[12]

The arguments continue today. William Safire, probably the most famous language authority in twentieth-century America, can be found delivering opinions both for and against the extended uses of *decimate*. He first considered the question in 1982: "to limit the word's meaning to 'one-tenth,'" he wrote then, "would be like limiting myriad to its literal 10000—time and usage have broadened the meaning of both words."[13] But by the time he revisited the question in 1991, he had become a hard-liner: "Sloppy writers use it as a confused intensifier after using *devastate*. . . . In time, unless purists persist, *decimate* will come to mean 'destroy a large part of.' "[14] Jan Freeman, writing in the *Boston Globe* in 2007, spotted Safire's inconsistency and called for a more permissive attitude: "decimate," she pointed out, "has always had a wider scope." She added, with the kind of common sense that's surprisingly rare among commentators on language, "we don't especially need a term that means 'kill one in 10.' "[15]

It's possible to quarrel with any individual instance of a word taking on extended meanings. Does *dilapidated* apply only to things made of stone, since its root is the Latin *lapis* 'stone'? Are we free to use an expression like *six-month anniversary*, even though the root is *annus* 'year'? Reasonable people can take either side. But to insist that etymologies must *always* determine meanings is seriously misguided. To limit every word's current meaning to the meaning of its root is to misunderstand the way language works. The word *nice* shows just how far a common word can drift from its etymon. The root is the Latin word *nescire* 'to be ignorant'; the *-sci-* root appears in words like *science, conscience,* and *omniscience,* and the *ne-* is a negation. When *nice* made its first appearance in English, around the year 1300, it meant "foolish, silly, simple." These senses died out in the seventeenth century, but along the way *nice* had picked up a new group of meanings, including "wanton, dissolute, lascivious" and "Precise or particular in matters of reputation or conduct; scrupulous, punctilious."

Starting late in the sixteenth century, the "scrupulous" meaning evolved into "Refined, cultured; associated with polite society," and then into "Respectable, virtuous, decent," a sense first cited from one of Jane Austen's letters from 1799: "The Biggs would call her a nice Woman." And shortly before Austen was born, *nice* also came to mean "That one derives pleasure or satisfaction from; agreeable, pleasant, satisfactory"; from there, it was only a short jump to "pleasant in manner, agreeable, good-natured," first attested in 1797, and the meaning that most people assume *nice* has always had. The *OED* offers more than three dozen distinct meanings of the adjective form of *nice* alone—"unimportant, trivial"; "slender, thin"; "pampered, luxurious"; "cowardly, unmanly";

"appetizing"; "strange, rare." Then there are the two adverbial meanings ("foolishly" or "pleasingly"), three meanings of a verb—"To be pleasant," "To do or perform well," "To be (excessively) nice or polite"—six phrases requiring separate definition, and nineteen "special uses." The point of this digression is that anyone who believes a word's meaning is necessarily restricted to its root is obliged to use *nice* only to mean "ignorant" or "foolish"—which would itself be ignorant and foolish.

MAYBE LATIN AND Greek roots aren't definitive; still, the answers may be found in Latin and Greek *grammar*. The supposed prohibition on ending a sentence with a preposition—as in "What are you looking for?" or "That's where I got it from"—derives from the fact that, in Latin, a preposition *must* go before its object. Some took it for granted that an English preposition, too, must always take the pre-position, and that sentence-ending prepositions are simply wrong.

Another dispute shows how classical grammar can be brought to bear on modern English. Consider the split infinitive: since the nineteenth century, there's been an argument against allowing an adverb to come between the particle *to* and the infinitive form of a verb. It's true that, through much of the history of the language, the *to* and the verb have tended to stick together. Sometime in the nineteenth century, though, when the split infinitive was very common in spoken and written English, infinitive-splitting became a sin. White was typical of his age in disparaging it: in *Every-Day English*, he approvingly quoted a correspondent who hoped "to get rid of that barbarism of speech which has lately come into vogue, introduced by our American journalists, of placing the adverb between the sign of the infinitive mood and the verb." This correspondent combined appeals to Latin grammar and to authorities when he insisted, "This collocation is grossly unclassical, not being found in any standard author of any age." (Not so: there's no shortage of split infinitives in the works of great English writers.) White was ready with an answer: "He is so clearly right about the placing of the adverb as to make comment unnecessary. Distinguished precedent might be shown for this construction," he wrote, "as for many other bad uses of language; but it is eminently un-English."[16]

THE USE OF "logic" or "reason" to justify some usages, and to blame others, is particularly troublesome, because it often flies in the face of widespread, even universal, practice. And Richard Grant White—an exceedingly devout, not to say zealous, worshiper at the altar of logic—was guilty of many of the transgressions that logic forces on language.

White had particular animus against the word *reliable*, placing it high on a list of "words that are not words. . . . That it is often heard merely shows that many persons have been led into the error of using it." What's the problem? Most of our adjectives with *-able* or *-ible* mean "that may be ——ed": *acceptable*, "that may be accepted"; *admirable*, "that may be admired." But "*reliable*," White insisted, "does not mean that may be relied, but is used to mean that may be relied *upon*, and that, therefore, it is not tolerable."[17] If *relyuponable* were a word, it might make the grade, but without the *upon*, it was, for White, mere nonsense. Logic said so.

Logic also prohibited the so-called double negative. In many languages, double negatives—actually multiple negations, since there's no reason to stop at two—serve to emphasize the negation. In Spanish, for instance, *no sé nada* can be literally translated as "I don't know nothing," but in practice means "I know nothing" or "I don't know anything." Similar constructions were once common in English. Middle English was loaded with multiple negatives: as Chaucer wrote of his Knight in *The Canterbury Tales*, not long before 1400, "He nevere yet no vileynye ne sayde / In al his lyf unto no manner wight," a quadruple negative that demonstrates an almost acrobatic degree of linguistic agility: "He never yet didn't say no villainy in all his life to no kind of person." Shakespeare and many other writers used multiple negation all the time.

Beginning in the seventeenth century, though, the English double negative fell out of favor, at least in more formal settings. And reason was used to justify this shift. Take the idiomatic Spanish phrase "I don't know nothing": logic says that if you *don't* know *nothing*, then you *must* know *something*. And it's true that treating two negatives as a positive can sometimes produce frustrating ambiguities: a sentence like "I couldn't do nothing" can mean either "I couldn't do anything" (treating the two negatives as intensifiers) or "I had to do something" (as in, "I couldn't just sit there doing nothing"). Though real confusion is rare, grammarians have long worked to expunge English of the dreaded double negative. Abner Alden, a Bostonian, decreed in 1811, "RULE XIII. Two negatives destroy each other, and are equivalent to an affirmative: as, I *don't* know *nothing* about it; is the same as, I do know *something* about it. He is *not never* willing to write; that is, he is always willing, &c. You *dont* [sic] eat *nothing*; that is, you eat something."[18]

White agreed with Alden, admitting that the double negative may have been widespread in earlier eras; still, it was illogical and therefore had to go. At some point in history, two negatives became an affirmative. This wasn't mere caprice: "it was chiefly owing to a deliberate conformity to the requirements of logic, which in the process of time was inevitable, and which, once attained, will never be abandoned."[19] Reason rules—and if it doesn't now, it will in the long run.

The problem with these claims is that what seems logical or reasonable to one person may not seem so to others. White was guilty of turning the *familiar* into the *natural*. He was convinced that logic—at least, logic as he saw it—was apparent to anyone with a brain; if "grammar," a word he despised, contradicted his logic, then grammar had to be tossed out. He even went so far as to declare, "Formal grammar is at war with common-sense." What, though, is "common-sense"? It's the ability to perceive "the practical relations" and, as it happens, "This faculty exists in a greater degree in some races than in others. The Anglo-Saxon race are distinguished by it; they are preëminently a people of common-sense."[20]

"Common-sense," it seems, is common only among people of the "Anglo-Saxon race." When other "races" make different choices in their own languages, they don't prompt White to rethink whether his "logic" is really universal; they simply prove that they lack the sense he is so proud of. So, for instance, "The grammar of the oldest written language known—the Sanskrit—is of all grammars the most complicated, and the rivals of Sanskrit in this respect are the languages of some utterly barbarous peoples."[21] It's clear that White is taking his own background—he was born and raised in an English-speaking country with Western values—and using it as the standard by which to measure all human experience. It's a sad instance of narrow-minded prejudice. There's no reason to single out White for particular racist ignominy; he was merely giving voice to beliefs common to many in his day. But his strict application of logic tends to wipe out many perfectly acceptable idioms.

AFTER THIS EXTENDED example of Victorian prescription, it's a pleasure to turn to a more thoughtful prescriptivist of the first half of the twentieth century, Henry Watson Fowler.

Fowler attended Rugby, one of the most distinguished public schools in England, where he studied the classical languages, French, and German. He thrived there, serving as the secretary of the debating society and taking the school's prize for English composition. From Rugby it was off to Balliol College, Oxford, but there his reputation lagged: no longer the biggest fish in a small pond, Fowler found himself competing with many serious thinkers. The master at Balliol was Benjamin Jowett, one of the legendary scholars of Victorian Oxford. A famous bit of doggerel, written by one of his students, captures both Jowett's polymathic range and his colossal ego:

> First come I; my name is Jowett.
> There's no knowledge but I know it.
> I am the Master of this College,
> What I don't know isn't knowledge.

Jowett thought well enough of Fowler; he found him "quite a gentleman in manner and feeling," with "good sense and good taste." This "very fair scholar," he wrote in his letter of reference, has "a natural aptitude for the profession of Schoolmaster."[22]

It hardly seems like enthusiastic praise, and with good reason: Fowler passed his exams, but his scores were unimpressive, and he probably wasn't suited for anything better than a schoolmaster's position. And so a schoolmaster he became, teaching at Sedbergh School in Yorkshire. His years there weren't particularly happy: he found the place "intellectually stagnant," and he became increasingly "sceptical about the good of ramming logic into the heads of small boys." To complicate matters, Fowler had by this time disavowed Christianity, which excluded him from many posts of responsibility in the school.[23]

Eventually he settled in London, where he began writing for magazines. But freelance writing was not enough to pay the bills, so Henry and his brother Frank sought more substantial literary employment. They proposed a translation of the satirical works of the Roman poet Lucian, whose works hadn't been available in English for decades. The Lucian translation was well received—as well received, at least, as a learned translation of a comparatively little-known classical satirist can be. Most important, it was enough to get the attention of Oxford University Press. The Fowlers began thinking of other projects they might publish with one of the oldest presses in the English-speaking world.

The first hint of what would eventually become *The King's English* came in a letter written December 19, 1904, which the Fowlers sent to Charles Cannan at Oxford University's Clarendon Press, offering him "a sort of English composition manual, from the negative point of view, for journalists & amateur writers." The idea was to collect examples of bad writing—taken from real published sources, and not made up for the purpose—and to display them "in terrorem," while offering "a few rules on common solecisms."[24] Three days later, Cannan replied in the affirmative. He, too, was disturbed by the "heap of filth" in the language and thought the Fowlers would be just the right people to remove it.

The brothers proposed a few titles for their planned book: *The New Solecist*, *A Book of Solecisms*, and *The Clarendon Press Book of Solecisms*.[25] None pleased the marketing division; eventually they settled on *The King's English*.

OFTEN THE FOWLERS' advice had little to do with "grammar" narrowly understood, and everything to do with clarity of expression. Even though their examples were mostly negative, *The King's English* marked a big change from most of the earlier *thou-shalt-not* guides. "Any one who wishes to become a good writer," they advised, "should endeavour, before he allows himself to be tempted by the more showy qualities, to be direct, simple, brief, vigorous, and lucid." They then expanded these adjectives into more practical advice:

> This general principle may be translated into practical rules in the domain of vocabulary as follows:—
> Prefer the familiar word to the far-fetched.
> Prefer the concrete word to the abstract.
> Prefer the single word to the circumlocution.
> Prefer the short word to the long.
> Prefer the Saxon word to the Romance.[26]

The Fowlers were smart enough to know that any guideline, if applied unintelligently, would produce bad results. While these five "practical rules" usually reinforce one another—"all five rules would be often found to give the same answer about the same word or set of words"—there are times when they conflict. A writer might decide to "Prefer the Saxon word to the Romance" on every occasion; "Observing that *translate* is derived from Latin," therefore, "and learning that the Elizabethans had another word for it, he will pull us up by *englishing* his quotations." Poppycock, said the brothers: "Such freaks should be left to the Germans, who have by this time succeeded in expelling as aliens a great many words that were good enough for Goethe." In general, though, sinning against one of the rules amounts to sinning against the lot, for bad writers tended to be far-fetched, abstract, and full of circumlocution and to use long and Romance-language words all at the same time. The Fowlers offered as an example of bad writing "*In the contemplated eventuality*," which they call "a phrase no worse than what any one can pick up for himself out of his paper's leading article for the day." This abomination "is at once the far-fetched, the abstract, the periphrastic, the long, and the Romance, for *if so*."[27]

After *The King's English*, the Fowler brothers teamed up again in 1911 to work on *The Concise Oxford English Dictionary*, an abridgment of the monumental *Oxford English Dictionary*, then still in progress. But the First World War interrupted their work; Frank, who volunteered even though he was well past the age of most soldiers, contracted tuberculosis in the army and died in 1918 at the age of forty-seven. Henry completed the dictionary alone before turning his attention to a new project—a kind of expansion of *The King's English*, a book with the same concern for blunders and solecisms, but much more extensive. The result was *A Dictionary of Modern English Usage*, published in 1926. Its 742 pages of double-columned small print offer advice on everything from the choice of *a* or *an* to the pronunciation of *zwieback*.

Sometimes, in both *The King's English* and *Modern English Usage*, Fowler repeated the grammarian's perennial complaints, especially those based on arguments from etymology. "There is no such thing as a mutual friend in the singular," for instance—Fowler knew that *mutual* comes from Latin *mutuus* 'reciprocal'; reciprocity involves more than one thing. "*Our mutual friend* is nonsense," he ruled in *The King's English*; "*mutual friends*, though not nonsense, is bad English, because it is tautological."[28] Or "uniqueness is a matter of yes or no only; no unique thing is more or less unique than another unique thing."[29] The verb *to aggravate* entered the language around 1530, when it meant—as its Latin root, *gravis*, suggests—"to make heavy; to load down." To *aggravate* was to make a situation worse; you can aggravate a situation, an affliction, an offense. But as early as 1611, people began using *aggravate* to refer to a person, using it as a synonym for *irritate* or *annoy*. Still, for Fowler, etymology gets the final say: this sense of *aggravate* "should be left to the uneducated," since it is nothing more than "a feminine or childish colloquialism."[30]

Usually, though, Fowler was reasonable and sought a middle ground between the permissive and the unforgiving. His prescriptions were conservative but rarely narrow-minded. And he was refreshingly aware that some problems have no solution, or at least no good solution. He looked, for instance, at the phrase *nom de plume* for "pen name." The problem is that this French term is not French—among Francophones, *nom de guerre* is preferred. Should English writers use *nom de plume* and risk alienating those who know the French? Should they opt for correct French and risk confusing Anglophone readers? No easy answer presents itself. "It is unfortunate," Henry and Frank wrote; "for we now have to choose between a blunder and a pedantry."[31] Fowler also usually knew when he was beaten. There were Victorian objections to the word *reliable*—since you don't *rely something* but *rely upon something*, it made no sense to form *reliable*; only *relyuponable* made good sense. Hooey, said Fowler; by 1926 it had been in the language for decades and was widely used among all classes. "It is clear," he wrote, "that the purists have not yet reconciled themselves to the inevitable."[32] *Norma loquendi* was making a comeback.

Fowler took a particular delight in shattering conventional wisdom on matters grammatical. On the split infinitive, he insisted that the happiest people of all were "those who neither know nor care what a split infinitive is."[33] He did find the split infinitive ugly, but there's nothing unusual about that: "it is one among several hundred ugly things, and the novice should not allow it to occupy his mind exclusively."[34] And on the famous prohibition on sentence-ending prepositions, he declared it "a cherished superstition."[35] Some reviewers were unhappy with his permissiveness: the *Times*, for instance, declared sentence-ending prepositions "inelegant." Fowler, frustrated by such attacks, wrote to the *OED*'s Henry Bradley:

> Earlier writers felt themselves (as we ought to) quite free
> to choose. Some (eighteenth-century?) grammarian made
> a rule on quite insufficient induction—as with many
> grammatical rules— . . . Grammatical parrots have re-
> peated it from generation to generation, not making any
> independent inquiry.[36]

Fowler also knew something that too few commentators have realized: that the written and the spoken languages are different things. "The interrogative *who* is often used for *whom*," wrote Fowler and his brother, as in, "*Who* did you see?" Rather than chastising the barbarity of those who say such things, they pointed out, "A distinction should here be made between conversation, written or spoken, and formal writing. Many educated people feel that in saying *It is I*, *Whom do you mean?* instead of *It's me*, *Who do you mean?* they will be talking like a book, and they justifiably prefer geniality to grammar." Even Fowler spoke casually; no one who knew him ever accused him of talking like a book. But writing and speaking aren't the same thing: "in print," he advised, "unless it is dialogue, the correct forms are advisable."[37]

He could give no good reason for his dislike of some other words and usages. On *bureaucrat*, a comparatively recent coinage, he lamented that "The formation is so barbarous that all attempt at self-respect in pronunciation may perhaps as well be abandoned."[38] He echoed his earlier objection that "The termination *-cracy* is now so freely applied that it is too late to complain of this except on the ground of ugliness."[39] The forms *quietened* and *quietening*, likewise, are ugly.[40] Judgments like this are based entirely on taste, but Fowler was clear about that: he didn't try to justify their preference in terms of "the genius of the language," logic, etymology, or anything else.

FOWLER DOMINATED THE British market for decades; to this day, more than a century after *The King's English*, the name "Fowler" can strike fear into British hearts. But Fowler's books never caught on in the United States. The newspapers and magazines through which Fowler trawled for examples would be familiar to readers in England, but who in America read the *Daily Telegraph* or the *Guernsey Evening Press*? Many of Fowler's recommendations, moreover, dealt with British spelling, British pronunciation, and British punctuation and had little to do with Yankee practice. Fowler was explicit about it: "The English and the American language and literature are both good things," he wrote in *The King's English*; "but they are better apart than mixed." He was adamant that "Americanisms are foreign words, and should be so treated," though he was careful to remind readers that "To say this is not to insult the American language."[41] A companion to *Modern English Usage*, H. W. Horwill's *Dictionary of Modern American Usage*, appeared in 1935 and tried to adapt Fowler's advice for audiences on the other side of the Atlantic, but it got little attention.[42]

That left room for a homegrown American guide to writing. The most famous example of the genre began not as a project of the great Clarendon Press, under the supervision of Oxford lexicographers, but as a tiny booklet, cheaply and privately printed in a small press run in 1918. Its author was an obscure professor of English at Cornell University in Ithaca, New York, who had published editions of *Macaulay's and Carlyle's Essays on Samuel Johnson*, John Dryden's dramatic criticism, James Fenimore Cooper's *Last of the Mohicans*, and the *Juliana* by the Old English poet Cynewulf. That's respectable work for a low-profile academic, but hardly the sort of thing that could lead to widespread fame. And yet this professor's name has been one of the most familiar in American university classrooms for decades: William Strunk Jr.

Strunk was both author and publisher of what he called *The Elements of Style*, though it was known on the Cornell campus simply as "the little book." And "little" was right: it was a pamphlet of just forty-three pages. The campus buzz led Strunk to issue a commercial edition in 1920, which in turn appeared in a revised edition in 1935, completed with the help of Edward A. Tenney, under a new title, *The Elements and Practice of Composition*. But it remained little known in the larger world until the late 1950s, when one of Strunk's former students, Elwyn Brooks White, decided to expand his late master's teaching notes and present them to the wider world.

White had taken an English class with Strunk in 1919 and went on to have a successful literary career, far more successful than Strunk himself: White teamed up with James Thurber to write *Is Sex Necessary?* in 1929, and he later wrote the children's classics *Stuart Little* (1945) and *Charlotte's Web* (1952). After Strunk's death in 1946, White published a recollection of his former professor in the *New Yorker*. "At the close of the first World War," he wrote, "when I was a student at Cornell, I took a course called English 8. My professor was William Strunk Jr." He described the required textbook, "a slim volume called *The Elements of Style*, whose author was the professor himself."[43] The article led a publisher to ask White to revise "the little book"; happy to pay homage to his late professor, he agreed. And so in 1959 there appeared *The Elements of Style*—the original title—now with two names on the title page. The book has been known to generations of students simply as "Strunk & White."

LIKE THE FOWLERS, Strunk and White managed to dispense stylistic advice, much of it still very useful today. More than half a century after its appearance, *The Elements of Style* continues to be one of the bestselling books on the English language, and with good reason. Their emphasis on clarity and precision is just what many writers need to learn, whether college freshmen or professional copywriters.

Strunk and White did, however, lapse into some of the errors that have plagued prescriptivists since the eighteenth century. Their biggest systematic mistake was issuing diktats on questions that are still open. Many people long for authoritative answers on what's right or wrong in usage, but there's a whole class of questions to which no definitive answer is possible. *The Elements of Style*, for instance, begins unambiguously: the first "Elementary Rule of Usage" is

1. *Form the possessive singular of nouns by adding 's.*
   Follow this rule whatever the final consonant. Thus write,

   >Charles's friend
   >Burns's poems
   >the witch's malice.[44]

But the appearance of an *s* after a single possessive ending in *s* is actually optional, with most book publishers favoring it (*Charles's friend, Burns's poems*) and most newspapers omitting it (*Charles' friend, Burns' poems*). To demand the *s* flatly as part of "rule 1" makes it sound as if the matter has been settled. Likewise the so-called serial comma, sometimes called the Oxford comma or the Harvard comma, the subject of rule number 2:

2. *In a series of three or more terms with a single conjunction, use a comma after each term except the last.*
   Thus write,

   >red, white, and blue
   >gold, silver, or copper.[45]

Once again, the serial comma is not mandatory. There's certainly nothing wrong with it, and it does occasionally lend clarity. A notorious book dedication—almost certainly apocryphal, but a good story nonetheless—supposedly thanks "my parents, Ayn Rand and God"; an extra comma would have gone a long way toward clearing up questions about the author's family tree. But some publishers prefer to omit the serial comma, and that's their prerogative. They're not wrong in any sense.

Questions like this can generate a lot of anger. Some argue passionately for the inclusion (or exclusion) of the *s* in possessives or the serial comma, asserting dogmatically that theirs is the only proper "grammar." But these are really matters of *house style*, which the *OED* defines as "the distinctive printing methods and regulations, including the preferred spellings and conventions of punctuation, of a publishing or printing business."

Many of the features identified as rules by prescriptive grammarians have at least the advantage of being accurate rules within the most privileged variety of English, the kind you find in most newspapers, magazines, books, and business writing. Most serious readers and writers would agree that *ain't* is likely to be out of place in a scientific paper or a Nobel Prize acceptance speech. That doesn't mean the word is bad in itself—only that it's not suited to the situations in which standard English is called for.

The problems with house style, though, are different in kind. They're purely arbitrary, and authors rarely have any say in them; it's the job of the publishers to settle all such questions. Some are matters of national style: most people are now familiar with the differences between British and American spellings, as with *colour* and *color*, *centre* and *center*. There are also national differences in punctuation. American publishers generally use "double quotations," and they always put commas and periods inside the quotation marks. British publishers, on the other hand, often use 'inverted commas', and they place periods or commas inside or outside them based on context.

Smart writers need to learn the virtues of tolerance, especially tolerance of diversity. Lynne Truss, like Strunk and White, manages to be both entertaining and informative in *Eats, Shoots & Leaves*. But her own subtitle violates a rule that's common in many house styles: she wrote *The Zero Tolerance Guide to Punctuation*, where many house styles would call for *The Zero-Tolerance Guide*, hyphenating multiword phrases when they serve as adjectives. David Crystal puts it well: "Zero tolerance? That is the language of crime prevention and political extremism. Are we really comfortable with the recommendation that we should all become linguistic fundamentalists?"[46] Truss and her kind would do well to exercise a little more tolerance.

CHAPTER 10

Sabotage in Springfield

PHILIP GOVE STOKES THE FLAMES

BY ALL ACCOUNTS, PHILIP BABCOCK Gove was a decent human being. History attributes to him no flagitious crimes—no genocides, no rapes, no murders. If he ever turned hungry orphans out into the snow, no such information survives in the historical record. No department store detective ever collared him for shoplifting. As far as we know, he wasn't in the habit of stealing money from the church collection plate or kicking puppies.

And yet future historians may be excused if they conclude from the documentary evidence that Gove was one of the wickedest men who ever walked the earth, a villain comparable to Adolf Hitler or Idi Amin. It was a strange turn of events for the mild-mannered, bespectacled lexicographer who spent most of his professional life in a small office in Springfield, Massachusetts: the great crime for which Gove has been condemned is that he edited a dictionary.

It was no ordinary dictionary. This was *Webster's Third New International Dictionary*, unabridged, and it was the most important lexicographical project of the middle of the twentieth century, issued by the most trusted name in American dictionaries. And yet it generated the kind of ire that one expects to see in quarrels between pro-lifers and pro-choicers, between jihadists and Zionists, or even between Red Sox and Yankees fans. As Bergen Evans put it in the pages of the *Atlantic*, "Never has a scholarly work of this stature been attacked with such unbridled fury and contempt."[1]

PHILIP GOVE WORKED for G. & C. Merriam Company and edited one of an unbroken line of dictionaries going back to the days of Noah Webster himself. After Webster's death in 1843, George and Charles Merriam took over the franchise and began publishing new versions of the most famous American dictionary. Their company survives today, now under the name Merriam-Webster.

Now these are the generations of Webster: Webster's *American Dictionary of the English Language* (1828) begat a second edition (1840); the second edition begat a new revised edition (1847); the new revised edition begat a royal quarto edition (1864); the royal quarto edition begat *Webster's International Dictionary* (1890); *Webster's International Dictionary* begat *Webster's New International Dictionary* (1909); *Webster's New International Dictionary* begat a second edition (1934); that second edition begat *Webster's Third New International Dictionary* (1961).[2] It was on this final dictionary in the series—still the most recent unabridged dictionary from Merriam-Webster—that Gove worked for more than a decade, and that made him famous, or infamous, not only among other lexicographers but among the public at large.

The company that had inherited Noah Webster's most important property decided in the late 1930s or '40s that *Webster's Second New International*, first published in 1934, needed not merely a light revision for its next edition but a substantial reconception as well. The result was *Webster's Third*, which appeared in September 1961. Most commentators praised at least some aspects of the new dictionary. They liked the newly added words, around 100,000 of them, though some objected to the fact that 150,000 obsolete terms were kicked out to make room for the new ones. The etymologies—the weakest part of Johnson's and Webster's dictionaries—represented the state of the art in thinking about the history of the language. Many reviewers admired the new style of definition, and most agreed the printing and layout were clear.

Other innovations got mixed notices. The reviewers split over whether the new system of representing pronunciation marked an improvement over the old one. More significantly, *Webster's Third* decided to eject all proper nouns, including biographical, geographical, mythological, and literary names. This "encyclopedic" information had been central to the Merriam Company's advertising strategies in the 1930s and '40s, when *Webster's Second* was touted in newspaper and magazine ads as an all-in-one reference book, but in the 1950s the lexicographers decided to restrict their attention to words alone. Some readers approved, arguing that such matters should be left to encyclopedias, biographical dictionaries, and gazetteers; some frowned, regretting the loss of a reference book for one-stop shopping.

But it was Gove's descriptive policy toward the language that drew most of the criticism, and turned the publication of a dictionary—normally a sedate affair, attracting a few sober reviews in learned journals, with perhaps a brief notice deep inside a few newspaper book review sections—into a cultural donnybrook that filled hundreds of column inches in the most influential magazines and newspapers in the country. Gove and his team published a dictionary that did not presume to tell people how they *should* speak and write; they instead offered an ostensibly objective report on how people *did* speak and write. Prescription, Gove argued, was not the job of a writer of dictionaries; he should only describe prevailing usage—the logical conclusion of the Horatian principle of *norma loquendi*. And this descriptivism of *Webster's Third* provoked what might be the bloodiest linguistic brawl of the twentieth century.

Webster's Third wasn't the first attempt to apply descriptivism to dictionary making—Johnson's *Dictionary* ended up being far more descriptive than most people expected, and *The Oxford English Dictionary* was every bit as descriptive as Gove's work. But three factors made the *OED*'s descriptivism seem less egregious to reviewers in 1961. First, the *OED* was a *historical* dictionary, and it made no sense to prescribe to people who died before Shakespeare was born. Second, by the 1960s, the descriptive information in much of the *OED* was nearly a century old, and readers could look back on Victorian foibles with a degree of equanimity they couldn't bring to modern ones. Finally, the first edition of the *OED* occupied thirteen volumes and cost several months' wages; it was for the most part available only in libraries, and few other than scholars worked with it regularly. Most people revered it but never saw it.

Besides, even the *OED* was never *entirely* descriptive. Murray and his co-workers, for all their protestations about an objective, scientific description of the language without value judgments, still sometimes offered praise or blame. It's evident in entries like *allude*, "Often used ignorantly as = *refer* in its general sense"; *anyways*, "*dial[ect]* or *illiterate*"; *boviculture*, "*Affected*"; *codger*, "*low colloq[uial]*"; *confectionary*, "Improperly used for CONFEC-TIONERY"; *eruscation*, "Ignorantly used for CORUSCATION"; *frequent*, "in illiterate use, as a real adv[erb] = Frequently, often"; *literally*, "Now often improperly used to indicate that some conventional metaphorical or hyperbolical phrase is to be taken in the strongest admissible sense"; *off*, verb: "To go off, make off (*illiterate*)"; *prognate*, "Innate, congenital (*pedantic*)"; *statute* used for *statue*, "Now only an illiterate blunder"; *testimonialize*, "Improperly, To ask for testimonials"; *them*, "Used for the nominative they. . . . Now only dial. or illiterate"; and so on. All these judgments—*ignorant, illiterate, pedantic, improper*—reveal that value judgments were never entirely abandoned.[3] It's no surprise, then, that many people, ignoring all the declarations of the lexicographers, decided to treat the *OED* as a prescriptive dictionary, turning to "the Oxford dictionary" to settle arguments. The authority inherent in the name of the medieval university was often enough to cow even the most unrepentant linguistic sinners into submission.

Webster's Third, though, was different. It wasn't a historical dictionary, and it wasn't confined to scholarly libraries. It was meant to be a dictionary for real people. True, it was big and expensive—its two volumes weighed in at 2,720 pages and retailed for $47.50, hardly an insignificant sum in 1961. But compared with the hundreds of dollars that the tens of thousands of pages of the *OED* cost, it was a bargain. Reviewers also knew it would serve as the basis for the cheaper abridged and collegiate dictionaries that would inevitably follow from the Merriam Company. Soon it would even trickle down into high schools. Scholars might be trusted to deal with description free of value judgments, said the traditional defenders of the language, but schoolboys needed the firm hand of discipline.

WHAT, THEN, WERE the traditionalists to make of claims like this, offered by advocates of *Webster's Third*?

> The function of grammars and dictionaries is to tell the truth about language. Not what somebody thinks ought to be the truth, nor what somebody wants to ram down somebody else's throat, nor what somebody wants to sell somebody else as being the "best" language, but what people actually do when they talk and write. Anything else is not the truth, but an untruth.[4]

That's not to say it's an easy matter to figure out "what people actually do when they talk and write." Which people? Surely it would be inadvisable to record the inarticulate babble of two-year-olds, or the conversational attempts of those in the first few weeks of their study of English as a foreign language. And it's impossible to include *everything* even adult native speakers do when they talk and write—every slip of the tongue, every stammer, every malapropism, every typo or spelling error.

But, said the descriptivists, if enough people made the same malapropism or spelling error, it eventually became part of the language. Still, it's not at all obvious how widespread an error has to be before it counts as standard usage. If one misguided writer confuses the words *allusion* and *illusion*, no sane lexicographer would list one as a synonym for the other. But what if ten writers do? a hundred? a thousand? What if a *majority* of writers and speakers put it the wrong way? At what point does it become the right way?

That's not likely to happen with *allusion* and *illusion* any time soon. There are words, however, that a majority use in a way that was once labeled wrong. The traditional meaning of *peruse*, for example, is "To examine in detail; to scrutinize, inspect, survey, oversee; to consider, to take heed of." The *per-* prefix means "thoroughly, completely," and earlier dictionaries were explicit: *peruse* meant "to read carefully," and nothing else. But *peruse* is increasingly being used to mean "to look over briefly or superficially; to browse"—so much so that most native English speakers are surprised to hear that *peruse* means the opposite of what they think it means. Does this mean that *peruse* now *really* means "skim," because most people think that's what it means? Does it retain its earlier meaning? Does it mean both things, or has it been drained of all meaning?

Not only do we not know the answers to these questions; we don't even know how to figure them out. Is it simply a matter of numbers? If 51 percent of people on the street use the word in a new sense, do they now authorize the new meaning? Or should the threshold be lower—say, 25 percent of speakers? And is it *any* speakers, or should we accept only the *best* users of language? If it's the latter, who gets to decide who's best? In our survey, should we include teenagers talking informally to their peers, or should we wait for approval from great literary stylists? Should we distinguish casual conversation from formal declarations? No dictionary can abandon prescription entirely, if for no other reason than the need to decide how widespread a linguistic habit must be before it constitutes an acceptable variant. It is impossible to include every spelling, definition, and usage assigned to every word by everyone who has ever used the language, and even the most fundamentalist descriptive linguist has to acknowledge that some uses of the language are simply wrong. If one person confuses *rein* and *reign*, no one rushes to revise a dictionary to reflect the new meanings. Former president George W. Bush declared, "We cannot let terrorists and rogue nations hold this nation hostile"; surely it does not follow that *hostile* is now a synonym for *hostage*. He also declared himself "mindful not only of preserving executive powers for myself, but for predecessors as well," but no dictionary will define *predecessor* as *successor*. *Peruse*, on the other hand, has reached the point where far more people use it to mean "skim" than "examine with great care."

For one group of prescriptivists, the most vocal enemies of *Webster's Third*, an error was an error no matter how widespread. Dwight Macdonald, for example, was convinced that numbers alone can't tell the story: "If nine-tenths of the citizens of the United States, including a recent President, were to use *inviduous*, the one-tenth who clung to *invidious* would still be right, and they would be doing a favor to the majority if they continued to maintain the point."[5] Gove couldn't resist replying to this, calling it "one of the most ridiculously mistaken statements that has been made during the year."[6] And so the team at the Merriam Company tore through one old-fashioned prescription after another, declaring that these supposed rules and distinctions were now dead and buried—and good riddance. People use *peruse* to mean "skim," and they use *unique* to mean "distinctive." People say *ain't*, even in decent company. They use *who* in place of *whom* without going blind, and use *like* for *as* without growing hair on their palms. Perhaps they shouldn't, but it's not a dictionary's job to tell readers what they *should* do.

FEW REVIEWERS, WHETHER their sympathies were with or against the Springfield lexicographers, could resist the temptation to break the rules that Gove and the others had declared moribund. Dozens of headlines sported an ostentatious *ain't*: SAYING AIN'T AIN'T WRONG: SEE WEBSTER, declared the *Chicago Tribune*; IT AIN'T NECESSARILY UNCOUTH, said the *Chicago Daily News*; and IT "AIN'T" GOOD appeared in the Washington *Sunday Star*—all within two days, and before the dictionary was officially published. (The quotation marks on that last *ain't* seem to offer reassurance to nervous readers: "Don't worry; we don't *really* use barbarisms like *ain't*.") More headlines followed in the next few months: SAY IT "AIN'T" SO, pleaded *Science*; IT AIN'T RIGHT, declared the *New Republic*. Other transgressions appeared in other papers: the *New York Times*, amused by the friendly treatment slang received in *Webster's Third*, invited readers to DIG THOSE WORDS; *Business Week* commented on the financial gamble taken by WEBSTER'S WAY OUT DICTIONARY. The hostile reviewers did it to point out the foolishness of a dictionary that authorized such transgressions, but even the more receptive commentators were clearly amused by the novelty of being allowed to use "wrong" words—in the newspaper, no less. Readers weren't sure what to make of this newfangled descriptivism. As Gove's biographer wrote, "what seems self-evident to lexicographers—that meaning depends on usage—makes many teachers, editors, and commentators on language uncomfortable."[7]

Other reviews bore less playful titles, and in these the serious accusations against Gove's project began to become clear. *Life*, for instance, called the book A NON-WORD DELUGE. Virginia's *Richmond News Leader* declared bluntly that WEBSTER'S LAYS AN EGG. Chicago's *Sun-Times* surveyed the scene and found ANARCHY IN LANGUAGE. The *Washington Post* distilled all the negative reviews of the new *Webster's* and offered readers this practical advice: KEEP YOUR OLD WEBSTER'S. ("If your old copy of the unabridged second edition . . . is battered and dog-eared," the reviewer advised, "don't throw it away. If you love truth, accuracy, and a little grammar to improve your speech or writing, hang on to it. You are not likely to find its virtues in the new third edition which has recently appeared.")[8] The *Atlantic Monthly*, the most alarmist of the lot, warned of SABOTAGE IN SPRINGFIELD.

Many critics objected to the sanctuary Gove offered to slang, ephemeral usage, and recent coinages not sanctioned by good literary examples. The reviewer for *Time* was pained by the "100,000 brand-new terms, from *astronaut, beatnik, boo-boo, countdown, den mother* and *drip-dry*, to *footsie, hard sell, mccarthyism, no-show, schlemiel, sit-in, wage dividend* and *zip gun.*" He objected that the editors of *Webster's Third* "*dig cool cats* who make *stacked chicks flip.* Without *drips* and *pads* and *junkies,* who *bug* victims for *bread* to buy *horse* for a *fix,* the dictionary of 1961 would not be *finalized.*"[9] Wilson Follett, writing in the *Atlantic Monthly,* was also unhappy with all the crazy jive: "the new dictionary was inevitably notorious for its unreserved acceptance as standard of *wise up, get hep* (it uses the second as a definition of the first), *ants in one's pants, one for the books; hugeous, nixie, passel, hepped up* (with *hepcat* and *hepster*), *anyplace, someplace,* and so forth. These and a swarm of their kind it admits to full canonical standing by the suppression of such qualifying status labels as *colloquial, slang, cant, facetious,* and *substandard.*"[10]

Not all the reviewers who stopped to comment on new words were so disapproving. Oliver Pritchett, writing about the new dictionary for the *Cardiff Western Mail,* began his search for new words "rather morbidly with 'fall-out' and 'radioactive,' " but was gladdened by the inclusion of " 'Rock 'n' Roll' ('jazz characterized by a strong beat and much repetition of simple phrases often with both blues and folk song elements'), 'dig' and 'cat,' " all of which "prove that Webster is 'with it.' "[11] Christopher Small, writing in the *Glasgow Herald,* professed pleasure at seeing the long list of specifically American neologisms:

> Hep, beatnik, hipster, square, in the groove, all are there (though not that universal imperative, dig); lush, palooka, jerk, schmo, slob, rummy, plonk, the rich vocabulary of American abuse is generously allowed for; jeep and bazooka and jerican and all the other words which came over here with the G.I.s 20 years ago have passed solidly into the language.[12]

A world where words like *beatnik, hep,* and *square* were still novelties may induce a rush of nostalgia in readers of a certain age. Other neologisms serve as reminders of just how much the world was changing in the late 1950s and early '60s, whether for good or ill: this is the era that gave us words like *astronaut*, *automation*, *blast-off*, *brainwashing* ("compare *menticide*"), *cybernetics*, *countdown*, *desegregation*, *McCarthyism*, *megaton*, *nuclear*, *occupational neurosis*, *red-baiting*, *sit-in*, and *Sovietologist*, all of which were noted by early reviewers. The social upheavals of the era—the cold war, the questioning of authority, racial desegregation, peace protests, free love—played out in many of the reviews of *Webster's Third*. The early 1960s saw the opening skirmishes of what were later christened the "culture wars." To many culturally conservative commentators writing in 1961, the breakdown of standards at the Merriam Company was a sign of larger breakdowns to come in society at large.

The linguistic culture wars of the '60s had begun even before *Webster's Third* appeared. The first battle may have taken place in 1957, when Random House published *A Dictionary of Contemporary American Usage* by a brother-and-sister team, Bergen and Cornelia Evans. It offered useful advice on thousands of grammatical, stylistic, lexical, and mechanical questions and generally took a moderate approach to all of them—holding the line on a few traditional issues but often telling readers they need no longer fear reprisals for breaking old-fashioned rules. Most early reviews were complimentary, and few seemed bothered by the perceived permissiveness. The review in the *New York Times* even noted that "the Evanses are purist in heart."[13]

But when Wilson Follett, a literary critic who specialized in the modern novel, read the Evanses, he saw only do-as-you-please permissivism, an utter abandonment of the standards he expected in a dictionary of usage. His frothy jeremiad appeared in the *Atlantic Monthly* in February 1960: under the bitterly sarcastic headline GRAMMAR IS OBSOLETE, he declared that newfangled linguistics was concerned only with "the abolition of standards" and devoted entirely to "an organized assumption that language good enough for anybody is good enough for everybody."[14]

Follett proposed to find out what would happen if a writer decided to follow all of Gove's suggestions. He devoted a full column of small type to putative solecisms, barbarisms, and other nasties supposedly sanctioned by the Evanses: "Ask whoever you see." "He had as much or more trouble than I did." "He works faster than me." "More unique." "Different than." "The reason is because." And so on. The list was clearly intended to provoke sudden gasps of astonishment: "Who [instead of *whom*] did you see?"—*surely not!* "Less [instead of *fewer*] than three"—*how can they be allowed to get away with such things?* "Very little [instead of *few*] data"—*they must be ashamed to show their faces in public!* Follett saw the book as a harbinger of impending cultural collapse. In a few generations, he feared, English wouldn't be capable of "producing an Irving, a Hawthorne, a Melville, a Henry James, a Howells, a Sarah Orne Jewett, a Willa Cather." And don't try telling Follett that Irving, Hawthorne, Melville, et alia committed some of those sins themselves. "Not everything ever written by a good writer," he lectured, "or even by quite a number of good writers, is good. . . . Every good writer has committed himself at one time or another to practices without which he would have been a better writer."[15]

GIVEN THESE CULTURAL and linguistic tensions in the America of 1961, it was perhaps inevitable that *Webster's Third* would provoke such hubbub. The *Nation* expressed its regret that Gove himself, a decent and thoughtful man, had become "a victim of the pseudo-egalitarianism of the times."[16] Dwight Macdonald's high-profile *New Yorker* review attributed the new dictionary's failure to a "scientific revolution" that "has meshed gears with a trend toward permissiveness, in the name of democracy."[17] And Sydney J. Harris told *Chicago Daily News* readers, "Relativism is the reigning philosophy of our day, in all fields. Not merely in language, but in ethics, in politics, in every field of human behavior." Perhaps, then, we were predestined to suffer through an abomination like *Webster's Third*: "It is not terribly important whether we use 'ain't,' or 'like' instead of 'as'—except as symptoms of a general decay in values."[18]

The Rt. Rev. Richard S. Emrich in the *Detroit News* likewise saw in *Webster's Third* the same breakdown in values that led to the social unrest of the early sixties: "The bolshevik spirit . . . is to be found everywhere, not just in Russia." His rhetoric rises to the level of an evangelical sermon against Bolshevism:

> Wherever our standards are discarded in family life, the care of the soul, art, literature, or education, there is the bolshevik spirit. Wherever men believe that what is, is right; wherever they discard discipline for an easy short-cut, there is bolshevism. It is a spirit that corrupts every-thing it touches.

As a result of this anarchic spirit, "the greatest of all American dictionaries has been corrupted at center. The greatest language on earth has lost a guardian. When the editors 'concretized' their philosophy and 'finalized' their policy, 'irregardless' was blessed. When it comes to a standardless dictionary, include me out."[19]

It's not difficult to hear the political echoes of the late 1950s and early 1960s in reviews of the dictionary. More than one reviewer latched on to the title of the notorious book, *Webster's Third New International*, and punned on the Third International of the Bolsheviks in 1919: thus were lexicographers drafted into the cold war. And not merely the cold war—sometimes the linguistic wars were hot. It's remarkable how often military metaphors show up in the critical discussions of *Webster's Third*. "If a sentry forsakes his post and places an army in danger," advised Emrich, "the penalty is severe. If a guardian ceases to guard and neglects his duty to children, there are few who would not condemn. If a great dictionary forsakes its post as the guardian of our language, how can one avoid disappointment?"[20] Wilson Follett saw *Webster's Third* not merely as a dereliction of duty but as an unauthorized attack on decent folk, a "fighting document" seeking to wipe out "every surviving influence that makes for the upholding of standards, every criterion for distinguishing between better usages and worse."[21] The reviewer for the *Richmond News Leader* saw it as a total war and called for willing conscripts to fight the good fight alongside other warriors "who believe in high standards of English usage."[22] And Dwight Macdonald saw not a fair fight but mass slaughter in the removal of old words: in his *New Yorker* review, he nearly swooned at the prospect that a quarter of a million words from *Webster's Second* had been removed to make room for the new entries, writing, "This incredible massacre—almost half the words in the English language seem to have disappeared between 1934 and 1961—is in fact incredible."[23] Lexicography had become genocide.

Soon "the sixties"—with all the term implies, including sexual experimentation, drug use, political protest, black power, women's lib, gay rights, and the whole turn-on-tune-in-drop-out worldview—would arrive; every negative review of *Webster's Third* now seems, in retrospect, to be announcing that a rough beast was slouching toward Springfield, Massachusetts. "Small wonder," wrote one reviewer, "that our English-speaking world, when it thus tolerates the debasement of its language, is having trouble with creatures like beatniks—not to mention Nikita Khrushchev and his kind—who are developing a style of writing that may best be described as literary anarchy, to use a polite word."[24] *Webster's Third* was blasted as a countercultural dictionary, the work of dope fiends and longhairs and fellow travelers. It was produced by Bolsheviks; it encouraged philosophical relativism; it came out of the same ethos that gave us sexual promiscuity. Macdonald likened *Webster's Third* to the Kinsey reports, in that both Gove and Alfred Kinsey took a "statistical, objective and non-evaluative" approach to their subject matters:

> The fatal mistake of both was to ignore, from an ambition to apply scientific method to a field in which it is not appropriate, the qualitative aspect. Sex and language are areas of human activity in which moral, or at least evaluative, judgments have always been made. Too much so in

the past, but this doesn't necessarily lead to the conclusion that no such judgments should be made now. . . .
Sexual experience cannot be reduced to figures any more
than linguistic experience can.[25]

MACDONALD'S APPROVING CITATION of *Webster's Second New
International* is typical of most of the *Third*'s critics, who looked
on the earlier dictionary as the model of lexicographical excellence and blasted Gove for sullying that masterpiece of 1934. As
Gove's biographer points out, *Webster's Second* "was more than
respected. It was accepted as the ultimate authority on meaning
and usage, and its preeminence was virtually unchallenged in the
United States. It did not provoke controversies; it settled them."[26]
But Gove and his defenders, irritated by the constant calls to return to *Webster's Second*, reminded those critics that many of the
words and senses they despised were actually approved by their
supposedly sacrosanct predecessor. Gove felt compelled to lecture
the *New York Times*, which had singled out *finalize*: "You will
find . . . that 'finalize' . . . is entered without stigma in the Second
Edition." He noted dozens of appearances "in highly reputable
places like Current History, Journal of Near Eastern Studies, Amer-
icana Annual, The New Republic and"—wait for it—"The Times
itself."[27]

Still the complaints came. *Life*'s reviewer was bothered by Gove's
refusal to keep intruders out of the language, though he disavowed
any desire to be "stuffy"; he was pleased to see new words like *beatnik* and *litterbug*. But lines had to be drawn: "that most monstrous
of all non-words—'irregardless'—is included. So is Madison Av-
enue's abomination of adding '-wise' to those nouns ('Yes, but how
is he wisdomwise?') which it hasn't already corrupted by adding
'-ize' ('As soon as we can concretize the program, we will finalize
it')." The implication? There's no way that "Lincoln could have
modeled his Gettysburg Address, or Churchill his immortal
speeches, on a word book so lax." After all, "even the following sentence could be concocted from words found in Webster's":

Irregardless of the enormity of the upsurge, none of us are able, governmentwise, in a time of normalcy, to act like we can ignore it; we don't mean to infer otherwise in saying so.[28]

That trick—formulating a monstrous sentence or paragraph that would supposedly pass muster in Springfield—was performed by many of the hostile reviewers. Here, for instance, is the pastiche Sydney J. Harris published in the *Chicago Daily News*:

> Lemme recommend a swell new book that has been in the works for 27 years and has just been finalized—no kidding—by the G. & C. Merriam Co. in Springfield, Mass.
>
> It's Webster's Third New International Dictionary, Unabridged, and wordwise it's a gasser. In this new edition, it turns out that good English ain't what we thought it was at all—good English, man, is whatever is popular.
>
> This is a nifty speak-as-you-go dictionary. Not like that moldy fig of a Second Edition, which tried to separate "standard English" from slang, bastardized formations, colloquialisms, and all the passing fads and fancies of spoken English.[29]

The *New York Times* had a similar parody:

> A passel of double-domes at the G. & C. Merriam Company joint in Springfield, Mass., have been confabbing and yakking for twenty-seven years—which is not intended to infer that they have not been doing plenty work—and now they have finalized Webster's Third New International Dictionary, Unabridged, a new edition of that swell and esteemed word book.

The *Times* writer pointed out that all these words appeared in the new dictionary without being stigmatized, and he concluded,

"Webster's has . . . surrendered to the permissive school that has been busily extending its beachhead on English instruction in the schools."[30]

This was too much for Gove, who felt obliged to reply in the pages of the *Times*: any dictionary, he said, could produce a "similar artificial monstrosity."[31] He maintained that traditional status and usage labels ("slang," "nonstandard," "dialect," "colloquial") could never indicate all the acceptable registers of the English language. He also wrote to *Life* after that magazine griped about the inclusion of a long catalog of unpleasant words and advised readers to stick with the second edition. "Won't you take another look at your Second and Third editions of Webster's New International Dictionary?" Gove demanded.

> You will find that *irregardless* is in Second and that Third calls it nonstandard; that *enormity* is not "approved" (nor even listed) in Third as a synonym for *enormousness*; that *normalcy*, *concretize* and *finalize* are in Second as well as in Third and that *wisdomwise* and *governmentwise* are in neither edition.[32]

SOME URGED THE Merriam Company to recant, to disavow its heresies, by correcting its many errors in a hastily issued revision— certainly before it was abridged for student use. But one group, convinced that the battle was lost, resolved to retreat, reorganize, and fight another day. James Parton, president of the American Heritage Publishing Company, declared to the world that G. & C. Merriam was "badly in need of guidance," and he generously offered to provide it—in the form of a hostile takeover. He began buying shares of the Merriam Company after it rebuffed his proposal for a joint publishing project, and shortly after *Webster's Third* appeared, he offered three hundred dollars a share to all shareholders. He was frank in declaring his intent: "We'd take the Third out of print! We'd go back to the Second International and speed ahead on the Fourth. It'd take us two or three years, and the company would lose some sales. But if Merriam keeps on the way it's going, they'll ruin their company."[33]

The takeover bid failed, but Parton refused to give up. He authorized a new dictionary to be published by his own company. The result was the *American Heritage Dictionary of the English Language*, first published in 1969 and now in its fourth edition. From the beginning it was conceived as a kind of antidote to the laissez-faire descriptivism of *Webster's Third*. The editors decided to refer controversial words and senses to a panel of "experts"— 105 writers, scholars, editors, and reporters in the first edition, now grown to more than 200—and ask their opinion. The dictionary would then offer a summary of the responses. Most members of the usage panel, especially those for the first edition, have been linguistically conservative and can usually be counted on to side with the traditionalists and against the descriptive linguists.

American Heritage was proudly, even defiantly, prescriptive in its declared intentions; still, the editors have managed to find one of the smarter approaches to prescription. Rather than delivering a simple verdict of yea or nay, guilty or not guilty, *American Heritage* presents the opinions of the whole panel, and it is up to readers to figure out what to make of that evidence. What's more, recent editions have made good use of corpus linguistics—huge electronic databases of published text, which allow the lexicographers to provide statistics on how often certain words or senses are used—and have grown more lenient. Here, for instance, is the entry on *nauseous* from *American Heritage*'s third edition, published in 1992:

> Traditionally, *nauseous* means "causing nausea"; *nauseated* means "suffering from nausea." The use of *nauseous* in the sense of *nauseated* is unacceptable to a great majority of the Usage Panel and should be avoided in writing.[34]

Words like *traditionally* suggest the possibility of change, but *unacceptable* sounds draconian, and *a great majority* suggests there's little room for disagreement. The fourth edition appeared just eight years later, and this time came across as more forgiving and more open to language change:

> Traditional critics have insisted that *nauseous* is properly used only to mean "causing nausea" and that it is incorrect to use it to mean "affected with nausea," as in *Roller coasters make me nauseous*. In this example, *nauseated* is preferred by 72 percent of the Usage Panel. Curiously, though, 88 percent of the Panelists prefer using nauseating in the sentence *The children looked a little green from too many candy apples and nauseating* (not *nauseous*) *rides*. Since there is a lot of evidence to show that *nauseous* is widely used to mean "feeling sick," it appears that people use *nauseous* mainly in the sense in which it is considered incorrect. In its "correct" sense it is being supplanted by *nauseating*.[35]

The American Heritage Dictionary gives readers a sense that words do not fall neatly into categories labeled "approved" and "forbidden." The book remains one of the most serious American rivals to the Merriam-Webster brand.

THE TWENTIETH CENTURY'S "dictionary wars" showed few of the combatants in a good light, and it's hard to think of a scholarly dispute in which straw men played a larger role. Appeals to literary authority were a favorite mode on both sides, with Webster's detractors recalling the glories of Shakespeare and Dickens and Melville, while Webster's defenders insisted Shakespeare and Dickens and Melville committed all the putative sins excoriated by the prescriptivists. There have been few scholarly battles in which the stakes were more exaggerated. For the descriptivists, declaring a preference in a dictionary was tantamount to linguistic fascism. For some conservatives, admitting *ain't* into the dictionary seemed tantamount to handing over America's nuclear launch codes to

Nikita Khrushchev. The real difficulty lay in the fact that Gove and many of his reviewers had fundamentally incompatible notions of what a dictionary is for.

The battle had to do with the authority dictionaries claim for themselves. The lexicographers at Merriam & Co. worked hard to convince the reading public that dictionaries *shouldn't* be authoritative. The critical reviewers missed the point, said Gove; they were betrayed by the absurd notion that dictionaries are supposed to set standards for usage.

Where on earth did lay readers get the ludicrous idea that dictionaries should be treated as authorities? Perhaps from advertisements for *Webster's Second New International Dictionary* through the 1930s, '40s, and '50s, declaring that the dictionary was an authoritative standard. In 1934, when *Webster's Second* was announced, major newspapers bore large display advertisements declaring, "Under the leadership of William Allan Neilson, President of Smith College, as Editor in Chief, the greatest corps of editors ever organized was created to make this volume and to maintain the Merriam-Webster reputation for 'supreme authority.' " The phrase "supreme authority" became the leading marketing slogan for *Webster's Second* and the dictionaries derived from it, and it appeared in virtually every advertisement. The company's newspaper ads from 1936 call the new book "indispensable to every one who wants power and accuracy in speech and writing." In 1940, the ads proclaimed, "whenever you need to *know*, you think of *Webster*, as the utmost in authority, the court of last appeal." The studious and retiring lexicographers at work in Merriam's editorial department, even in 1934, were probably much more diffident in their conceptions of themselves, and may not have wanted to be anyone's "court of last appeal," but the people in the marketing department knew that authority—even authoritarianism—sold dictionaries. They did everything they could to promote the widespread attitudes that, just a few years later, resulted in the attacks on the third edition. Merriam has to take some of the blame for that, even if the claims came from the marketing department rather than the editorial division.

Gove & Co. were right that the language comes in an almost infinite number of registers and that any simple set of usage labels reduces all that richness to a short list of boxes to be ticked mechanically. But they didn't recognize—or refused to recognize, or pretended not to recognize—that many people turn to dictionaries for guidance with their own writing because they're aiming at one particular register, one that holds a special place in modern society. The variety of English used in most business writing can afford a little room for variation, but there are many little shibboleths a business writer has to avoid in order to escape a scolding from bosses or customers. From the point of view of descriptive linguistics, this variety of English is just one register among many. To the people who buy dictionaries, it's the only register they need a book to figure out. Native speakers of English are confident enough in their use of the other varieties of the language; no dictionary entry, no matter how harshly phrased, will frighten working-class people from using *ain't* at the pool hall or the pub. But there are some contested points of usage on which native speakers actively seek advice, matters on which they feel their lack of familiarity.

People turn to dictionaries for two main reasons, and *Webster's Third* served one of them very well, the other very badly. People open a dictionary when they encounter a word they don't know, or aren't sure they know, and want to know how it's being used—for that, *Webster's Third* was superb and provided more information (and more-accurate information) than any other dictionary. But people also open a dictionary when they have to *use* words and aren't sure how they'll be received. By pretending standard English was merely one register among many—nothing special—Gove and his assistants neglected the needs of the many people who wanted authoritative guidance. The attempt to bring the principles of modern, scientific linguistics to dictionary making was admirable, but Gove and his colleagues found themselves caught in a strange paradox: they refused to prescribe how to use *due to* or *different than*, but they did prescribe how to use a dictionary. It was no longer to be a source for inquisitive, even insecure, writers and speakers who wanted to know what's preferred in the realms of experience where formal English and business English are spoken.

WHILE GOVE AND the other Webster editors were sometimes wrong, their detractors were—to use a word that they would likely resist but that appears without comment in *Webster's Third*—wronger. The critics of *Webster's Third* had an absurdly overinflated estimation of the influence scholars have over the language. Implicit in all their attacks on descriptive lexicography were a pair of notions: first, that good writers have ever felt "authorized" or "forbidden" to use a word on the basis of a dictionary entry; second, that the acceptance of "bad" words into a dictionary will force the rest of the world to use them against their better judgment. Hoke Norris, in his *Chicago Sun-Times* review, noted that the dictionary's definition of *ain't* "seems not only 'permissive' but downright 'encouraging,' and, finally, erroneous. 'Ain't' is not only substandard; it fully deserves the labels 'illiterate' and 'dialect' as applied by the Second."[36] Did he sincerely believe that people who use *ain't* await permission to do so, or that people who would otherwise virtuously resist *ain't*'s siren song would be won over to the dark side simply because a dictionary blessed it with approval?

The reviewers who had warned the world about creeping permissivism in *Webster's Third* spent the 1970s and '80s repeating "told ya so!" In 1970, Jean Stafford delivered a lecture at Barnard College:

> Besides the neologisms that are splashed all over the body of the American language like the daubings of a chimpanzee turned loose with finger paints, the poor thing has had its parts of speech broken to smithereens: . . . now verbs are used as nouns and nouns are used as verbs. . . . Upon its aching back [the language] carries an astonishing burden of lumber piled on by the sociologists and the psychologists and the sociopsychologists and the

psychosociologists, the Pentagon, the admen, and, lately, the alleged robbers and bug planters of Watergate.

"The prognosis for the ailing language is not good," she said. "I predict that it will not die in my lifetime, but I fear that it will be assailed by countless cerebral accidents and massive strokes and gross insults to the brain and finally no one will be able to sit up in bed and take nourishment by mouth."[37]

But here we are, forty or fifty years after Cassandra's predictions of apocalypse, and still society has not collapsed. The linguistic conservatives have almost to a man—and the large majority have been men, though prescriptivists do count some women among their ranks—mistaken language change for language decay. Virtually all the words, senses, and usages that induce apoplexy among purists today—*who* for *whom*, singular *they*, *more unique*—will probably become standard English in another generation or two, and most people will never know that our age worried about them. That's the natural course of things. In the 1930s, purists fulminated over *electrocute*, criticizing it as a meaningless hybrid—the ending *-cute*, apparently lifted from *execute*, does not mean "kill." Today virtually no one finds *electrocute* linguistically offensive. It's reasonable to assume that most of the modern shibboleths, the ones that the critics of *Webster's Third* railed against in the 1960s, will eventually become perfectly standard, and the world will be none the worse for it.

CHAPTER 11

Expletive Deleted

GEORGE CARLIN VEXES THE CENSORS

THE EDITORS OF *THE OXFORD English Dictionary* dreamed of being comprehensive, but they didn't include *every* word in the language. As we've seen, there's room for disagreement over the size of the English vocabulary, and whole classes of words were omitted: foreign words, proper nouns, technical terms. The compilers also simply missed some words—any human undertaking is bound to be imperfect. The *OED* readers accumulated examples of the word *bondmaid*, for instance, but the slips containing the quotations were misplaced, and the word did not appear in the first edition.[1]

But only a few out of the hundreds of thousands of English words were omitted on *moral* grounds. James Dixon, a surgeon who contributed many slips to the *OED*, was shocked when he came across references to "an article called a Cundum"—an older spelling of *condom*—which he glossed for James Murray as "a contrivance used by fornicators, to save themselves from a well-deserved clap; also by others who wish to enjoy copulation without the possibility of impregnation." Disturbed by this "very obscene subject," Dixon made the case that the word was "too utterly obscene" for inclusion in the dictionary. He got his way: the word *condom* was omitted from the first edition of the *OED*.[2]

A handful of similar words, shocking, perhaps, to Victorian sensibilities, hardly raise an eyebrow among jaded moderns. But two words omitted from the first edition of the *OED* are still powerful enough to cause trouble. As noted by A. S. C. Ross, who reviewed the first *Supplement* in 1933, "the perpetuation of a Victorian prudishness . . . led to the omission of some of the commonest words in the English language"—above all, *fuck* and *cunt*. Both were studiously excluded from *The Oxford English Dictionary* until the supplement of 1972.

Not everyone approved of the omissions, even in the Victorian era. One contributor, John Hamilton, challenged Murray's decision to expunge what we now euphemize as the "C-word." "It is an old English word of Teutonic origin," he insisted, "& is just as good English (though by the nature of things not so much used in polite society) as the words, leg, arm, heart, stomach, & other parts of the body. . . . It is no more vulgar than bowels or womb."[3] But Hamilton knew better, or should have: the word *cunt* really is more vulgar than *bowels* or *womb*, and every reader knows it too. A special class of words deserves special treatment. This chapter looks at some of the attempts to purge the language of "bad words"—not bad in the sense of "ungrammatical" or "illegitimate," but offensive words that should never be spoken or written by anyone.

THERE'S NO END of ways to get into legal or moral trouble with language. Depending on the jurisdiction and the era, you might be punished for saying "The prime minister is a knave" or "The president is a fool"; for denying the divinity of Jesus; for ridiculing Muhammad; for inciting a riot; for lying under oath; for making a death threat. You can be punished for falsely accusing someone of crimes, or even for publicizing true information if the law says it should be protected, as with medical records, privileged communications, and state secrets.

In these cases, though, it's not the *language* that's the problem, but the *message*. A physician who illegally revealed a patient's medical condition would be in trouble no matter how he or she said it: "Smith has herpes," "Smith is infected with the herpes virus," "Tests for herpes simplex in Smith have come back positive," and so on. But there are situations in which the message is acceptable even though the words in which it is delivered render it unspeakable. "Smith is a stupid idiot" may be impolite but is unlikely to lead to legal trouble. "Smith is a stupid cunt," on the other hand, is enough to land you in jail if you say it in the wrong place. From one point of view there's no difference between "Smith has an unnatural predilection to copulate with farm animals" and "Smith is a goat-fucker"; from another, they're completely different statements.

The notion that particular words are taboo can probably be traced back to primitive beliefs about sympathetic magic, in which language can be used to injure people at a distance. It's telling that many of our unseemly words are known as *curses*, since the conception of offensive language seems to have derived from a belief in the power of a malefactor to place a curse on an enemy. Many cultures also have prohibitions on invoking the gods. In the Jewish religious tradition, for instance, it is forbidden to pronounce the personal name of God, which is represented in print as YHWH and often known as the Tetragrammaton ("four letters"). When the Torah is read aloud, the reader must not speak the name. Instead he pronounces the word *adonai*, or "lord."

The Christian tradition shares many Jewish concerns—the third commandment, "Thou shalt not take the name of the LORD thy God in vain; for the LORD will not hold him guiltless that taketh his name in vain,"[4] applies in both faiths—but Christians established their own interdictions on profane language. "Fornication, and all uncleanness, or covetousness," St. Paul instructed the Ephesians, "let it not be once named among you."[5] Note that Paul doesn't merely instruct the Ephesians to avoid fornication; they are not to *name* it either.

The Christian homiletic tradition is filled with exhortations to avoid the sin of swearing; for centuries there has been a kind of religious cottage industry in castigating the foul-mouthed. Early in the eighteenth century one preacher addressed a sermon to "Her

Majesty's Fleet," providing evidence that "swearing like a sailor" is no modern phenomenon. Thinking of phrases like *damn you*, he begged his listeners "to consider, what a Wildness it is to dally and trifle with that Judgment, upon which the Eternal Doom of all Creatures depend."[6]

George Whitefield—one of the most inspiring preachers of the eighteenth century, and one of the founders of Methodism— delivered his own sermon titled *The Heinous Sin of Profane Cursing and Swearing* in 1738. For him, England was particularly guilty in this respect: "Among the many heinous Sins for which this Nation is grown infamous, perhaps there is no one more crying, but withal more common, than the abominable Custom of Profane *Swearing* and *Cursing*." It's impossible to walk around London, he charged, without hearing profanity: "Our Streets abound with Persons of all Degrees and Qualities, who are continually provoking the Holy One of *Israel* to Anger by their detestable Oaths and Blasphemies."[7] Whitefield was neither the first nor the last to single out Britain as a nation of swearers. "The nation's time-honoured reputation for swearing," writes one scholar of offensive language, "reaches back at least to the time of Joan of Arc, when the French termed them 'les Goddems.' Their modern descendants have maintained the tradition by acquiring (from the same quarter) the sobriquet of 'les fuckoffs.' "[8]

WE CAN EXPLAIN some linguistic taboos with reference to oaths and blasphemies, but not all offensive words violate the third commandment. The earliest uses of the word *swear*—and it's one of the oldest words in the language, appearing before the year 900— mean "To make a solemn declaration or statement with an appeal to God or a superhuman being." But by the fifteenth century, *swear* could mean "To utter a form of oath lightly or irreverently, as a mere intensive, or an expression of anger," and by the end of the nineteenth century, a *swear-word* could be any "profane word." (It was Mark Twain who coined the related *cuss-word*.) And some of those profanities have only the loosest connections with the name of God. As the anthropologist Ashley Montagu put it in *The Anatomy of Swearing*, a kind of anti-Bible of crude language, "Of all the words in the English swearer's vocabulary one has probably been worked harder than all the rest put together. It is the word *bloody*."[9]

The adjective *bloody*, meaning "Of the nature of, composed of, or like blood," showed up before the year 1000. A related sense, "Covered, smeared, stained, with blood" (as in *bloody nose*), followed a little more than a century later; we see "Accompanied by or involving the flowing or spilling of blood" (as in *bloody battle*) starting around 1385. But *bloody* as an epithet first showed up in 1676, in George Etherege's play *The Man of Mode*: "Not without he will promise to be bloody drunk."

No one knows where the coarse sense of *bloody* came from. Some have suggested that an oath by the Virgin Mary, *by our Lady*, became *by'r Lady*, which in turn became *bloody*. Others suggest it comes from *'s blood*, an oath in which the speaker swears *by God's blood*. Etymologists are skeptical. The *OED* notes that "there is good reason to think that it was at first a reference to the habits of the 'bloods' or aristocratic rowdies of the end of the 17th and beginning of the 18th c. The phrase 'bloody drunk' was apparently = 'as drunk as a blood' (cf. 'as drunk as a lord'); thence it was extended to kindred expressions, and at length to others."

Whatever its origin, *bloody* shocked consciences in many parts of the English-speaking world; and once it began appearing in print, moralists queued up for the chance to attack it. The Victorian critic Julian Sharman gave a few pages to the word *bloody* in his *Cursory History of Swearing* (1884). His distaste for "the ungainly adjective" is palpable: "Drunkards hiccup it as they wallow on ale-house floors," he wrote. "Morose porters bandy it about on quays and landing-stages. From the low-lying quarters of the towns the word buzzes in your ear with the confusion of a Babel. In the cramped narrow streets you are deafened by its whirr and din, as it rises from the throats of the chaffering multitude, from besotted men defiant and vain-glorious in their drink, from shrewish women hissing out rancour in their harsh querulous talk."[10]

Through most of the nineteenth century, though, *bloody* was confined to ale-house floors, quays, and landing stages—meaning, it rarely appeared in print or in polite conversation. That's not to say no aristocratic toff ever spoke it, but it was still a transgression, not something said in public. When George Bernard Shaw wrote *Pygmalion* in 1913, though, he gave moralists an opportunity to show their disgust. In act 3, Freddy Eynsford-Hill asks Eliza Doolittle if she plans to walk across the park. "Walk!" she replies. "Not bloody likely." (A significant stage direction follows: "[Sensation].") Was *that* word actually to be spoken in the public theater? On April 11, 1914, the *Daily Sketch* buzzed with excitement at the prospect:

TONIGHT'S "PYGMALION" IN WHICH MRS
PATRICK CAMPBELL IS EXPECTED TO
CAUSE THE BIGGEST THEATRICAL
SENSATION FOR MANY YEARS . . .
One word in Shaw's new play will cause sensation.
Mr Shaw introduces a certain forbidden word.
WILL MRS PATRICK CAMPBELL SPEAK IT?
Has the censor stepped in or will the word spread?
If he does not forbid it, then anything might happen!
It is a word which, although held by many to be merely a
meaningless vulgarism, is certainly not used in
decent society.
It is a word which the *Daily Sketch* cannot possibly
print, and tonight
it is to be uttered on the stage.[11]

Editorialists predicted the collapse of society in a series of newspaper headlines: THREATS BY DECENCY LEAGUE, said one; THEATRE TO BE BOYCOTTED, said another.[12]

Despite its prominence on the English stage owing to an Irish playwright, *bloody* found its spiritual home in the antipodes. So common is *bloody* Down Under that some have dubbed it the "Australian adjective," a position of distinction it has held for more than a century and a half. An English traveler in Australia, Alexander Marjoribanks, noted in 1847, "The word bloody is the favourite oath in that country. One man will tell you that he married a bloody young wife, another, a bloody old one; and a bushranger will call out, 'Stop, or I'll blow your bloody brains out.'" Marjoribanks "once had the curiosity to count the number of times that a bullock driver used this word in the course of a quarter of an hour," and enumerated twenty-five *bloody*s in fifteen minutes. He began performing the calculations: "I gave him eight hours in the day to sleep, and six to be silent, thus leaving ten hours for conversation. I supposed that he had commenced at twenty and continued till seventy years of age . . . and found that in the course of that time he must have pronounced this disgusting word no less than 18,200,000 times."[13]

THE WORD BLOODY is now not nearly so scurrilous and can be heard routinely on television and radio. But some taboos persist, and a few words are never heard on American broadcast television, even today.

The canonical list of filthy words was formulated by the American comic George Carlin, who in 1972 performed a monologue called "Seven Words You Can Never Say on Television." "There are four hundred thousand words in the English language," he began,

> and there are *seven* of them that you can't say on television. What a ratio that is: three hundred and ninety-nine thousand, nine hundred and ninety-three—to seven. They must *really* be bad. They'd have to be *outrageous* to be separated from a group that large. "All of you over here, you seven—*bad words!*" That's what they told us they were, remember? "That's a bad word." Aww—there are no bad words. Bad thoughts; bad intentions.

It was time for defiance. And so came the famous roster, delivered with the rapidity of a memorized poem: *shit, piss, fuck, cunt, cocksucker*, *motherfucker*, and *tits*. These malefactors—"the heavy seven," Carlin called them—"are the ones that will infect your soul, curve your spine, and keep the country from winning the war."

Carlin made up that list of obscenities himself; when he insisted you can't say them on television, he wasn't reporting on the law— there was no law. But when a radio station played Carlin's "Filthy Words" routine in 1973, the Federal Communications Commission fined the station for violating public indecency statutes. The opinion of the U.S. Supreme Court in *FCC* v. *Pacifica Foundation* gave informal precedents the force of law: the justices held that the FCC had the power to determine what constituted indecency. As it happens, Carlin's list became the de facto standard of what really couldn't be said on the public airwaves. It's a strange paradox that a foulmouthed champion of free speech should have been instrumental in writing the law prohibiting those same words in the public airwaves.

ALL SEVEN OF Carlin's words—*shit*, *piss*, *fuck*, *cunt*, *cocksucker*, *motherfucker*, and *tits*—retain their indecent status, though words do move on and off the list of unspeakables. Some of these words weren't particularly wicked when they entered the language. The verb *to shit*, for instance, goes all the way back to 1308, when it was no more offensive than a clinical term like *defecate*. In 1484, William Caxton, the man who brought printing to England, published his own translation of Aesop's *Fables*, in which appeared the sentence "I dyde shyte thre grete toordes"—"I did shit three great turds"—and no one seemed to mind. Only later was *shit* nudged out of decent language. Ditto *piss*, which has a long history even in somber contexts. A little before 1400, Chaucer included it in his *Wife of Bath's Tale*—"Xantippa caste pisse vpon his heed"—and a serious medical textbook written just before 1500 included advice for a poor man "that pissith blood." Perhaps most remarkably, a version of the Bible from around the year 1395 included this translation of 2 Kings 18:27: "Y schulde speke these wordis, . . . that thei ete her toordis and drynke her pisse"—that is, "I should speak these words, . . . that they eat their turds and drink their piss." By 1611, when the more familiar King James Version appeared, it had been toned down a little; *toordis* had become *dung*—"that they may eat their own dung"—but even in the King James Bible, these men "drink their own piss." (Many modern editions of the King James Version silently replace the word without editorial comment.) There was nothing improper about *piss*; it was simply the common word for urine. Only in 1788 did a minor writer, Ebeneezer Picken, hide the word *piss* behind its first letter, producing the euphemism *pee*.

But two of Carlin's words—three if we count the compound form—have been classed among the most lewd words in the English language from the very beginning. The first known appearance of the word *fuck* in written English shows how powerful it was. A satirical poem written sometime around the year 1475, *Flen Flyys*—"Fleas and Flies"—is composed in "macaronic" verse, a mixture of Latin and English. Sometimes the two languages can mingle in a single line, even in a single word—English words might get Latin endings and vice versa. The poem is an attack on the monks of Ely in Cambridgeshire. Among their many failings, the author explains, "Non sunt in cœli, quia gxddbov xxkxzt pg ifmk."

The first part is easy for anyone who survived first-year Latin: "They are not in heaven, because." But the rest—"gxddbov xxkxzt pg ifmk"—makes no more sense in Latin than it does in English. That's because it's in code. Either the author or the scribe concealed the real text behind a cipher known as the "Caesar shift," named after Julius Caesar. Each letter of the message is replaced with the following letter in the alphabet: the name Caesar, for instance, would become *Dbftbs*. To decode the message, you simply reverse the operation.

What, then, can be made of "gxddbov xxkxzt pg ifmk"? The letter before g is f; that's easy enough. But the letter before x is w, and no English word begins *fw*-. Here the problem is that our alphabet isn't exactly identical to the one in use in 1475. In the Latin alphabet, *w* wasn't a separate letter—it was, as the name suggests, two *u*'s—and *u* and *v* were considered the same letter. So the letter before *x* in this code is actually *u*. The rest follows easily: before *d* is *c*; before *b* is *a*; before *o* is *n*; before *v* (which is the same as *u*) is *t*, and so on. This gives us "fuccant uuiuys of heli." Since the *-ant* ending is the third-person plural ending on many Latin verbs, we can render the passage as "They are not in heaven, because *fuccant* [they fuck] the wives of Ely." (Later in the poem, another obscenity, *swive*—once nearly as filthy as *fuck*, now forgotten—is encoded the same way: "Fratres cum knyvys goth about and txxkxzv nfookt xxzxkt." Similarly deciphered, translated, and rendered into modern spelling, that gives us "The Friars with knives go about and swive men's wives.")

History does not record whether the Carmelite brothers were any more given to illicit wife-swiving than anyone else, but this bizarre bit of naughty cryptography tells us that the word *fuck* was offensive enough in 1475 that it had to be hidden. Where did the word come from before that? This is one of the great mysteries, and exercises etymologists in their more speculative moods. *The Oxford English Dictionary*, after pointedly omitting the word in its first edition, now has a note running to more than six hundred words—nearly two pages in a book this size—offering all sorts of learned meditations. "Probably cognate," the musings begin, "with Dutch *fokken* to mock (15th cent.), to strike (1591), to fool, gull (1623), to beget children (1637), to have sexual intercourse with (1657), to grow, cultivate (1772)." Earlier than that? There was a word in the long-lost Proto-Indo-European language, the ancestor of most of the European languages, that meant "to strike"; it gives us words like the Latin *pugnus* 'fist', the Old Icelandic *feykja* 'to blow, drive away', and the Middle High German *fochen* 'to hiss, to blow'. There's also a Middle High German word *ficken* 'to rub', which by the sixteenth century had evolved into the modern German obscenity *ficken*. But the connections are far from certain, and the first paragraph of the *OED*'s etymology reads, "the exact nature of any relationship is unclear."[14]

The origin of the other big no-no—the C-word—is a little clearer. The Middle English word *cunte* or *counte* is related to a series of words in the Northern European languages—Old Norse, Norwegian, Swedish, Danish, Middle Dutch—where forms like *kunta* and *kunte* are common. They apparently come from the old Germanic word *kunton*, which in turn probably comes from a Proto-Indo-European root meaning "hollow space." These may be distant cousins of words like *cove*, *cottage*, and *keel*, all of which describe hollow spaces. Still, all of this is just guessing. The great difficulty with telling the story of indecent words is that, however widespread they may once have been in speech, they were rarely written down, and without written evidence, it's hard for scholars to make reliable claims.

ONE OF THE curiosities of the history of lexicography is that some words now universally condemned as offensive appeared, without comment, in early dictionaries. John Florio's Italian–English dictionary, *A Worlde of Wordes*, appeared in 1598; next to the Italian word *fottere*, he offered several English translations: "to jape, to sard, to fucke, to swiue, to occupy" (*jape* and *sard*, both obsolete, mean to deceive; we also see *swive* again; and *occupy* had smutty overtones).[15] And Stephen Skinner's *Etymologicon Linguae Anglicanae*, published in 1671, offered a learned disquisition on the obscene etymology. Nathan Bailey's *Universal Etymological English Dictionary*, first published in 1721, follows Skinner in offering a learned meditation: "*foutre*, F. *foutere*, Ital. *futuo*, L. . . . but Dr. *Th. H.* derives it from *Fuycken, Fucken, Du.* to thrust or knock; others from *Foder, Du.* to beget," before giving a brief but cryptic definition, "*Fœminam Subagitare*"—"to lie illicitly with a woman."[16]

As dictionaries became authoritative reference works, though, some began to worry that the inclusion of bad words would harm impressionable readers. Samuel Johnson's handling of obscene words in his *Dictionary* is illuminating. The real-life Johnson was no prude; according to one story, when asked what was the greatest pleasure on earth, "Johnson answered f—ing and the second was drinking. And therefore he wondered why there were not more drunkards, for all could drink though all could not f—k."[17]

In print, though, he was far more decorous, and the prurient will not find *fuck*, *cunt*, or *shit* in his pages. His exclusion of these words from the *Dictionary* gave Johnson an opportunity to exercise his famous wit. Johnson visited two ladies "soon after the publication of his immortal dictionary," and these ladies "very much commended the omission of all *naughty* words. 'What, my dears! then you have been looking for them?' said the moralist. The ladies, confused at being thus caught, dropped the subject of the dictionary."[18]

Nearly every dictionary followed Johnson's practice until the 1960s. There's a long history of schoolboys taking their cue from Johnson's female acquaintances and opening their dictionaries to the end of the *c*'s, the end of the *f*'s, or the middle of the *s*'s to see whether *those words* are there. The schoolboys usually go away disappointed, though perhaps having inadvertently learned a little about *cuneiform* and *cupboards*, *fuchsia* and *fugues*, *shirtwaists* and *shivarees* along the way.

WE THINK OF the aversion to racy language as "Victorian," but even Victorian Britain couldn't compete with the prudery found in nineteenth-century America. When the novelist Frances Milton Trollope (mother of the more famous Anthony Trollope) visited the United States in 1832, she struck up a conversation with a local about her country's greatest playwright and was unprepared for his reaction: "Shakspeare, Madam, is obscene," he insisted, "and, thank God, WE are sufficiently advanced to have found it out! If we must have the abomination of stage plays, let them at least be marked by the refinement of the age in which we live."[19]

To be fair to the hyperventilating gentleman, Shakespeare often *is* obscene; his bawdry prompted Henrietta Maria Bowdler to republish his works without the offensive bits in 1807.[20] But seven years after Trollope's visit, another British traveler in the United States discovered that American fussiness went much further. Captain Frederick Marryat's 1839 *Diary in America* described an encounter with a young lady at Niagara Falls. When the lady slipped from a rock and barked her shin, Marryat asked, "Did you hurt your leg much?" The lady "turned from me," he recorded, "evidently much shocked, or much offended." Marryat, "not being aware that [he] had committed any very heinous offence," asked "the reason of her displeasure." The lady could hardly bring herself to speak the word, but she finally explained, in an embarrassed whisper, "that the word *leg* was never mentioned before ladies." Marryat, amazed that a word as innocent as *leg* could provoke gasps, finally asked "by what name [he] might mention them without shocking the company. Her reply was, that the word *limb* was used." He was later surprised to hear someone else refer to "a square piano-forte with four *limbs*"—even to see a piano on which a woman had "dressed all these four limbs in modest little trousers, with frills at the bottom of them!"[21]

It's possible that Marryat was pulling his readers' limbs and that Victorian-era pianos weren't quite so modest as this suggests. His story has been widely repeated and gained the status of an urban legend, but there's little contemporary evidence, other than his say-so, that a cottage industry of piano-leg coverings had arisen in nineteenth-century America. But there's no denying that the age was notable for its very clear notions that some words were proper and others were not.

UNTIL FAIRLY LATE in the twentieth century, the grossest obscenities were rarely seen in print. A learned article on the history of the so-called four-letter words, written by the distinguished American linguist Allen Walker Read, appeared in the scholarly journal *American Speech* in 1934; remarkably, the words themselves never appear at all. We do read about "the most disreputable of all English words—the colloquial verb and noun, universally known by speakers of English, designating the sex act,"[22] which, from that point, is coded as "our word"—but we never read the word itself.

To avoid using the obscenities, people have developed a long list of euphemistic equivalents, often derived from a similarity of sound: *pee* (first attested in 1788) for *piss; darn* (1789) or *dang*

(1793) for *damn; doggone* (1851) for *goddamn; heck* (1887) for *hell; oh, sugar!* (1883) for *oh, shit!*; and *eff* (1943) or *feck* (1980) for *fuck*. When Norman Mailer submitted *The Naked and the Dead* in 1948, his publisher convinced him to change every appearance of *fuck* to *fug*; Mailer reluctantly agreed. A widely reported story has Mailer meeting Dorothy Parker, who said, "So you're the young man who can't spell *fuck*."[23]

Other substitutions are more inventive. After Shaw's play caused a stir, it was fashionable to euphemize *bloody* with the word *pygmalion*, as in "Not pygmalion likely." The cultural historian Paul Fussell writes that troops in the Second World War sometimes "wearied of *fucking* and tried substituting equivalents like *conjugal* or *matrimonial*, as in 'Where's the conjugal NAAFI in this camp?' or 'What the matrimonial bloody hell do you think you're doing?' "[24] Even more curious than these euphemisms are the ways of reporting on profane language that simply omit a letter or two, leaving no doubt what the intended word is, but stopping short of putting the wicked letters on the page. "The practice of using asterisks to denote omissions," notes linguist Geoffrey Hughes, "was established by the early eighteenth century and continued to the early part of this [the twentieth], the abbreviations *f****, *f**k*, *f*ck* then being commonly encountered."[25]

This technique has survived into the age of electronic media, where the visual blank is replaced by the audible bleep. The bleep was born in the mid-1960s, when the counterculture was finding its way onto television. Networks were eager for the young viewers that cutting-edge programs brought, but they also feared government crackdowns and advertiser boycotts; they therefore turned to technology for a solution. The word *blip*, both noun and verb, shows up in the *New York Times* in the mid-sixties, but the more familiar form of the word, *bleep*, first appears in the April 1968 edition of *Life* magazine.

Live television and radio pose special challenges; skilled technicians keep their fingers hovering over the bleep button, listening for every offense, ready to expunge the unsavory sounds with the benefit of just a seven-second broadcast delay. Prerecorded material—films shown on television, for instance—can be censored at leisure, and a skillful bleeper can leave in just enough of the offending word to inform every listener of the obscenity without actually allowing the entire word to be heard. When it's well done, audiences can make out *motherf-* before the bleep and *-cker* after it, but the network, never having broadcast the dreadful vowel *u*, gets off scot-free. And just as nineteenth-century wags began using the word *blank* as a comic euphemism—"I wouldn't give a blank for such a blank blank"[26]—moderns sometimes use *bleep* to stand in for words that can't be spoken, as when Special Prosecutor Patrick Fitzgerald quoted Illinois governor Rod Blagojevich's taped discussions: "Fire all those bleeping people. Get them the bleep out of there."[27]

ALTHOUGH NEWSPAPERS DON'T face the same censorship restrictions as network television, some papers have similar policies on coarse language. And yet the ubiquity of the words in the larger culture have made it almost impossible to exclude them altogether. The worst obscenities have not appeared in the *New York Times*, for instance, with a single exception: on September 12, 1998, the *Times* directly quoted Monica Lewinsky's testimony from the Starr Report. The *Washington Post* has only three occurrences of *fuck* in its history: a quotation from a death-row inmate in 1992, another extract from the Starr Report in 1998, and a bon mot delivered by U.S. vice president Dick Cheney on the floor of the Senate in 2004.[28]

That foulmouthed Dick, though, pales in comparison with an earlier Dick, one who had once occupied the same office of the vice president. In bringing offensive words into many forums where they had long been excluded, Richard M. Nixon gave us a new phrase, *expletive deleted*, with which newspapers sought to explain omissions from their transcriptions of the famous White House tapes. Terence Moran was surprised to find that "the pious companion of the Reverend Billy Graham and Dr. Norman Vincent Peale who so publicly chastised President Truman's use of 'bad language' was a facade behind which a sewer of characterizations and expletives and adjectives flowed." He noted, "In the first one hundred pages of transcripts, Mr. Nixon uses 59 expletives that are deleted and 11 characterizations that are omitted. Considering that the typists left in such words as *hell*, *damn*, *sons of bitches*, *crap*, and *by golly*, it is intriguing to speculate on the empty slots that need filling."[29] One result was angry protesters waving banners reading IMPEACH THE [EXPLETIVE DELETED]!

EVEN NIXON, THOUGH, was a mediocre swearer at best. The tapes reveal a foulmouthed and paranoid racist, but his oaths lack flair. The most inventive swearers raise obscenity to an art form, delivering virtuoso performances and presenting a set of variations on a theme, all in language certain to bring a blush to modest cheeks.

Carlin's original "Seven Words" routine became famous among his fans, leading him to offer a more comprehensive list:

> We start out lightly with *heck*, *hell*, *damn*, *goddamn*, *bitch*, *bastard*, and *crud*. And then we get right into *crap*, *turd*, *shit*, *dingleberry*, *piss*, *piddle*, *leak*, *mung cheese*, *laying some cable*, *pinching a loaf*, and *dropping a load*. *Ass*, *booty*, *butt*, *hiney*, *tuchus*, *bum*, *buns*, *rump*, *cheeks*, *tits*, *jugs*, *bazoombas*, *knockers*, *knobs*, *lungs*, *balloons*, *brown eyes*, *balls*, *nuts*, *onions*, *jewels*, *rocks*, *stones* . . .

So far, Carlin was just warming up. After a few more, he settled into a groove: "Here we go now," he said, and launched into a long rhythmic incantation, with obscenities coming with the melody of a nursery rhyme: "*Fuck*, *screw*, *lay*, *diddle*, *push*, *plow*, *hump*, *cut*, *bang*, *poke*, *batter*, *wham*, *beef injection*. *Vitamin F*, *knock up*, *put out*, *dip your wick*, *hide the salami* . . ." The monologue ran more than five minutes, with its hundreds of terms handily organized into categories: the male organ, the female organ, coitus, fellatio. The routine derives much of its comic force from Carlin's *oh-no-he-didn't!* lewdness, but even more from his sheer joy in playing with the language. Between a selection of words for menstruation and another on erections, he paused: "Some of these," he said to the audience, "border on poetry."

Carlin was a strange kind of poet, of course—a demotic bard whose medium was smut. But others have also found a kind of poetry in the unspeakable. "Once, on a misty Scottish airfield," wrote the Canadian folklorist Anthony Hopkins, "an airman was changing the magneto on the engine of a Wellington bomber. Suddenly his wrench slipped and he flung it on the grass and snarled, 'Fuck! the fucking fucker's fucked.' The bystanders were all quite well aware that he had stripped a bolt and skinned his knuckles."[30] There are also some wonderful comic scenes predicated on the incongruity and inappropriateness of the language for the situation. Paul Fussell puts it well: "One RAF sergeant-major was renowned for his vigorous abusive word-hoard. 'As he led the squad into the church door, he stepped aside,' a witness remembers, 'but kept the left, right, left, right cadence as we proceeded inside. A sergeant in front of me tried to enter wearing his cap but the sergeant-major snatched it off his head roaring, "Take yer fuckin' 'at off in the 'ouse of God, cunt!" ' "[31]

For as long as such language was suppressed in polite company, it may have been possible to believe it was limited to schoolyards in bad neighborhoods, dockside warehouses, and army barracks. But the late twentieth century saw the opening of the floodgates, as the taboos fell in publishing and film. One industrious viewer watched Quentin Tarantino's film *Pulp Fiction* and tallied the word *fuck* and its derivatives 265 times. Since the film is 154 minutes long, that's roughly once every thirty-five seconds.[32] It may seem that our culture has reached the point at which it's impossible to be offended by words.

BUT STILL OFFENSES come, though it's often a different crowd that takes offense. Attacks on obscenities, such as those on Carlin's list, have been mostly from the conservative side of the spectrum, but linguistic moralizing is not strictly the province of the cultural right. The left has had its own concerns about the offensive potential of some of the darker corners of the language.

The biggest concern for liberals is what's known as "hate speech." We can learn much about a culture by watching the taboos change over time. Blasphemy and profaning the name of the Lord once gave the greatest offense; later obscenity—especially references to sex acts, excretion, and the body parts associated with them—became the paradigmatic dirty words. In recent decades, the ideals of inclusive language have made racial, ethnic, and sexual slurs the most disturbing. It's telling that at the beginning of the twenty-first century, the "N-word" has usurped the traditional place of the "F-word" as the single most objectionable word in American English. As one of the prosecutors pointed out in O. J. Simpson's murder trial, when defense attorney Johnnie Cochran introduced evidence that a police detective had used the word *nigger* in conversation, "If you allow Mr. Cochran to use this word and play the race card, the direction and focus of the case changes: it is a race case now. . . . It's the filthiest, dirtiest, nastiest word in the English language."[33]

It's easy to forget how widespread *nigger* once was even in polite company. Randall Kennedy notes its appearance in courtrooms, in legal documents, in political speeches. As recently as 1973, when Hank Aaron was poised to break Babe Ruth's record for career home runs, he received letters like the following:

> Dear Mr. Nigger,
>   I hope you don't brak the Babe's record. How can I tell my kids that a nigger did it?

> Dear Nigger,
>   You can hit all dem home runs over dem short fences, but you can't take dat black off yo face.

> Dear Nigger Henry,
>   You are [not] going to break this record established by the great Babe Ruth if you can help it. . . . Whites are far

more superior than jungle bunnies. . . . My gun is watching your every black move.[34]

There's no question that the Neanderthals who wrote these letters were subliterate cretins. Paradoxically, though, they were also very effective writers—they knew that words have the power to wound. They knew full well that no word in the English language could have caused more pain.

In the United States, *nigger* remains the most egregious ethnic slur, but there's no shortage of disparaging terms for ethnicities. Irving Lewis Allen offers a list of more than a thousand derogatory terms for ethnic and racial groups.[35] Words like *chink*, *dago*, *jap*, *kraut*, *nip*, *paddy*, *paki*, *spic*, *wetback*, and *wop* demean people on the basis of their ethnicity; others—*bitch*, *fag*, *dyke*, *kike*, *papist*, *redneck*, *towelhead*—single out religions, regional identities, gender, and sexual preference. In some quarters they can arouse more ire than a thousand *fuck*s.

The word *Jew* is an illuminating case, because it stands for an ethnicity, a religion, and a culture at the same time and has been used as both a neutral and a derogatory term. A history of many centuries of ill-will between Christians and Jews in Europe has given the word a unique set of resonances. Even the word *Jew* itself, as a noun, can be enough to provoke discomfort; many people who are comfortable saying *a Christian*, *a Buddhist*, or *a Muslim* might still say *a Jewish person*, out of a conviction that *a Jew* is a put-down. The creators of the taboo-shattering animated series *South Park* played on the word's strange double character:

> CARTMAN: Kyle, all those times I called you a stupid
>   Jew, I didn't mean it. You're not a Jew.
> KYLE: Yes I am, Cartman! I *am* a Jew!
> CARTMAN: No, no, don't be so hard on yourself.[36]

Still, many of the extended meanings of *Jew* are unambiguously derogatory: using *jew* to accuse someone of being cheap, or the verb *to jew*, "To cheat or overreach, in the way attributed to

Jewish traders or usurers. Also, to drive a hard bargain, and . . . to haggle. Phr. *to jew down*, to beat down in price." Just as lexicographers fret over how to handle obscenities, they wring their hands over racially and ethnically insensitive terms, apparently out of a belief that their appearance in a reference book amounts to a kind of approval. The grammarian Richard Grant White, writing in 1880, pointed out "that an esteemed Jewish gentleman requested the publishers of Webster's and Worcester's dictionaries to omit from those books the verb *to jew*," apparently with success in the case of Worcester's. Curious readers asked White for his opinion, which he found "an unwelcome task." And here his tone became cringe-inducing as he resorted to the some-of-my-best-friends-are-Jewish mode of arguing:

> among the most intelligent, the most polite, the most trustworthy, and the most benevolent men that I have ever met, I reckon no small proportion of the few Hebrews of my acquaintance. And in particular I have had occasion to remark not only their probity in matters of money, but their fairness and kindliness of dealing.[37]

And yet he had to agree that the word belonged in dictionaries. The derogatory meanings, however distasteful even to the lexicographers, are part of the language.

Lexicographers live in perpetual fear that, despite their protestations that their works are objective records of the language as it is used, and not advice on how it *should* be used, people will turn to dictionaries to regulate their own language. The Fowlers confronted this as they worked on their dictionary.[38] It came up again in October 1930, when London's *Sunday Express* announced that "uncomplimentary synonyms given under the word 'Jew' had been omitted in a new edition of the *Thesaurus* published in the United States"; the headline read WHAT THE WORD "JEW" MEANS: OFFENSIVE TERMS CUT FROM A BOOK.[39]

When Robert Burchfield took over editing the supplementary volumes to the *OED* in the 1950s, the concern was still very much alive.[40] In 1969, for instance, a Jewish businessman, Marcus Schloimovitz, argued that the dictionary entries for *Jew*, both noun and verb, were "abusive and insulting and reflected a deplorable attitude towards Jewry." He wrote many newspapers, politicians, and religious leaders, campaigning to expunge the word from the language. Oxford refused to make the requested changes, and Shloimovitz filed a legal action against Clarendon Press, calling the *OED*'s definitions "derogatory, defamatory, and deplorable," "a part of the slow poison of hatred in our midst." "Every Jew," he argued, "who reads these dictionaries is defamed."[41] Burchfield made the case that many dictionary writers had made before him: "It is the duty of lexicographers to record actual usage, as shown by collected examples, not to express moral approval or disapproval of usage; dictionaries cannot be regulative in matters of social, political, and religious attitude."[42] And on this occasion he carried the day: in July 1973 the case was decided in favor of Clarendon Press.

That doesn't stop people from complaining. *Merriam-Webster's Collegiate Dictionary* had long defined *nigger* as "a Negro—usually taken to be offensive"; by the 1980s, when *Negro* had fallen out of favor, it was replaced by "black person." In 1993, the dictionary went further, adding that the word "now ranks as perhaps the most offensive and inflammatory racial slur in English" and is "expressive of racial hatred and bigotry." But the usage note was not enough for some. In 1997 Kathryn Williams, the curator of the Museum of African American History in Flint, Michigan, began collecting signatures on a petition urging Merriam-Webster to remove the entry from its dictionaries altogether. "The definition is simply not accurate," insisted Williams. "That is not what the word means." Around the same time, Delphine Abraham, a computer operator in Michigan, began a petition drive of her own. "I can't believe that in 1997 you can look up 'nigger' in the dictionary," said Abraham, "and it says 'a black person.'"[43] By October 1997, the president of the NAACP, Kweisi Mfume, began a nationwide letter-writing campaign to convince Merriam-Webster either to change the definition or to drop the entry. His plea was backed up with a threat: "Mfume warned that if the company did not bend, the NAACP would urge colleges and school systems not to buy its dictionaries."[44] Merriam-Webster responded with a written statement, echoing the earlier protestations of Fowler and Burchfield: "We have made it clear that the use of this word as a racial slur is abhorrent to us, but it is nonetheless part of the language, and as such, it is our duty as dictionary makers to report on it. . . . To do less would simply mislead people by creating the false impression that racial slurs are no longer a part of our culture; and that, tragically, is not the case."[45]

ATTEMPTS TO CASTRATE the lexicon continue from the left, the right, and the center—and not only to banish the really offensive words. Each time a new dictionary comes out, the McDonald's Corporation objects to words like *McJob*, defined by the *OED* as "An unstimulating, low-paid job with few prospects, *esp.* one created by the expansion of the service sector." It now shows up in *Merriam-Webster's Collegiate Dictionary*, 11th edition, the *OED*, the *Collins English Dictionary*, *The American Heritage Dictionary*, and *Random House Webster's Dictionary*; with each new appearance, a corporate representative of the McDonald's Corporation is ready with a statement. When *McJob* showed up in a Merriam-Webster dictionary in 2003, the chief executive officer of McDonald's fired off an angry letter. "On behalf of every individual who proudly waits a table, cooks the food, washes a dish, or seats a party at a restaurant, let's agree to stop giving this term any more exposure," the CEO demanded. The real definition of *McJob*, he insisted, should be "teaches opportunity."[46] Of course a big corporation wants to resist the transformation of its name into a byword for "worthless" in words like *McDonaldization* ("the spread of the influence of American culture"), *McMansion* ("a modern house built on a large and imposing scale, but regarded as ostentatious and lacking architectural integrity"), *McPaper* (used to dismiss *USA Today* as "journalistic junk food"), even *McDoctor*, *McPoliceman*, and *McTherapy*. But it's unlikely any serious dictionary will yield to corporate pressure, at least as long as the words continue to be in use.

THE ATTEMPTS AT regulating offensive language have had limited success—there are still words that aren't heard on broadcast television or seen in most newspapers—but the regulations are much looser than what the censors would like. What's more, their mission is probably futile, because the very attempt to eliminate offensive words is what gives those words their power. Lenny Bruce, a comic who was one of George Carlin's greatest influences, made the point memorably in a performance in the early 1960s. He paused in one of his long, rambling monologues in a nightclub to ask a question of the audience: "By the way, are there any niggers here tonight?" The room immediately fell silent—this was a comedian known for his liberal politics, and he was using that sort of redneck language? Bruce assumed the voice of a shocked audience member: "What did he say?" he hissed into the microphone. " 'Are there any niggers here tonight?' Jesus Christ! Does he have to get that low for laughs?" Resuming his own voice, he began looking around the room, trying out a variety of offensive terms as he identified audience members: "Between those two niggers sits one kike—man, thank God for the kike! Uh, two kikes." Then, as if taking stock: "That's two kikes, and three niggers, and one spic. One spic—two, three spics. One mick. One mick, one spic, one hick, thick, funky, spunky boogey." Tempers in the room were rising, and Bruce may well have been putting his safety in danger, since racial insults and two-drink-minimum nightclubs can be a dangerous combination. After ratcheting up the tension as high as it could go, though, he paused again, and delivered the moral of the story:

> The point? That the word's suppression gives it the power, the violence, the viciousness. If President Kennedy got on television and said, "Tonight I'd like to introduce the niggers in my cabinet," and he yelled "niggerniggerniggerniggerniggerniggernigger" at every nigger he saw . . .

till nigger didn't mean anything any more, till nigger lost
its meaning—you'd never make any four-year-old nigger
cry when he came home from school.[47]

The relief in the nightclub was palpable, and the audience realized
that he wasn't being gratuitously offensive; he was being offensive
for a good reason. Bruce was no linguist, but with the central insight of that passage—"the word's suppression gives it the
power"—he showed that he understood far more about how "offensive words" work than most of the moralists who've hoped to
control our unruly language.

CHAPTER 12

Grammar, and Nonsense, and Learning

WE LOOK TO THE FUTURE

GUESSING WHAT THE LANGUAGE will look like in a century's time is a mug's game: three-card monte offers better odds. No responsible commentator would be so bold as to guess which words, senses, and grammatical features will appear or disappear. But while we can't predict specific changes, we can think about the kinds of forces that might influence the language in the next few decades. And if history provides any clues to the future, it's likely that two features above all others will shape the English language over the course of the twenty-first century: technology and globalization.

TECHNOLOGY WILL ALMOST certainly continue to shape the language. *Continue* is the right word: technology's influence on language is nothing new. Long before mobile phones and the Internet, technologies transmitted, mediated, and even altered the language.[1] One very old technology, the book, offers some insights into how our relationship with language can change. The oldest surviving writings were done on stone monuments or clay tablets. (Other media may have been used earlier—leaves, maybe, or tree bark— but if so, they don't survive.) A work too long to fit onto a single clay tablet simply became a collection of loose tablets. By the time the ancient Egyptians developed their own writing system around 3200 B.C., though, they had begun using a different medium, papyrus, made from plant matter. Its thinness and flexibility meant that pieces could be stitched together and the whole rolled up into a compact form: long works could now be stored on a single scroll rather than dozens of heavy clay tablets. The ease of transmitting and storing works of literature inevitably shaped the works of literature themselves. The medium was becoming the message.

The scroll marked a number of advances on the old loose tablets, but there were still problems. Because scrolls were made up of one continuous stream of text, it was difficult to find something in the middle of a long work. A reader eager to discover some favorite sentence would have to start at the beginning of the scroll and unroll it until he reached the desired passage. Sometime around the third or fourth century A.D., though, the codex—the more familiar kind of book, with separate pages bound together against a spine—began to take over from the scroll. The new kind of book was revolutionary in enabling rapid reference to any part of the text, an analogy to what computer scientists call "random-access memory," since it's possible to go to any passage without having to start at the beginning. And a new set of technologies emerged in the Middle Ages to take advantage of this new property of books: page numbers, tables of contents, indexes, footnotes, and marginal notes all made it possible to read out of sequence, and they changed the experience of reading in fundamental ways.

The most famous technology of the word came at the very end of the Middle Ages, and played a large role in bringing about the cultural "rebirth" known as the Renaissance. After about 1450, when the German goldsmith Johannes Gutenberg developed movable type, printed books began to do the work that manuscripts had done for the previous millennia. The print revolution happened quickly: within just a few years of Gutenberg's invention, writers in Europe were taking advantage of the technological novelty.

OTHER TECHNOLOGIES OF the word have done almost as much to shape the language. The nineteenth century brought first the telegraph, then the telephone; sound recording, radio, motion pictures, and television followed in quick succession. Every one of these inventions exerted its influence on the language. The word *hello*, for instance, was a rare variant on *hollo* and *hallo* when it was coined in the early nineteenth century, but after Thomas Edison proposed its use on the newly invented telephone, it found a new life. (Alexander Graham Bell, the telephone's inventor, had been rooting for *ahoy!* as the proper greeting, but it never caught on.) The high-tech science of telephony turned *hello* from an obscure regionalism into one of the most common greetings in the language—and in many languages, for that matter, since you can now hear *hello* in dozens of countries.

The most important technologies reshaping the language today are computers. They've given us new words (*byte*, *modem*), new senses for old words (*mouse*, *network*), and new abbreviations (LAN, DSL). But they've also made more subtle, and more far-reaching, changes than simply adding a few entries to the dictionary. The transformation of the computer from number-cruncher to symbol-manipulator has to count as one of the most significant developments of the second half of the twentieth century. As the name suggests, the first electronic computers were built to do numerical calculations. The pioneers of electronic computing—John von Neumann, Alan Turing—were mathematicians, and one of the contenders for the title of "first electronic digital computer" is ENIAC, Electronic Numerical Integrator and Computer. The word *numerical*, too, makes it clear that numbers were at the heart of early computing. ENIAC had been commissioned by the U.S. Army's Ballistic Research Laboratory to produce tables of figures for firing heavy artillery, a job that had once been done by scores of people, mostly women (since the men were serving in the military) with mathematics degrees, who were known as "human computers." ENIAC was unveiled in February 1946, too late to be of any use for its intended purpose, but it soon found new applications. With its 17,480 vacuum tubes performing a hundred thousand operations a second—orders of magnitude more powerful than anything the world had seen before—ENIAC was in nearly continuous use from 1946 to 1955. And all the work it did was mathematical. Computers computed.

It didn't take long, though, for programmers to realize that these new devices were not actually manipulators of *numbers*, but rather of *symbols*—anything that can be reduced to a finite set of signs can be stored, moved, compared, and transformed. And the written language lends itself very easily to representation as signs. By the late 1950s, computers were being used to help the printing process, for typesetting and page layout, and they became almost universal among publishers in the late 1960s. In the 1970s, some pioneering literary scholars were using mainframe computers to do textual analysis, such as attributing the various anonymous *Federalist* papers to their authors, or sorting through the variants in early editions of Shakespeare. Concordances—lists of every word in a text such as the Bible, with references to where the words appear in that work, allowing readers to find every occurrence of every word—had been prepared with quill pens and index cards for generations, but in the electronic age it was possible to turn out these word indexes in a tiny fraction of the time. Other technological breakthroughs followed rapidly. The first spelling checker was developed around 1961 at the Massachusetts Institute of Technology, and in the 1970s programmers began to experiment with style and grammar checkers. Now both are standard in every commercial word processor. They were made possible by the realization that computers don't care which symbols they are manipulating, and that machines designed to crunch numbers can crunch words just as easily.

The other revolutionary change in computing had to do with scale and availability. Until the 1970s, the influence of computers on language was limited by the tiny number of computers on the planet. The personal computer changed all that. The technological visionary Theodor Holm Nelson, who is usually credited with the idea of "hypertext" that makes the World Wide Web possible, also helped to popularize the term "personal computer" at a time when it sounded as exotic as "personal atom-smasher." In Woody

Allen's *Take the Money and Run*, con man Virgil Starkwell hopes to secure a job in an office. When the interviewer asks, "Have you ever had any experience in running a high-speed digital electronic computer?" Starkwell decides to bluff: "Yes, I have." "Where?" "My aunt has one." That line got big laughs in 1969, so improbable did it seem. Today, of course, it would be noteworthy if Virgil's aunt didn't own a computer of some sort.

NOT ALL THE effects of computers have been unambiguously positive. Once upon a time, when people read printed material, it had been copyedited, typeset, and proofread by professionals. Handwritten notes were one thing—no one was surprised by erratic spelling, punctuation, and grammar there—but if something appeared in print, it had almost always undergone several stages of vetting. Heaven knows it wasn't always perfect, but it had received at least some superficial attention.

The technological transformations of the last few decades have changed that, apparently forever. Now, thanks to the phenomenon known as "desktop publishing"—a term coined by Paul Brainerd, the founder of Aldus Corporation, to describe the PageMaker software package he released in 1985—anyone has the power to do what only professional typesetters could do before. There are many advantages to giving the masses easier access to the printed word, but there are also downsides. Under the old dispensation, typesetters and proofreaders were expected to learn an elaborate protocol about when punctuation goes inside or outside quotation marks, when to use italics, how to set ordinal numbers (1st or 1st, 2nd or 2nd), how far to indent new paragraphs, where to hyphenate words across lines, whether it's *U.S.A.* or *USA*, whether it's a *well known president* or a *well-known President*, whether it's *flower pot*, *flowerpot*, or *flowerpot*, whether it should be *pages 123–124*, *pages 123–24*, or *pages 123–4*, how long that dash between the digits should be (*123-24, 123–24, 123—24*), and so on. The handbooks spelling out the rules for such matters—*The Chicago Manual of Style* is one of the most famous—stretch to hundreds of pages, describing the minutiae of typesetting practice. You didn't get to make those decisions until you'd served an apprenticeship in the publishing business and demonstrated a mastery of the rules.

Today, though, anyone with access to even a cheap computer and a printer can reproduce the superficial appearance of a printed book, without training in how to handle all the special cases. And sometimes the results are nervous-making. The "greengrocer's apostrophe"—the stray apostrophe before the plural-marker *s* found on signs advertising *banana's* and *tomato's*—used to be limited to hand-printed signs. Nowadays we see it all the time in blogs and in e-mail, and it's even creeping into professionally printed books and magazines. The technology made it possible to skip the apprenticeship, and now even the marginally literate can publish. It's not necessarily a bad thing, but it is one way in which technology is changing the language—or, to be more precise, in which the social changes made possible by technology are changing the language.

DESKTOP PUBLISHING IS one technological revolution, but the more important one is the connection of computers to one another. J. C. R. Licklider, an MIT professor working for the U.S. Department of Defense's Advanced Research Projects Agency (ARPA) in 1962, proposed something he facetiously called the "intergalactic computer network," which was one of the first plans for a large network of connected computers. Licklider laid the groundwork for the ARPANET network, which in 1969 had just four host computers but was the beginning of what eventually became known as the Internet. Originally designed to allow communication among defense contractors, the network has expanded to the point where now 20 percent of the world's population has access to it. And the "killer app"—the invention that taught the rest of the world that the new technology was worthwhile—was the World Wide Web, first developed by Tim Berners-Lee in 1989, released to the public in 1992, and discovered by the multitudes in the mid-1990s. The multitudes have been busily writing and reading on the Internet ever since.

It's not hard to find dire assessments of the state of the language in the Internet age. One complaint—typical in its concerns, but more elegant than most in its expression—comes from John Humphrys, long the main presenter on BBC TV's *Nine O'Clock News* and a regular on BBC Radio 4's *Today*. Humphrys has spent many years fighting the dumbing down of popular culture, especially in so-called reality television and soap operas. One of his perennial concerns is the health of the language; he has even been recognized by the Plain English Campaign with the silver platter award for Crystal Clear Broadcasting. And one of his recurring bêtes noires is tech-speak.

In London's conservative *Daily Mail* in 2007, Humphrys published an impassioned screed titled "I H8 Txt Msgs: How Texting Is Wrecking Our Language." He confessed to feeling the fetishistic pleasures of hard copy when he praised "the physical sensation—the feel and smell of good paper," and he took almost the same sensuous pleasure in a well-turned sentence. But the language is now going all to hell, he insisted, and technology is one of the leading culprits. A distinct impression of nausea comes through in his description of "those absurd little smiley faces with which texters litter their messages." "It is the relentless onward march of the texters," he wrote, "the SMS (Short Message Service) vandals who are doing to our language what Genghis Khan did to his neighbours eight hundred years ago." And the modern barbarians are little better than the original Mongol hordes: "They are destroying [the language]: pillaging our punctuation; savaging our sentences; raping our vocabulary. And they must be stopped." Even his beloved paper dictionaries are beginning to show signs of decay. The *Shorter Oxford English Dictionary* had long been among his favorites, but now his "lifetime love affair with the OED is at risk. The sixth edition has just been published and—I feel a small shudder as I write these words—it has fallen victim to fashion." The shudder-inducing offense? "It has removed the hyphen from no fewer than 16,000 words." In this dystopian vision of the future, "we are required to spell pigeon-hole, for instance, as pigeonhole and leap-frog as leapfrog. In other cases we have two words instead of one. Pot-belly shall henceforth be pot belly."

(Why Humphrys believed a new edition of a book from Oxford University Press would "require" anyone to spell differently is unclear; Oxford has never claimed that authority for itself, so it's odd that Humphrys should be so eager to give it to the press.)

David Crystal, on the other hand, is unfazed by the prospect of mobile-phone-wielding barbarians at the gates. He quotes John Sutherland of University College London, who in 2002 called this kind of text-message language "bleak, bald, sad shorthand. Drab shrinktalk . . . Linguistically it's all pig's ear . . . it masks dyslexia, poor spelling and mental laziness. Texting is penmanship for illiterates." Crystal thinks the anxiety is misplaced. In fact it's a welcome sign of verbal inventiveness in the younger generation. He even goes so far as to point to "increasing evidence that it helps rather than hinders literacy." Texting, he writes, "has added a new dimension to language use, but its long-term impact is negligible. It is not a disaster."[2]

Crystal begins by pointing out that "the early media hysteria about the novelty (and thus the dangers) of text messaging" was entirely unwarranted. Doomsayers have convinced themselves that "youngsters use nothing else but abbreviations when they text, such as the reports in 2003 that a teenager had written an essay so full of textspeak that her teacher was unable to understand it." Of course, as is often the way with these friend-of-a-friend stories, "no one was ever able to track down the entire essay," meaning "it was probably a hoax." Crystal even cites a study in which "less than 20% of the text messages looked at showed abbreviated forms of any kind— about three per message"; the ratio in other kinds of writing, including student essays, would be much, much lower.

And so what, Crystal asks, if they do use abbreviations? We've been abbreviating for centuries. Traditionalists reach for the smelling salts when they see something like *imho* for "in my humble opinion" and *btw* for "by the way," but, Crystal says, "the use of initial letters for whole words . . . is not at all new. People have been initialising common phrases for ages. IOU is known from 1618. There is no difference, apart from the medium of communication, between a modern kid's 'lol' ('laughing out loud') and an earlier generation's 'Swalk' ('sealed with a loving kiss')." Let's not forget *ASAP, HQ, COD, CIA, Ph.D.*, and innumerable other initialisms, even *OK*. And some of the abbreviations in text messages and e-mail—*cul8r*, for example—show an impressive degree of verbal proficiency and inventiveness, the sort of thing people should be encouraging in the young. "The most noticeable feature," Crystal writes of these messages, "is the use of single letters, numerals, and symbols to represent words or parts of words, as with b 'be' and 2 'to'. They are called rebuses, and they go back centuries. Adults who condemn a 'c u' in a young person's texting have forgotten that they once did the same thing themselves (though not on a mobile phone)." He points to published puzzles like this that once featured in newspapers:

YY U R YY U B I C U R YY 4 ME

"Too wise you are," Crystal hints, for those who don't get it at first glance.

Texters also mangle grammar—though here, too, it's intentional, done partly to save time and space, and partly to play with the language. We see the same thing on blogs, newsgroups, Twitter messages, e-mail, and many other electronic media, though grammar butchery is perhaps most extreme in the "lolcat" phenomenon. As Lev Grossman described "lolcats" to the uninitiated in *Time*:

> Take a picture of a cat doing something cute. Then make up a caption—something witty that the cat would be saying if cats could talk. Bear in mind that cats can't spell all that well and that they're not so hot on subject–verb agreement either. Photoshop the caption onto the image, and post your creation on a blog. What you get is lolcats: lol for laugh out loud, cats for cats.[3]

Thus we see a cat staring into an open refrigerator, announcing "IM IN UR FRIDGE EATIN UR FOODZ," or another examining its sharp claws, musing "If Iz knot loud to kil tings, why Iz got dese

tings for??!!" Once again, traditionalists see in these messages a society on the verge of collapse—young people can't spell, they don't
know grammar, they don't know punctuation! But this misses the
point entirely. Yes, the writers of these things violate the rules of
spelling, grammar, and punctuation—but they do so *intentionally*.
The comic effect comes not from an ignorance of the rules, but
from a willful flouting of the rules. If the authors and their audiences didn't know what proper spelling and grammar were, these
passages would lose all their force. In a way, playful lolcatters and
texters aren't ignoring the traditional rules of English; they're depending on the existence of those rules in order to raise a laugh.

Still the forecasts of cataclysm keep coming. A good example
of a gloomy anti-texting rant comes from Ireland's Department of
Education. "Text messaging," its April 2007 report announced,
"with its use of phonetic spelling and little or no punctuation,
seems to pose a threat to traditional conventions in writing. . . .
The emergence of the mobile phone and the rise of text messaging
as a popular means of communication would appear to have impacted on standards of writing as evidenced in the responses of
candidates." (Actually many of the lolcatters have a better ear for
the language than the author of a leaden phrase like "would appear to have impacted on standards of writing as evidenced in the
responses of candidates." Blech. It's a sentence only a bureaucrat
could love.) The glum article was accompanied by a more playful
sidebar, asking, "W@ would da gr8 poet William Butler Y8s have
made of da news dat txt spk is chngin da way da yung ppl rite?"
But even in the jovial passages the angst is clear.[4]

Crystal, once again, keeps a level head: "Texters use deviant
spellings—and they know they are deviant. But they are by no
means the first to use such nonstandard forms as cos 'because',
wot 'what', or gissa 'give us a'. Several of these are so much part of
English literary tradition that they have been given entries in the
Oxford English Dictionary. 'Cos' is there from 1828 and 'wot' from
1829." Crystal's summary is probably the wisest take on the whole
phenomenon of extravagantly nonstandard English in electronic
forums. "Some people dislike texting," he says. "Some are bemused

by it. But it is merely the latest manifestation of the human ability to be linguistically creative and to adapt language to suit the demands of diverse settings. There is no disaster pending. We will not see a new generation of adults growing up unable to write proper English. The language as a whole will not decline. In texting what we are seeing, in a small way, is language in evolution."[5]

ANOTHER LANGUAGE-SHAPING FORCE may prove even more influential than technology. The first letter in *www* reminds us that the Web is an international forum: people now have pen pals from around the world. English, already an international language, continues to expand its global range. And all the signs point to a fundamentally reconfigured world in which what we now think of as the English-speaking world will eventually lose its effective control of the English language.

This won't be the first time English has relocated its spiritual home. We've already seen that Noah Webster heralded a change in the language's center of gravity, as the language of a small island off the northwest coast of Europe began to transform itself into a world language. Since the late nineteenth century, the United States has had more native English speakers than any other country, including the birthplace of the language, England itself. But the United States, while it still has the most native English speakers, can no longer claim majority status. The spread of English around the globe is unprecedented. English today is a majority language in Ireland, Canada, Australia, New Zealand, South Africa, Guyana, Belize, Bermuda, the Bahamas, and Jamaica. In many other countries—Ghana, India, Liberia, Nigeria, Sri Lanka, Zimbabwe—it is an official language, albeit not the first language of the majority. Nigeria boasts more than seventy-five million English speakers, more than in the United Kingdom or Canada; there are more than forty million in the Philippines, and thirty-six million in Germany.

Britain's long involvement in India—especially from 1757, when the East India Company assumed control of the subcontinent, until 1947, when India gained its independence from the British

THE LEXICOGRAPHER'S DILEMMA

Empire—has made English one of the most important languages in that country of a billion people. English is the first language of only a minority of Indians, but it is a second or third language of nearly a hundred million. China, too, is making tremendous strides into the "Anglosphere," especially as the nation of 1.3 billion people becomes more and more involved in global commerce.

It is easy to look on these foreign Englishes as imperfect imitations of the more proper varieties; Web sites and magazine columns do a brisk traffic in reprinting unintentionally funny passages from countries where English is still on the rise. Someone cleverly coined the word *Hinglish* for the kind of English used by native speakers of Hindi, which often strikes Britons and Americans as quaint. A recent newspaper article collected some examples: "Sexual harassment . . . is known as 'Eve-teasing.' Mourners don't give condolences, they 'condole.' And then there's 'pre-pone,' the logical but nonexistent opposite of 'post-pone': 'I'm busy for dinner. Can we pre-pone for lunch instead?' "[6] We sometimes smirk and sometimes scoff at such usages, but this is exactly the kind of condescension that eighteenth- and nineteenth-century Britons turned on Americans. Population growth eventually made their complaints irrelevant: by 1850 there were more Americans than Britons, and what had once been dismissed as obscure provincial barbarisms eventually became the norm. The same thing is likely to happen to American English, as more and more speakers of the language are in other parts of the world. To call *pre-pone* a "non-existent" word misses the point: it exists now. It may strike speakers of British and American English as foolish, inconsistent, ugly, or illogical, but it's now part of global English. As the number of English speakers grows, it will become increasingly difficult to view these varieties as debased imitations of proper English.

TECHNOLOGY AND GLOBALIZATION, then, have been two of the most powerful forces on the language in recent years, and they promise to continue exerting their influence for decades, maybe centuries, to come—that much is fairly safe, as predictions about the language go. And as the hostile reactions to the new developments in this chapter make clear, it's possible to make another prediction: as the English language continues to change, people will continue to worry about it.

When an individual violates linguistic norms, it's common to blame the individual—he's an idiot, she's uneducated. When a whole group departs from the standard variety of the language, though, it's too easy to blame the group—to dismiss the lot as ignorant, backwards, barbarous, uncultivated, or even congenitally stupid. We see it over and over again: every time a new variety of English begins to impinge on the public consciousness, there's a struggle over whether it's "legitimate." It happened when American English began to diverge from British English; it happened as each immigrant community began speaking English; it's happening now as English is spreading to new parts of the world. And in the United States, one of the most recent high-profile battles has been over just this question—whether the speakers of one variety of English are competent speakers. Linguists had long called that variety Black English, though African American Vernacular English (AAVE) is now the more common term. But when it made the papers, it was known as Ebonics.

The name *Ebonics* was coined by the psychologist Robert Williams in 1973 and featured in the title of his 1975 book, *Ebonics: The True Language of Black Folks*. There he defined the word:

> Ebonics may be defined as "the linguistic and paralinguistic features which on a concentric continuum represent the communicative competence of the West African, Caribbean, and United States slave descendant of African origin. It includes the various idioms, patois, argots, idiolects, and social dialects of black people" especially those who have adapted to colonial circumstances. Ebonics derives its form from ebony (black) and phonics (sound, the study of sound) and refers to the study of the language of black people in all its cultural uniqueness.[7]

But few outside linguistics and sociology departments heard the word before December 1996, when the school board of Oakland, California, passed a resolution that became infamous across America and the world. Taking it as settled that "African Language Systems are genetically based and not a dialect of English" and that "such West and Niger-Congo African languages have been officially recognized and addressed in the mainstream community as worth [*sic*] of study, understanding or appreciation of its principles, laws, and structures for the benefit of African-American students both in terms of positive appreciation of the language and these students' acquisition and mastery of English language skills," the committee therefore resolved "that the Board of Education officially recognizes the existence, and the cultural and historical bases of West and Niger-Congo African Language Systems, and each language as the predominant primary language of African-American students."[8]

Much is controversial here—linguists question whether the distinctive features of African American Vernacular English derive from West and Niger-Congo African languages or whether they're homegrown. And the motives for some of these assertions prompted suspicion. Some speculated that Oakland was eager to declare Ebonics a "language" rather than a dialect to get federal money set aside for bilingual education. Most linguists agree that AAVE is a form of English, not a language in its own right: linguist John Baugh insists that "American slave descendants speak English and not a distinctive African language. However, vernacular African American English has incontrovertible African influences."[9]

Whatever its origin, though, AAVE is a full-fledged variety of English in its own right, not an imperfect attempt to use standard English; from the point of view of professional linguists, it's not "inferior" to any other variety of English. Many seem to fear that it's an impoverished version of the "real" language, incapable of expressing fundamental thoughts, but there's no such thing as a "primitive language." Black English has the capacity to be every bit as sophisticated as Jane Austen's English. It's not standard English, of course, and there are occasions when standard English is called for. There's a long tradition of African Americans trying to get ahead by mastering standard English: the ex-slave Frederick Douglass asserted his identity as a free man by becoming a great writer, and Malcolm X famously read an entire dictionary when he was locked away in Norfolk Prison. "I saw that the best thing I could do," he recollected in his *Autobiography*, "was get hold of a dictionary—to study, to learn some words." He read it, even copied it by hand, word for word, into a series of notebooks.[10] There are situations where all nonstandard varieties of the language, including AAVE, are inappropriate. But it's nonsense to say they're *bad* English.

You wouldn't guess it from the media coverage of the Oakland school board's resolution, which was often hysterical in tone. The LexisNexis database shows nearly two hundred newspaper articles in just the first month after the resolution was passed, and the headlines sometimes crackled with sarcasm and contempt: "EBONICS" EARNS A FAILING GRADE, said the *Washington Times*; DON'T GET HOOKED ON EBONICS, advised the *New York Daily News*. Too often the discussion smacked of racism. The journalist David Hinckley listened to a fair amount of conservative talk radio and noticed a recurring pattern among the detractors of Ebonics: "Some hosts and callers . . . seem to feel the best way to articulate their opposition to the Oakland decision is to mimic black English themselves." Hinckley summarized: "The idea is this: If they say something really stupid in an exaggerated 'black' accent, it proves that recognizing Ebonics is also really stupid."[11]

Ridicule—often racist ridicule—was all too common in the public discussions of Ebonics. An early online service called the Ebonics Translator invited people to submit a passage of standard English and get a "translation" back. The Lord's Prayer was translated to become "Bid Daddy's Rap":

> Yo, Bid Daddy upstairs,
> You be chillin'
> So be yo hood
> You be sayin' it, I be doin' it

> In dis 'ere hood yo's
> Gimme some eats
> And cut me some slack, Blood
> Sos I be doin' it dem dat trespass against us
> don't be pushing me into no jive
> and keep dem Crips away
> 'Cause you always be da Man
> Das right.

As Baugh put it, "In the name of humor, this so-called translation offends blacks and Christians simultaneously."[12]

Things may have been even worse overseas. In a satirical article titled YO, HOMEYS! ENGLISH HAS GOT A FAT NEW FLAVA, NOME SAME? John Carlin took the opening sentence of Jane Austen's *Pride and Prejudice*—now retitled *Dap and Diss*—and changed it from "It is a truth universally acknowledged, that a single man in possession of a good fortune, must be in want of a wife," to the supposed Ebonic "It be droppin' science that a dawg mad with slamming cream must be hurtin' for a bitch."[13] And in the *Irish Times*, Joe Carroll wrote, under the headline TO IS OR NOT TO IS, THAT BE THE QUESTION, "The peace and good will of the Christmas season was disrupted by a noisy debate over how African Americans speak English. Or don't speak it. Ebonics, in other words." Carroll casts his mind back to the good old days: "In Ireland," he recalled, "there was a time when you would get a clip on the ear from the teacher for saying 'I do be going home' or 'I axed him.'" Ah, yes— the time when you could strike a child for reversing the *s* and *k* sounds in *ask*. Carroll might have been surprised to discover that Geoffrey Chaucer, like most Middle English authors, spelled it *axe*, as in "I axe, why the fyfte man Was nought housbond to the Samaritan?" and "Now lovyeres axe I this question"; Chaucer might have been glad to box the adult Carroll on the ears for the absurd blunder of *ask*.[14] For Carroll, though, this history counts for nothing. In his youth, if you committed a sin as heinous as "I do be going home," "You did not think to console yourself that this was an Anglo Saxon form or an example of Elizabethan

English brought over by settlers."[15] You simply braced yourself for a beating and vowed never again to announce your intention to go home.

ONE EXAMPLE FROM AAVE makes the point clearly. The verb *to diss*—in the words of the *OED*, "To show disrespect for by using insulting language or dismissive behaviour; to abuse or insult, usually verbally"—had probably been circulating orally among urban African Americans for some time in the 1970s, but it gained new attention in 1980 when Gabriel Jackson, an early hip-hop singer who performed under the name Spoonie Gee, released a recording called "Spoonin' Rap." The song referred to the "sucker-sucker dudes who commit a crime," those who "wanna be dissed and then . . . wanna be a crook."

After 1980, *to diss* continued to be used by African Americans, but it also became increasingly popular among other populations, particularly among the young. It even began showing up in more somber mainstream publications, as when London's *Independent* newspaper reported in May 2000 on an employee of Britain's Ministry of Agriculture who saw "his life's work in pesticide research being dissed by the organic lobby."[16] Most commentators, though, showed little equanimity when confronted with this unwelcome addition to the language, and letters to the editor began to pour forth, with calls to fend off the invaders. Many managed to combine disapproval of the verb with disapproval of the culture that produced it, and turned their critiques into attacks on urban African Americans as a whole.

Some objected to the clipping of the word, reducing the three syllables of *disrespect* into one—out of sloth, many said. It's only to be expected, they argued, that kids on the street too lazy to get a job should be too lazy to finish even a simple word like *disrespect*. They forget abbreviation has been a common feature of English word-formation for a millennium, even though people have been whining about it for nearly as long. We've seen Swift dissing the word *mob*, preferring the longer *mobile vulgus*. It has nothing to do with laziness—even the most meticulous use abbreviations all the time. Perhaps there are still a few diehards who take the *omnibus* and suffer from *influenza*; the rest of us take the *bus* and catch the *flu*. These purists are probably the same people who have never opened a *fridge*, entered a *lab*, worked out in a *gym*, taken an *exam*, filled a tank with *gas*, played a *piano* or a *cello*, worn a *bra*, seen a *movie* or a *sitcom*, taken a *plane*, dialed a *phone*, written a *memo*, or visited a *zoo*—all abbreviated forms of longer words.

Other enemies of *diss*, apparently more sophisticated, professed they had no trouble with the shortening of words. Their objection, they said, was strictly *grammatical* and had to do with parts of speech: *disrespect* is "not a verb!" cried the guardians of the language. When the boxer Mike Tyson used *disrespect*, a writer for the *Times* of London sarcastically professed to find it "a most engaging example of a substantive metamorphosing into a verb," a disregard of linguistic rules only to be expected from someone who disregarded the rules of decent society. The writer mused facetiously about "Mr Tyson's view of grammar," particularly "whether he is a firm prescriptivist or one who welcomes the breaking of the ancient bonds."[17] Another reader composed a letter to the editor of the *Toronto Sun*: "I don't have a problem with slang if its usage helps to make a point," he conceded, but went on to object that "disrespect is not a verb, it is a noun, and this will never change no matter how many rap songs misuse the word. I love the English language too much to see this subcultural colloquialism further diminish a beautiful language."[18]

An admirable sentiment—except that *disrespect* was a verb before it was a noun. *Disrespect* has been a verb at least since 1614, when the poet George Whither wrote, "Here can I smile to see . . . how the mean mans suit is dis-respected." The earliest recorded appearance of the noun is 1631, nearly two decades later. Had the newspaper reader's belief that the part of speech "will never change" held true in the early seventeenth century, we'd have *only* the verb form: you could *disrespect* someone, but it would be absurd to *show disrespect*.

While that same reader was convinced the word was a

"subcultural colloquialism," it has been used by some very distinguished writers; and while the Australian newspaper writer Evan Williams refers to "that strange American verb,"[19] it has a long pedigree in the mother country as well. The verb has been used by bishops ("If he love the one he must disrespect the other"—Joseph Hall, *A Plaine and Familiar Explication . . . of All the Hard Texts of the Whole Divine Scripture*, 1633), by famous poets ("How huff'd and cuff'd and disrespecket!"—Robert Burns, "The Twa Dogs," 1786), by political theorists ("Reflecting how wretched was the condition of a disrespected man"—Tom Paine, *The Rights of Man*, 1791), and by major novelists ("You will judge whether he disrespects me"—George Meredith, *Diana of the Crossways*, 1885). And even if it lacked the seventeenth-century pedigree or the certificate of authenticity provided by big-name authors, there would be no principled reason to object to transformation of a noun into a verb—it happens all the time, and has been doing so for many centuries.

The real objection has little to do with "protecting the language" and everything to do with who is using it in new ways. Russell Baker, usually a genial commentator, reveals some of his own bias in this remark on the word *diss* from 1991: "Street children, who have taken to murdering each other with insouciance, sometimes do it because they don't get any respect. 'He dissed me,' a young killer may say of his victim, turning disrespect into a verb after lopping off its last two syllables."[20] "Street children"?—who are they? And "have taken to murdering each other with insouciance," with its own writerly insouciance (signaled in part by his choice of the word *insouciance*), assumes an air of superiority to these "street children" whose deaths aren't as important as "ours," whoever "we" are. Even "lopping off," applied to a verb, suggests an entire class of people is naturally violent, whether they're hacking apart bodies or sentences.

But similar class biases have shown up over and over again throughout the history of proper English. The Victorian grammarian Henry Alford believed that even minor variations in pronunciation can signal moral, intellectual, and spiritual degeneracy. The dropping of *h* where in standard English it should be

sounded, and inserting it where standard English leaves it silent—
think of *Pygmalion*'s and *My Fair Lady*'s "In 'ertford, 'ereford and
'ampshire, 'urricanes 'ardly hever 'appen!"—provoked particular
horror among the Victorian educated classes. Alford found it the
"worst of all faults": the habit of "leaving out of the aspirate
where it ought to be, and putting it in where it ought not to be" is
"a vulgarism" that "surely stamps a man as below the mark in in-
telligence, self-respect, and energy." And he left no doubt that the
lower classes gave him the creeps. He explained that he wrote this
passage "while waiting in a refreshment-room at Reading, between a Great-Western and a South-Eastern train," where he had
heard a conversation between "two commercial gentlemen, from a
neighbouring table." When Alford describes how one told the
other that "his *ed* used to *hake* ready to burst,"[21] we get the impression that Alford's own head is ready to burst because of his
proximity to people who have to work for a living.

HAVING MADE A few predictions in this chapter—that the language will continue to change, largely thanks to technology and
globalization, and that people will continue to complain about
it—I'll hazard one more guess about the future: these complaints
will have very little effect. And this final prediction sums up the
thesis of this book as a whole.

  In the first chapter I noted that a prominent educator, L. B. R.
Briggs, bemoaned the state of the language among Harvard students in 1888:

> Spelling is bad, and probably always will be: *loose* for
> *lose* is so nearly universal that *lose* begins to look wrong;
> *sentance* prevails; *dissapointed* and *facinating* are not un-
> usual. . . . Punctuation is frequently inaccurate—that is
> to say, unintelligent and misleading. The apostrophe is
> nearly as often a sign of the plural as of the possessive;
> the semicolon, if used at all, is a spasmodic ornament
> rather than a help to the understanding; and—worst of

all—the comma does duty for the period, so that even interesting writers run sentence into sentence without the
formality of full stop or of capital.[22]

English instructors continue to kvetch about exactly the same
things, more than 120 years later. You'd think that more than a
century of concerted effort on the part of thousands of teachers in
the best schools and universities across the English-speaking world
would have cleaned up comma splices, and yet the more rule-
bound proselytizers have remarkably little to show for their effort.
It's amazing how little impact the myriad prescriptivists, working
on behalf of the language for nearly three centuries, have had.

We can see some big changes happening in our lifetimes, and
they make the case that linguistic conservatives have a terrible
record of arresting change. Individual words come and go, of
course, but actual grammatical changes are very rare. In recent decades, though, the word *whom*, which has been part of the language
for more than a thousand years, has been undergoing a serious decline. Today it survives only in the writing of the highly educated—
virtually no one learns when to use *who* and when to use *whom*
from casual conversations in the real world; people learn it, if they
learn it at all, from reading grammar books, attending classes, and
being chastised when they're wrong. Even though hardly anybody
says it in casual speech, students are taught that there's an essential
distinction between *who* and *whom*.

A betting man should not place much money on the prospect of
whom lasting out the twenty-first century. Already it's common
for *who* to appear in place of *whom* in newspapers, magazines,
even presidential speeches. The highly educated themselves sometimes fall into errors like *Whom shall I say is calling?* (it should,
according to the traditional usage, be *who*). It may be heartening,
then, to realize that, even as early as in 1795, many people couldn't
tell the difference between *who* and *whom*.[23] The endless lectures
from prescriptivists have done next to nothing, and the distinction
is nearly dead: *whom* is doomed.

But so what? The language won't be any poorer for it. It's not a corruption of proper English, but an evolution. It doesn't demand a rearguard action to stave off the attackers; it doesn't call for guardians of the language to rush to the barricades. In fact English doesn't need protection. It's been doing remarkably well over the last fifteen hundred years, and is likely to outlive us all.

That's not to say prescription is always futile; there's still room for prescription of a kind. Clarity has to remain paramount; anything that interferes with clarity or precision of expression is a genuine obstacle to communication, and a sensitive teacher can give useful advice to beginners on these matters. And even the schoolmarmish rules can be valuable in the right context. A teacher who allows improper spellings, run-on sentences, and misused semicolons to pass unnoticed in students' papers is doing those students·an injustice: they need to become proficient in the standard form of the language, since it gives them access to power. Chapter 2 traced the origin of some of our beliefs about language to the prospect of social mobility, as people from the middle of the class hierarchy sought ways into the upper strata. The situation hasn't changed in the last three centuries: a thorough knowledge of the "prestige" forms and constructions of English still provides a way into the powerful social circles. A young person who uses *diss* in a corporate job interview, or pronounces *ask* as *ax*, will likely find the offer goes to another candidate. But the important thing they need to learn—both the educators and the learners—is that the version of the language that's taught in schools isn't *correct* English, but *appropriate* English—English suited to the occasion. David Crystal, who has been a kind of guiding spirit throughout this book, is smart on this point too. "The main aim of language education," he writes, must be "the instilling into children of a sense of linguistic appropriateness—when to use one variety or style rather than another, and when to appreciate the way in which other people have used one variety or style rather than another."[24]

SAMUEL JOHNSON ONCE said of the two major political parties of his day, "A wise Tory and a wise Whig, I believe, will agree. Their principles are the same, though their modes of thinking are different."[25] The same can be said of the two camps of language commentators—a wise prescriptivist and a wise descriptivist will agree, despite all the differences in their modes of thinking. The problem is that the people shouting loudest about language are rarely wise. The more extreme prescriptivists routinely make the mistake of assuming that standard English, which usually means the language of a certain social class from the previous generation, is the only acceptable English. The more extreme descriptivists make the mistake of assuming that there's nothing special about standard English, that it's merely one variety among many. A balanced approach would acknowledge that change happens—has always happened and will always happen, despite the best efforts of the guardians of the language—and that we should all learn to stop worrying and love language change.

But that approach would also recognize that some forms of the language, while not inherently better than others, do carry more cachet, and that standard English—with all its stupid rules and irrational regulations—is still the form that's used in the corridors of power. Refusing to use it will exclude you from those corridors, even though the exclusion is often for dumb and prejudicial reasons. Pretending the social prejudices don't exist, or trying to wish them away, won't help; refusing to teach beginners about the standard forms is a dereliction of duty. A good writer will recognize that readers come with various hang-ups, preconceptions, and biases, and that the only way to write effectively is to write with these prejudices in mind. A good writer, therefore, won't wantonly split infinitives—not because infinitives can't be split, not because it's some moral outrage, and certainly not because the English language needs to be protected, but simply because split infinitives might distract readers who've been taught that they're wrong. At the same time, a good writer won't let these rules get in the way of real communication. Grace and clarity should always trump pedantry.

THERE'S LITTLE REASON, though, to think the situation will improve any time soon. The struggle between the prescriptivists and the English language often feels like a confrontation between the unstoppable force and the immovable object. Culture warriors have been working quixotically to regulate a language that has rejected virtually all attempts to regulate it, and they show no signs of throwing in the towel.

Oliver Goldsmith—a friend of Samuel Johnson and a playwright, novelist, and historian in his own right—included a drinking song in his most famous play, *She Stoops to Conquer*:

> Let school-masters puzzle their brain,
>> With grammar, and nonsense, and learning;
> Good liquor, I stoutly maintain,
>> Gives *genus* a better discerning.
> Let them brag of their Heathenish Gods,
>> Their Lethes, their Styxes, and Stygians;
> Their Quis, and their Quæs, and their Quods,
>> They're all but a parcel of Pigeons.
>> *Toroddle, toroddle, toroll.*[26]

"Grammar, and nonsense, and learning": grammar has a frustrating habit of spending more time with nonsense than with learning. Goldsmith knew that proper words have their places, but that sometimes it's healthiest just to ignore the more foolish prescriptions. His *Toroddle, toroddle, toroll* may be the best way to conclude. Speaking and writing our own language shouldn't be a chore; we should resist all attempts to make us feel ashamed of speaking the way the rest of the world speaks. Using the language should be an opportunity for inventiveness, even playfulness. It's the only way to retain our sanity as we grapple with this big, messy, arbitrary, illogical, inconsistent, often infuriating but always fascinating language of ours.

Acknowledgments

I owe thanks to many friends and colleagues. H. Bruce Franklin, James O'Donnell, John Straus, and David Wallace all helped out with queries; Kaitlyn Bonsell came to my aid in providing some apropos quotations. I met David Wolman when he was working on *Righting the Mother Tongue*, and he helped me think through the character of English spelling. And the students in my classes have given me the opportunity to clarify my own thinking about many of these questions.

Face-to-face contact is wonderful, but I've also come to rely on several electronic forums for my research. I owe thanks to the members of Kevin Berland's C18-L, including Joel Berson, David Brewer, Dwight Codr, Timothy Erwin, Dale Katherine Ireland, Laura Miller, Sean D. Moore, Andrew O'Malley, Brad Pasanek, Betty Rizzo, Arby Ted Siraki, and Ian Small; likewise to participants in the SHAKSPER discussion group, including David Crystal, J. D. Markel, and Jason Rhode. And I can't forget the members of the MozartCafe, including Mimi Ezust, Janos Gereben, Steve Gustafson, Walter Meyer, Doug Purl, and Zeke Zubrow.

I began thinking about this project as I wrote my own guide to grammar, style, and usage, which appeared first online, then in print as *The English Language: A User's Guide*. I therefore owe thanks to the multitudes who have used and made suggestions about the guide, and especially to Ron Pullins of Focus Publishing, who helped turn the electronic resource into a book.

I've really come to enjoy working with the staff at Walker &

Company, including, above all, George Gibson and Michele Lee Amundsen.

Chapter 4, on Samuel Johnson, grew out of a series of lectures I've given to the Athenæum of Philadelphia, the National Archives, and the English-Speaking Union chapters in New Brunswick and Princeton; my conversations with those audiences helped me clarify my ideas. Finally, parts of chapter 6 first appeared as "A System of Our Own, in Language as Well as Government" in *Colonial Williamsburg: The Journal of the Colonial Williamsburg Foundation* 30, no. 1 (winter 2008): 34–38. I'm grateful to Dennis Montgomery, the journal's editor, for his support.

Notes

INTRODUCTION

1. Sampson, *English for the English*, p. 41.

CHAPTER 1: Vulgarities of Speech

1. Charles Hall Grandgent, *Imitation and Other Essays* (Cambridge, Mass.: Harvard University Press, 1933), p. 16, cited in Montagu, *The Anatomy of Swearing*, p. 6.
2. Noam Chomsky, *Language and Problems of Knowledge*, p. 183. See also Johansson, *Origins of Language*, pp. 2–3.
3. A useful summary of the archaeological and anthropological information appears in Fischer, *A History of Language*, chapter 2.
4. Hester Thrale, *Anecdotes of Samuel Johnson*, in Hill, *Johnsonian Miscellanies*, 1:187.
5. Fussell, "Can Graham Greene Write English?" pp. 97–100.
6. Mencken, *A Carnival of Buncombe*, p. 42.
7. *The Vulgarities of Speech Corrected*, pp. 23–24.
8. Judg. 12:5–6.
9. Brightland, *Reasons for an English Education*, p. 2.
10. Wilson, *The Many Advantages of a Good Language*, pp. 24, 12–13.
11. Gedoyn, "Dissertation," p. 413.
12. Dwight Macdonald, "The String Untuned," *New Yorker*, March 10, 1962, in Sledd and Ebbitt, ed., *Dictionaries and That Dictionary*, p. 166.
13. Alford, *A Plea for the Queen's English*, p. 49.
14. Chomsky, *Syntactic Structures*, p. 15.

15. Quoted from Sheffield, "Jackdaw." Sheffield also wickedly points out, "The jacket blurb informs us that this is the author's 'most accessible book to date.'"

16. *The Sacco-Vanzetti Case*, 5:4904.

17. The *OED* gives its earliest citation from 1958 (s.v. *go* B.III.44.a), but it can be found in an anonymous American poem from 1867, "Trotty," in *Littell's Living Age*, 4th series, 7 (October–December 1867): 438, as well as dozens of other early sources from around the English-speaking world.

18. All the selections come from http://crofsblogs.typepad.com/english/2005/08/went_missing.html.

19. Pope, *The Iliad of Homer*, 1:18 (*Iliad* 1.343–46).

20. Briggs, "The Harvard Admission Examination in English," pp. 23–24.

CHAPTER 2: The Age in Which I Live

1. Dryden, *Astræa Redux*, p. 14.

2. See my *Becoming Shakespeare*, chapter 1, for a discussion of the politics of the Restoration theater.

3. Johnson, *Life of Dryden*, in *Lives of the Most Eminent English Poets*, 2:118.

4. Dryden, *Critical and Miscellaneous Prose Works*, ed. Malone, 2:136.

5. See ibid., 2:138.

6. Crystal, *The Fight for English*, p. 111.

7. See, for instance, Beal, *English in Modern Times*, p. 110.

8. Dryden, *Letters*, p. 34. Walsh's text appears in *A Dialogue concerning Women*, p. 1.

9. Skelton, *The Boke of Phyllyp Sparowe*, sig. C3^r.

10. Boorde, *The Fyrst Boke of the Introduction of Knowledge*, sig. B2^r.

11. Evelyn, *Diary*, p. 312.

12. Defoe, *Essays upon Several Projects*, p. 237.

13. *Examiner* 13, in Swift, *The Works of the Rev. Dr. Jonathan Swift*, 3:6.

14. Defoe, *Robinson Crusoe*, p. 4.

15. The link between language and etiquette is alive and well even today: after the tremendous success of *Eats, Shoots & Leaves: The Zero Tolerance Approach to Punctuation* in 2003, Lynne Truss followed it up with *Talk to the Hand: The Utter Bloody Rudeness of the World Today, or Six Good Reasons to Stay Home and Bolt the Door*.

16. Samuel Richardson, *Letters Written to and for Particular Friends*, p. 5.

17. Ibid., p. 43.

18. Ibid., p. 99.
19. Defoe, *The Complete English Tradesman*, p. 25.
20. Ibid., p. 28.
21. *The Art of Letter-Writing*, pp. 1–2, 4.
22. *The Compleat Letter Writer*, sig. A2^r, A2^v.
23. Cooke, *The Universal Letter-Writer*, title page.
24. Defoe, *The Complete English Gentleman*, quoted in Novak, *Daniel Defoe*, p. 43.
25. Crystal, *The Fight for English*, pp. 81–82.

CHAPTER 3: Proper Words in Proper Places

1. Locke, *An Essay Concerning Human Understanding*, p. 408 (3.2.8).
2. Chaucer, *Troilus and Criseyde*, 2.22–26.
3. Caxton, *Eneydos*, sig. A1^v.
4. Pope, *An Essay on Criticism*, p. 24 (lines 482–83).
5. See Shippey and Arnold, *Appropriating the Middle Ages*, p. 44; and Considine, *Dictionaries in Early Modern Europe*, p. 230.
6. Waller, *Poems*, pp. 236–37.
7. In Boyle, *Dr. Bentley's Dissertations*, pp. 69–70, 71. The book was published under the name of Charles Boyle, Earl of Orrery, though Atterbury was the real author.
8. R. H., *New Atlantis*, p. 43.
9. Ibid., p. 92.
10. Scot, *The Tillage of Light*, p. 24.
11. Sprat, *History of the Royal-Society*, pp. 1–2.
12. Ibid., pp. 112, 413.
13. Ibid., p. 113.
14. Evelyn, letters to Samuel Pepys (1689) and Sir Peter Wyche (1665), in Spingarn, *Critical Essays of the Seventeenth Century*, 2:328, 311.
15. See Crystal, *The Fight for English*, p. 68.
16. Defoe, *Essays upon Several Projects*, pp. 227, 228.
17. Ibid., pp. 233, 236–37. David Crystal calls this "the earliest mention I have encountered . . . of an association between bad usage and crime. Defoe would doubtless be the patron saint of zero tolerance" (*The Fight for English*, pp. 70–71). Others have revisited the theme of counterfeiting: in 1776, George Campbell wrote that "many words and idioms prevail among the populace, which, notwithstanding a use pretty uniform and extensive, are considered as corrupt, and like counterfeit money, though common, not valued" (*The Philosophy of Rhetoric*, 1:347). In 1962, the American Bar Association rejected

the permissive editorial policies of *Webster's Third New International Dictionary* by asserting, "The analogy between language and coinage extends farther than merely to the metaphor, 'to coin a word.' Monetary currency is a medium of exchange in commercial transactions, and as such each unit must have a value which is widely and clearly understood. . . . Surely opening the floodgates to every word that is used, no matter how or by whom, and regardless of its propriety, is like the printing of paper money backed by no sound value. This is verbal inflation, which has the inevitable effect of debasing the currency of words" ("Logomachy—Debased Verbal Currency," *American Bar Association Journal*, January 1962, in Sledd and Ebbitt, ed., *Dictionaries and That Dictionary*, pp. 105–8).

18. Swift, *A Letter to a Young Gentleman*, pp. 5–6.
19. Ibid., pp. 6, 11.
20. *The Tatler*, 4:179.
21. Ibid., 4:180.
22. Swift, *Works* (1824), 9:46 n.
23. Swift, *Proposal*, pp. 8, 14.
24. Ibid., pp. 16, 15.
25. Ibid., pp. 16–17.
26. Ibid., p. 29.
27. Ibid., pp. 20, 21.
28. Ibid., p. 22. Swift wasn't alone in his complaints about English monosyllables and consonant clusters. In 1752, the scholar George Harris offered this advice: "we ought to make it an invariable Rule, *never to abbreviate any Word in our prose Writings by the Omission even of a Single Letter, altho the Place of it is supplied by an Apostrophe.* Abbreviations are destructive of Language" (Harris, *Observations upon the English Language*, p. 12). Apparently *altho* gets some special dispensation, which Harris had no time to explain.
29. Swift, *Proposal*, pp. 30–31.
30. Ibid., p. 34.
31. Oldmixon, *Reflections on Dr. Swift's Letter*, pp. 25, 2.
32. Ibid., p. 4.
33. John Adams to the president of Congress, September 5, 1780, in Sparks, ed., *The Diplomatic Correspondence of the American Revolution*, 5:324–25. See also Mencken, *The American Language*, 1:7–10, 49–50.
34. Allen Walker Read pointed out the paradox of the liberty-loving Americans striving for an authoritarian power to prevent linguistic revolutions: "Two forces are always at work in a language—one

licentious, tending towards a disregard of regulation and convention; and the other conservative, tending to hold the language within bounds and to keep it neat and tidy." The United States, he noted, is usually imagined "as being under the influence of the former, because our exuberant linguistic creations very readily attract attention. Yet there is a strong current in the opposite direction" ("American Projects for an Academy," p. 1141).

35. Wilson, *The Many Advantages of a Good Language*, p. 5.
36. http://www.academie-francaise.fr/dictionnaire.

CHAPTER 4: Enchaining Syllables, Lashing the Wind

1. Mulcaster, *The First Part of the Elementarie*, p. 166.
2. Evelyn, *Diary*, pp. 310, 311.
3. Dryden, *Troilus and Cressida*, sig. A3^r.
4. Dryden, *The Satires of Decimus Junius Juvenalis*, p. li.
5. Hume, "Of Liberty and Despotism," in *Essays, Moral and Political*, p. 179.
6. Warburton, preface, in Shakespeare, *Works*, ed. Johnson, 1:clxii.
7. Boswell, *The Life of Samuel Johnson*, 1:145–47.
8. Ibid., 1:76–77.
9. Ibid., 3:460.
10. Behn, *The Feign'd Curtizans*, sig. A2^{r-v}.
11. Dryden, *The State of Innocence and the Fall of Man*, sig. A1^{r-v}.
12. Johnson, *Lives of the Most Eminent English Poets*, 2:43, 92.
13. Johnson, *Samuel Johnson's Dictionary*, p. 578.
14. Ibid., p. 39.
15. Ibid., p. 32.
16. See my "Johnson's Encyclopedia."
17. *World* 2 (1754): 601.
18. Boswell, *The Life of Samuel Johnson*, 1:259.
19. Johnson, *Letters*, 1:95–97.
20. Kernan, *Printing Technology, Letters, & Samuel Johnson*, p. 105.
21. Johnson, *Samuel Johnson's Dictionary*, p. 579.
22. Warton, *An Essay on the Writings and Genius of Pope*, 1:155.
23. Johnson, *Samuel Johnson's Dictionary*, p. 42.
24. Boswell, *The Life of Samuel Johnson*, 1:186.
25. See my *Becoming Shakespeare*, chapter 3.
26. Boswell, *The Life of Samuel Johnson*, 3:38.
27. Johnson, *Samuel Johnson's Dictionary*, p. 37.
28. Ibid., p. 41.

CHAPTER 5: The Art of Using Words Properly

1. *Merriam-Webster's Dictionary of English Usage*, s.v. *flat adverbs*.
2. Sonnet 142.
3. *New-England Magazine* 7 (1834): 469.
4. *Academy*, April 3, 1897, p. 371, cited in the *OED*.
5. Curme, "The Split Infinitive," p. 341.
6. Block, *Legal Writing*, p. 69.
7. Valli and Lucas, *Linguistics of American Sign Language*, p. 224. Other attributions of the split-infinitive "rule" to eighteenth-century grammarians are Thomason and Kaufman, *Language Contact*, p. 78; and Stockwell, *Sociolinguistics*, p. 98 (where the rule is called "another of Bishop Lowth's prohibitions").
8. Pinker, "The Language Mavens," p. 5.
9. Priestley, *Experiments and Observations on Different Kinds of Air*, 2:31.
10. Robert Schofield, "Joseph Priestley," in *The Oxford Dictionary of National Biography*.
11. Priestley, *Memoirs*, p. 20.
12. Priestley, *Miscellaneous Observations relating to Education*, pp. 44–47.
13. Priestley, *The Rudiments of English Grammar*, pp. iii, iv.
14. Ibid., p. 1.
15. Lily, *Institutio compendiaria totius grammaticae*, sig. B1^r.
16. Priestley, *The Rudiments of English Grammar*, p. 14.
17. Priestley, *The Rudiments of English Grammar*, 2nd ed., p. 80.
18. Priestley, *The Rudiments of English Grammar*, p. 37.
19. Ibid., p. vi.
20. Ibid., p. vii.
21. Ibid., pp. 45–46 n.
22. Ibid., pp. 56, 57, 33.
23. Lowth, *A Short Introduction to English Grammar*, pp. i–ii.
24. Johnson, *Samuel Johnson's Dictionary*, p. 42.
25. Priestley, *The Rudiments of English Grammar*, p. vii.
26. Lowth, *A Short Introduction to English Grammar*, pp. x, 48, 75 n.
27. Ibid., pp. iii, 64.
28. Ibid., pp. 127–28.
29. Priestley made a similarly descriptive statement: "Prepositions generally precede their substantives," he wrote; "as *He went to London*: but sometimes a verb more elegantly parts them; as *This is the*

thing with which *I am pleased*; or, *This is the thing* which *I am pleased* with" (*The Rudiments of English Grammar*, p. 34 n).

30. Ingrid Tieken-Boon van Ostade, "Murray, Lindley," in *The Oxford Dictionary of National Biography*. Murray's domination of the field also attracted criticism: a parody of his *Grammar* appeared in 1840 as *The Comic English Grammar*, and 1868 saw the appearance of *The Bad English of Lindley Murray and Other Writers on the English Language*.

31. Lindley Murray, *English Grammar*, p. iv.

32. Ibid., pp. 55–56.

33. Ibid., p. 103.

34. Ibid., pp. 110–11.

35. It's curious that many of the biggest complaints about linguistic novelty come from conservatives, who are usually keenest on letting the economy do its thing without outside intervention. But in most Western democracies the conservative parties have called for laissez-faire in economic matters but stronger regulation in social affairs—drugs, sexuality, and so on. This suggests that the culturally conservative crusaders against abuses of the English language actually view the transgressors as the verbal equivalents of junkies and polygamists.

36. Dwight Macdonald, "Three Questions for Structural Linguists, or Webster 3 Revisited," in Sledd and Ebbitt, ed., *Dictionaries and That Dictionary*, p. 262.

37. Pinker, "The Language Mavens," p. 4.

38. Simon, "The Corruption of English," pp. 37, 42. See also Milroy and Milroy, *Authority in Language*, p. 8.

39. Pinker, "The Language Mavens," p. 14.

40. Ps. 119:121.

41. A personal confession. When I was twelve, my middle school English teacher, Mr. Gallo, declared that the *t* in *often* is silent: *offin* is not only an acceptable pronunciation, but the *only* acceptable pronunciation. Decades later, despite countless hours of research that have taught me that both pronunciations are perfectly standard, I still find that *often* with the *t* sounds *wrong* to me, and I have to bite my tongue to stop myself from correcting those who use it.

CHAPTER 6: The People in These States

1. Sheridan, *A Course of Lectures on Elocution*, pp. 32–33.

2. Hume, *The Philosophical Works*, 1:cxxv–cxxix.

3. Lyttelton to Hume, October 12, 1761, in *Letters of Eminent Persons, Addressed to David Hume*, p. 21.

4. Boswell, *The Life of Samuel Johnson*, 3:178, 378.

5. Ibid., 2:75, 1:425.

6. Ibid., 2:312.

7. Basker, "Samuel Johnson and the American Common Reader," pp. 6–7.

8. Jefferson, *Writings*, p. 741.

9. Witherspoon, reprinted in Matthews, *The Beginnings of American English*, p. 17. See also Mencken, *The American Language*, 1:1–12.

10. Cited in Richard Bailey, "American English Abroad," p. 479.

11. Webster to Thomas Dawes, December 20, 1808, in NYPL NN-1, cited in Monaghan, *A Common Heritage*, p. 23.

12. Jones, *History of New York*, p. 3.

13. Webster to David Ramsay, October 1807, in Webster, *Letters*, p. 284; Webster to David Ramsay, October 1807, in Webster, *Letters*, p. 289.

14. Horne Tooke, Επεα Πτεροεντα, pp. 267–68 n.

15. Richardson, *Illustrations of English Philology*, p. 17.

16. James A. H. Murray, *The Evolution of English Lexicography*, p. 44.

17. Cited in Micklethwait, *Noah Webster and the American Dictionary*, p. 54.

18. Webster, *An American Selection*, pp. 5–6, 154, 156.

19. Webster to Benjamin Franklin, May 24, 1786, in Webster, *Letters*, p. 51; Webster, *Dissertations on the English Language*, p. 20.

20. Webster, *A Collection of Essays and Fugitiv Writings*, p. 4. For the proposals of other national languages instead of English, see Shoemaker, *Noah Webster*, pp. 249–50.

21. Webster, *Dissertations on the English Language*, pp. 22–23, 171.

22. Webster to Timothy Pickering, May 25, 1786, in Webster, *Letters*, p. 52.

23. Webster to Thomas Dawes, July 25, 1809, in Webster, *Letters*, p. 324; Webster to Dawes, August 5, 1809, in Webster, *Letters*, p. 329.

24. Webster, *An American Dictionary of the English Language*, preface.

25. Reed, "Noah Webster's Debt to Samuel Johnson," p. 98.

26. Webster to David Ramsay, October 1807, in Webster, *Letters*, p. 288; Webster to Thomas Dawes, August 5, 1809, in *Letters*, p. 330; Webster to David Ramsay, October 1807, in *Letters*, pp. 286–87; *An American Dictionary of the English Language*, preface.

27. Webster to Benjamin Franklin, May 24, 1786, in Webster, *Letters*, p. 50; *A Collection of Essays and Fugitiv Writings*, p. ix.

28. Webster to Thomas Dawes, August 5, 1809, in Webster, *Letters*, p. 329.

29. For more on Webster's influence on American spelling, see Mencken, *The American Language*, 1:379–88.

30. See Friend, *Development*, p. 55.

31. Webster to John Canfield, January 6, 1783, in Webster, *Letters*, p. 4; Webster to Benjamin Franklin, May 24, 1786, in *Letters*, p. 50.

32. Webster to the Governors . . . , January 1798, in Webster, *Letters*, p. 177; Stiles, *Literary Diary*, 1:73; Webster to Samuel Lee, December 20, 1824, in Webster, *Letters*, pp. 412–13.

33. See Commager, introduction to Webster, *Noah Webster's American Spelling Book*; and Warfel, *Noah Webster*, p. 3.

34. *British Critic* 35 (1810): 182; Lambert, *Travels through Lower Canada*, 3:480; both cited in Bailey, "American English Abroad," pp. 482–83.

35. E. V. Knox, "Cinema English," *Living Age* 338 (1930): 188, cited in Bailey, "American English Abroad," p. 493.

36. Bailey, "American English Abroad," p. 495.

37. Review of Ingersoll's *Inchiquin*, in *Quarterly Review* 10 (1810): 523, cited in Bailey, "American English Abroad," pp. 483–84.

38. See Mencken, *The American Language*, 1:vi, 31.

39. Baugh and Cable, *A History of the English Language*, p. 389.

40. Lighter, "Slang," p. 219.

41. See Read, "The First Stage in the History of 'O.K.'"

42. Lederer, *A Man of My Words*, p. 65.

CHAPTER 7: Words, Words, Words

1. Trusler, *The Difference, between Words*, 1:78.

2. Piozzi, *British Synonymy*, 1:174–75.

3. Roget, *Thesaurus*, pp. iii, ix.

4. Ibid., pp. iii–iv.

5. Trench, *On Some Deficiencies in Our English Dictionaries*, pp. 3, 6.

6. K. M. Elizabeth Murray, *Caught in the Web of Words*, p. 137.

7. Ibid., pp. 11, 32.

8. Mugglestone, *Lost for Words*, p. 1.

9. Payack, *A Million Words and Counting*, pp. 4–6.

10. Butterfield, *Damp Squid*, p. 11.

11. Johnson, *Samuel Johnson's Dictionary*, pp. 30–31.

12. Walpole was not the only prodigious noncewordizer. Lewis Carroll composed "Jabberwocky," made up almost entirely of words

invented for the occasion, and the master of these nonce words was James Joyce, whose playful approach to language led him to fill his final masterpiece, *Finnegans Wake*, with tens of thousands of newly coined words, many of them complicated multilingual puns.

13. Mugglestone discusses the place of scientific language in the *OED* in *Lost for Words*, chapter 4.

14. *Astragal*, a kind of molding; *furdown*, a dropped ceiling; *plancier*, a soffit or the underside of a cornice; *bruxism*, grinding of the teeth; *frenum*, a fold of tissue between the lip or cheek and the gum; *occlusal*, the grinding surface of the teeth; *chaptalization*, the addition of sugar to fermenting wine; *maderize*, oxygenate; *remuage*, rotating champagne bottles to let the sediment settle; *hypoeutectoid*, steel made with less than 0.8 percent carbon; *nitriding*, a technique for hardening a steel surface; *spheroidizing*, heating steel to the point where the cementite particles become spherical.

15. Crystal, *The Stories of English*, p. 455.

16. James A. H. Murray et al., "General Explanations," in *OED1*, 1:xxvii.

17. James A. H. Murray, "Ninth Annual Address," p. 131.

18. James A. H. Murray et al., "General Explanations," in *OED1*, 1:xxvii.

19. Ibid., 1:xxviii.

20. Ibid.

21. Trench, *On Some Deficiencies in Our English Dictionaries*, pp. 4–5.

22. Burchfield, "The *Oxford English Dictionary* and Its Historical Principles," p. 168.

23. Willinsky gives a useful overview of Burchfield's editorship in *Empire of Words*, chapter 8.

24. See Willinsky, *Empire of Words*, chapter 10.

25. Gledhill, "OED Editors Never at a Loss for Words."

CHAPTER 8: The Taste and Fancy of the Speller

1. It's *kluff*, *broom* or *brome*, and *hoe-ton*.

2. See http://www.spellingsociety.org/journals/pamflets/ses1.php#rip.

3. Wolman, *Righting the Mother Tongue*, p. 3.

4. Ibid., p. 11.

5. Crystal, *The Fight for English*, p. 20.

6. Dickens, *Pickwick Papers*, p. 530.

7. Scragg offers a catalog of other etymological spellings in *A History of English Spelling*, pp. 54–55.

8. See http://www.spellingsociety.org/journals/pamflets/ses1.php#rip.
9. Hart, *An Orthographie*, fol. 2ʳ.
10. Evelyn, *Diary*, p. 310.
11. *Right Spelling Very Much Improved*, sig. A3ʳ.
12. Franklin, "A Scheme for a New Alphabet," pp. 468–69. For more on early American schemes to reform spelling, see Mencken, *The American Language*, 1:397–407.
13. Coulmas, *Writing Systems*, p. 240. The essay is often attributed to Mark Twain, but it appears nowhere in his works. A similar piece by W. K. Lessing was published in *Astounding Science Fiction* in 1946.
14. Shaw, *George Bernard Shaw on Language*, pp. 4, 115.
15. Ibid., p. 12.
16. Ibid., pp. 26, 28.
17. Johnson, "A Grammar of the English Tongue," in *A Dictionary of the English Language*, n.p.
18. Johnson, *Samuel Johnson's Dictionary*, p. 28.
19. Ibid.
20. Ibid.

CHAPTER 9: Direct, Simple, Brief, Vigorous, and Lucid

1. For a few attempts to redeem the reputation of some eighteenth-century grammarians, see Beal, *English in Modern Times*, pp. 105–7.
2. Bunce, *Don't*, pp. 5, 50–51.
3. Richard Grant White, *Words and Their Uses*, 1st ed., p. 3.
4. Mencken, *The American Language*, 1:61.
5. Richard Grant White, *Words and Their Uses*, 1st ed., pp. 4–6, 13–14.
6. Ibid., pp. 24, 26–27.
7. Ibid., pp. 112–13.
8. Ibid., pp. 206, 128, 150.
9. Franklin, *Autobiography*, pp. 15–16.
10. Richard Grant White, *Words and Their Uses*, 1st ed., pp. 25, 67–68, 114.
11. Plutarch, *Lives*, 5:178.
12. Richard Grant White, *Words and Their Uses*, 1st ed., p. 106.
13. Safire, "Words at War"; reprinted in *Take My Word for It*, p. 317.
14. Safire, "Balloon Goes Up on War Words."
15. Freeman, "When in Rome."
16. Richard Grant White, *Every-Day English*, pp. 447–48.

17. Richard Grant White, *Words and Their Uses*, 1st ed., pp. 221–22.

18. Alden, *Grammar Made Easy*, p. 92.

19. Richard Grant White, *Words and Their Uses*, 1st ed., pp. 414–15.

20. Richard Grant White, *Every-Day English*, pp. 278, 273–74.

21. Ibid., p. 274.

22. McMorris, *The Warden of English*, p. 12.

23. Ibid., pp. 27, 13.

24. Burchfield, "The Fowlers," p. 131; McMorris, *The Warden of English*, p. 58.

25. McMorris, *The Warden of English*, pp. 58, 61.

26. Fowler and Fowler, *The King's English*, p. 11.

27. Ibid., pp. 11–13.

28. Ibid., *The King's English*, p. 65.

29. Fowler, *A Dictionary of Modern English Usage*, s.v. *unique*.

30. Ibid., s.v. *aggravate, aggravation*.

31. Fowler and Fowler, *The King's English*, p. 43.

32. Fowler, *A Dictionary of Modern English Usage*, s.v. *reliable*.

33. Ibid., s.v. *split infinitive*.

34. Fowler and Fowler, *The King's English*, p. 329.

35. Fowler, *A Dictionary of Modern English Usage*, s.v. *preposition at end*.

36. McMorris, *The Warden of English*, pp. 65–66.

37. Fowler and Fowler, *The King's English*, p. 70.

38. Fowler, *A Dictionary of Modern English Usage*, s.v. *bureaucrat*.

39. Fowler and Fowler, *The King's English*, p. 56.

40. Fowler, *A Dictionary of Modern English Usage*, s.v. *-en verbs from adjectives*.

41. Fowler and Fowler, *The King's English*, pp. 35, 33.

42. Horwill's *Dictionary* was not the only companion to Fowler's *Modern English Usage*. Eric Partridge's *Usage and Abusage* was "designed, not to compete with H. W. Fowler's *Modern English Usage* (that would be a fatuous attempt—and impossible), but to supplement it and to complement it, and also to deal with usage of the period since 1926" (Partridge, *Usage and Abusage*, p. 5). Wilson Follett published his own *Modern American Usage*, modeled on Fowler's, in 1966, and a new version, revised by Erik Wensberg, was published in 1998; it's a useful American version of Fowler's comprehensive alphabetical guide, though it lacks some of the quirky charm of the original.

43. White, introduction to *The Elements of Style*, p. xi.

44. Strunk and White, *The Elements of Style*, p. 1.
45. Ibid., p. 2.
46. Crystal, *The Fight for English*, p. viii.

CHAPTER 10: Sabotage in Springfield

1. Bergen Evans, "But What's a Dictionary For?" *Atlantic Monthly*, May 1962, in Sledd and Ebbitt, ed., *Dictionaries and That Dictionary*, p. 238.
2. Many of these big dictionaries were later issued in abridged versions, student versions, and so on, but most of the serious lexicographical work went on in these unabridged editions. Morton provides an overview in *The Story of Webster's Third*, chapter 3.
3. Lynda Mugglestone offers other examples of prescriptivism in " 'An Historian Not a Critic,' " p. 199.
4. Robert A. Hall Jr., in Harold B. Allen et al., "Webster's Third: A Symposium," p. 434.
5. Dwight Macdonald, "The String Untuned," *New Yorker*, March 10, 1962, in Sledd and Ebbitt, ed., *Dictionaries and That Dictionary*, p. 187.
6. Gove, "Lexicography and the Teacher of English," p. 346.
7. Morton, *The Story of Webster's Third*, p. 85.
8. "Keep Your Old Webster's," *Washington Post*, January 17, 1962, in Sledd and Ebbitt, ed., *Dictionaries and That Dictionary*, p. 125.
9. "Vox Populi, Vox Webster," *Time*, October 6, 1961, in Sledd and Ebbitt, ed., *Dictionaries and That Dictionary*, pp. 76–77.
10. Wilson Follett, "Sabotage in Springfield," *Atlantic Monthly*, January 1962, in Sledd and Ebbitt, ed., *Dictionaries and That Dictionary*, p. 113.
11. Oliver Pritchett, "Words, Words, Words!" *Cardiff Western Mail*, March 3, 1962, in Sledd and Ebbitt, ed., *Dictionaries and That Dictionary*, p. 155.
12. Christopher Small, review of *Webster's Third*, *Glasgow Herald*, February 27, 1962, in Sledd and Ebbitt, ed., *Dictionaries and That Dictionary*, pp. 137–38.
13. Dempsey, "According to Evans."
14. Follett, "Grammar Is Obsolete," p. 73.
15. Ibid., pp. 74–75.
16. "English Spoken," *Nation*, March 10, 1962, in Sledd and Ebbitt, ed., *Dictionaries and That Dictionary*, p. 163.

17. Dwight Macdonald, "The String Untuned," *New Yorker*, March 10, 1962, in Sledd and Ebbitt, ed., *Dictionaries and That Dictionary*, p. 166.

18. Sydney J. Harris, "Good English Ain't What We Thought," *Chicago Daily News*, October 20, 1961, in Sledd and Ebbitt, ed., *Dictionaries and That Dictionary*, p. 81.

19. Richard S. Emrich, "New Dictionary Cheap, Corrupt," *Detroit News*, February 10, 1962, in Sledd and Ebbitt, ed., *Dictionaries and That Dictionary*, p. 129.

20. Ibid., pp. 127–28.

21. Wilson Follett, "Sabotage in Springfield," *Atlantic Monthly*, January 1962, in Sledd and Ebbitt, ed., *Dictionaries and That Dictionary*, pp. 112–13.

22. "Webster's Lays an Egg," *Richmond News Leader*, January 3, 1962, in Sledd and Ebbitt, ed., *Dictionaries and That Dictionary*, p. 122.

23. Dwight Macdonald, "The String Untuned," *New Yorker*, March 10, 1962, in Sledd and Ebbitt, ed., *Dictionaries and That Dictionary*, p. 170.

24. "It 'Ain't' Good," *Washington Sunday Star*, September 10, 1961, in Sledd and Ebbitt, ed., *Dictionaries and That Dictionary*, p. 56.

25. Dwight Macdonald, "Three Questions for Structural Linguists, or Webster 3 Revisited," in Sledd and Ebbitt, ed., *Dictionaries and That Dictionary*, p. 264.

26. Morton, *The Story of Webster's Third*, pp. 1–2. See also his observation that "A way of showing sophistication is to toss off the comment, when an opportunity arises, 'Of course, I use *Webster's Second*' " (p. 201).

27. Philip Gove, letter to the editor, *New York Times*, November 5, 1961, in Sledd and Ebbitt, ed., *Dictionaries and That Dictionary*, pp. 88–89.

28. "A Non-Word Deluge," *Life*, October 27, 1961, in Sledd and Ebbitt, ed., *Dictionaries and That Dictionary*, p. 85.

29. Sydney J. Harris, "Good English Ain't What We Thought," *Chicago Daily News*, October 20, 1961, in Sledd and Ebbitt, ed., *Dictionaries and That Dictionary*, pp. 80–81.

30. "Webster's New Word Book," *New York Times*, October 12, 1961, in Sledd and Ebbitt, ed., *Dictionaries and That Dictionary*, p. 78.

31. Philip Gove, letter to the editor, *New York Times*, November 5, 1961, in Sledd and Ebbitt, ed., *Dictionaries and That Dictionary*, p. 88.

32. Philip Gove, letter to the editor, *Life*, November 17, 1961, in Sledd and Ebbitt, ed., *Dictionaries and That Dictionary*, pp. 91–92.

33. "Dictionaries: The Most Unique," *Newsweek*, March 12, 1962, in Sledd and Ebbitt, ed., *Dictionaries and That Dictionary*, pp. 193–94.
34. *American Heritage Dictionary*, 3rd ed., s.v. *nauseous*.
35. *American Heritage Dictionary*, 4th ed., s.v. *nauseous*.
36. Hoke Norris, "Anarchy in Language," *Chicago Sun-Times*, March 30, 1962, in Sledd and Ebbitt, ed., *Dictionaries and That Dictionary*, p. 201.
37. Stafford, "Plight of the American Language," p. 14.

CHAPTER 11: Expletive Deleted

1. Curzan, "The Compass of the Vocabulary," p. 100.
2. Mugglestone, *Lost for Words*, p. 84.
3. Mugglestone, " 'Pioneers in the Untrodden Forest,' " p. 11.
4. Ex. 20:7; see also Deut. 5:11. Protestants consider this the third commandment, but the traditional Roman Catholic system of numbering the commandments makes this number two.
5. Eph. 5:3–4.
6. Robinson, *A Sermon against Prophane Cursing and Swearing*, p. 16.
7. Whitefield, *The Heinous Sin of Profane Cursing and Swearing*, p. 1.
8. Hughes, *Swearing*, p. 1.
9. Montagu, *The Anatomy of Swearing*, p. 239.
10. Sharman, *A Cursory History of Swearing*, pp. 179–80.
11. Hughes, *Swearing*, p. 186.
12. Ibid., pp. 186–87.
13. Marjoribanks, *Travels in New South Wales*, pp. 57–58. For some Australians, a mere eighteen million lifetime *bloody*s would be a disappointment. The Australian comic Dennis Bryant, for instance, performs under the name Kevin Bloody Wilson. In 2006, Australia's official tourism board ran a television advertisement featuring a bikini-clad woman asking viewers, "So where the bloody hell are you?"
14. *The F-Word* is an alphabetical survey, from *absofuckinglutely* to *titfuck*, extracted from J. E. Lighter's in-progress *Historical Dictionary of American Slang*; Lighter, who disavowed the spin-off volume, refused to put his name on it, and Jesse Sheidlower stepped in as editor.
15. Florio, *A Worlde of Wordes*. Florio also includes the past participle, *fottuto*, defined as "iaped, occupied, sarded, swiued, fuckt." Allen Walker Read notes that *occupy* "was once one of the most obscene words in the language" ("An Obscenity Symbol," p. 276).

16. Bailey, *Universal Etymological English Dictionary*, s.v. *fuck*. John Ash's *New and Complete Dictionary of the English Language* appeared in 1775, twenty years after Johnson's *Dictionary*, but he also includes the word: "Fuck (*v. t.*, *a low vulgar word*) To perform the act of generation, to have to do with a woman."

17. Thomas Campbell, *Dr. Campbell's Diary*, p. 68. Boswell provides an abbreviated version of the same story; see *Boswell: The Ominous Years*, p. 114.

18. H. D. Best, from *Personal and Literary Memorials*, in Hill, *Johnsonian Miscellanies*, 2:390.

19. Trollope, *Domestic Manners of the Americans*, 1:127.

20. For the story of the Bowdlers, see my *Becoming Shakespeare*, pp. 171–92.

21. Marryat, *A Diary in America*, 2:245–47. Richard Grant White records this odd preference in his entry for "LIMB.—A squeamishness, which I am really ashamed to notice, leads many persons to use this word exclusively instead of *leg*" (*Words and Their Uses*, 1st ed., p. 181).

22. Read, "An Obscenity Symbol," p. 267.

23. The story is often repeated and often mutated: the quip has been attributed not only to Dorothy Parker but also to Tallulah Bankhead and Mae West. Mailer's euphemism did provide the name for the raucous sixties-era rock band the Fugs; before they began recording, the lead singer, Ed Sanders, was the editor of *Fuck You/A Magazine of the Arts*.

24. Fussell, *Wartime*, p. 95.

25. Hughes, *Swearing*, p. 18.

26. Ibid., p. 19.

27. Argetsinger and Roberts, "Excuse Us, May We See Your ID?"

28. American papers are more squeamish than those in other parts of the Anglophone world: the *Times* of London held off on printing *fuck* until the mid-1980s, but the word now appears from time to time; Melbourne's *Age* and the *Irish Times* are comparatively free in their use of obscenities.

29. Moran, "Public Doublespeak," p. 690.

30. Anthony Hopkins, *Songs from the Front and Rear: Canadian Servicemen's Songs of the Second World War* (Edmonton: Hurtig, 1979), p. 11, cited in Fussell, *Wartime*, p. 95.

31. Fussell, *Wartime*, p. 94.

32. Internet Movie Database.

33. Noble, "Issue of Racism Erupts in Simpson Trial."

34. Kennedy, *Nigger*, pp. 24–25.

35. Allen, *The Language of Ethnic Conflict*, p. 39.

36. Internet Movie Database.

37. Richard Grant White, *Every-Day English*, pp. 380–81.

38. McMorris, *The Warden of English*, p. 154.

39. Emblen, *Peter Mark Roget*, p. 278.

40. Burchfield, "The Treatment of Controversial Vocabulary," p. 102.

41. Burchfield, "The Turn of the Screw," p. 113; Howard, "Dictionary Definition of 'Jew' Action Fails."

42. Burchfield, "The Turn of the Screw," p. 113.

43. Fletcher, "Furor Erupts over Racial Epithet."

44. Fletcher, "Offensive Words May Get Less-Offending Definitions."

45. Fletcher, "Furor Erupts over Racial Epithet."

46. Dunford, "Boiling McMad."

47. Bruce, *The Essential Lenny Bruce*, pp. 83–84.

CHAPTER 12: Grammar, and Nonsense, and Learning

1. Fischer offers a valuable overview in *A History of Reading* and *A History of Writing*. See also Senner, ed., *The Origins of Writing*, especially chapters 1 and 2.

2. Crystal, "2B or Not 2B?"

3. Grossman, "Cashing In on Cute Cats."

4. Flynn, "Texting Damages Standards in English."

5. Crystal, "2B or Not 2B?"

6. Baldauf, "A Hindi–English Jumble."

7. Robert Williams, *Ebonics*, p. vi.

8. Lakoff, *The Language War*, p. 230.

9. John Baugh, *Beyond Ebonics*, p. 95. See also DeBose, "The Ebonics Phenomenon," p. 36.

10. Malcolm X, *Autobiography*, p. 187.

11. Hinckley, "Talk Radio Hooked on Ebonics Debate."

12. John Baugh, *Beyond Ebonics*, p. 88.

13. John Carlin, "Yo, Homeys!"

14. Linguists call the transposition of consonant sounds *metathesis*; *ax* to *ask* is a famous example. Another is the word *bird*. When it first appeared in an English text—sometime before the year A.D. 800—it was spelled and pronounced *brid*. By the fourteenth century, though, the two sounds in the middle, the *r* and the *i*, had reversed places.

15. Carroll, "To Is or Not to Is."

16. Hirst, "Why Not Sprinkle Organic Soil on Your Vegetables?"

17. Levin, "Pinched Buttock Stops Here."
18. Ivan Petkovsky, letter to the editor, *Toronto Sun*, March 28, 2002, p. 14.
19. Evan Williams, "Mob Rules in Amusing Mix."
20. Baker, "Dis and Gat."
21. Alford, *A Plea for the Queen's English*, pp. 40–41.
22. Briggs, "The Harvard Admission Examination in English," pp. 23–24.
23. Lindley Murray, *English Grammar*, p. 113.
24. Crystal, *The Fight for English*, p. 104.
25. Boswell, *The Life of Samuel Johnson*, 4:117.
26. Goldsmith, *She Stoops to Conquer*, p. 10.

Bibliography

Adamson, Robin. *The Defence of French: A Language in Crisis?* Cleve-
    don, England, and Buffalo, N.Y.: Multilingual Matters, 2007.

Alden, Abner. *Grammar Made Easy; or, A Practical Grammar of the En-
    glish Language.* Boston, 1811.

Alford, Henry. *A Plea for the Queen's English: Stray Notes on Speaking
    and Spelling.* 2nd ed. New York, 1881.

Algeo, John, ed. *The Cambridge History of the English Language.* Vol.
    6, *English in North America.* Cambridge: Cambridge University
    Press, 2001.

Allen, Harold B., et al. "*Webster's Third New International Dictionary*:
    A Symposium." *Quarterly Journal of Speech* 48 (1962): 431–40.

Allen, Irving L. *The Language of Ethnic Conflict: Social Organization
    and Lexical Culture.* New York: Columbia University Press, 1983.

The American Heritage Book of English Usage. Boston: Houghton Mif-
    flin, 1996.

The American Heritage Dictionary of the English Language. 3rd ed.
    Boston: Houghton Mifflin, 1992.

The American Heritage Dictionary of the English Language. 4th ed.
    Boston: Houghton Mifflin, 2000.

Argetsinger, Amy, and Roxanne Roberts. "Excuse Us, May We See Your
    ID?" *Washington Post*, December 10, 2008, p. C3.

*The Art of Letter-Writing, Divided into Two Parts: The First, Containing
    Rules and Directions for Writing Letters on All Sorts of Subjects . . .
    The Second, a Collection of Letters on the Most Interesting Occa-
    sions in Life.* London, 1762.

Ash, John. *The New and Complete Dictionary of the English Language . . .
    to Which Is Prefixed, a Comprehensive Grammar.* 2 vols. London,
    1775.

Bailey, Nathan. *An Universal Etymological English Dictionary.* 2nd ed. London, 1724.

Bailey, Richard W. "American English Abroad." In Algeo, *The Cambridge History of the English Language,* pp. 456–96.

Baker, Russell. "Dis and Gat." *New York Times,* April 20, 1991, p. 23.

Baldauf, Scott. "A Hindi–English Jumble, Spoken by 350 Million." *Christian Science Monitor,* November 23, 2004.

Barzun, Jacques. *A Word or Two Before You Go.* Middletown, Conn.: Wesleyan University Press, 1986.

Basker, James G. "Samuel Johnson and the American Common Reader." *The Age of Johnson: A Scholarly Annual* 6 (1994): 3–30.

Baugh, Albert C., and Thomas Cable. *A History of the English Language.* 4th ed. Englewood Cliffs, N.J.: Prentice-Hall; London: Routledge, 1993.

Baugh, John. *Beyond Ebonics: Linguistic Pride and Racial Prejudice.* New York: Oxford University Press, 2000.

Beal, John C. *English in Modern Times, 1700–1945.* London: Arnold, 2004.

Behn, Aphra. *The Feign'd Curtizans; or, A Nights Intrigue: A Comedy.* 2nd ed. London, 1679.

Bernstein, Theodore. *The Careful Writer: A Modern Guide to English Usage.* New York: Atheneum, 1965.

———. *Dos, Don'ts & Maybes of English Usage.* New York: Times Books, 1977.

———. *Miss Thistlebottom's Hobgoblins: The Careful Writer's Guide to the Taboos, Bugbears, and Outmoded Rules of English Usage.* New York: Farrar, Straus and Giroux, 1971.

———. *More Language That Needs Watching: Second Aid for Writers and Editors, Emanating from the News Room of the "New York Times."* Manhasset, N.Y.: Channel Press, 1962.

———. *Watch Your Language: A Lively, Informal Guide to Better Writing, Emanating from the News Room of the "New York Times."* Great Neck, N.Y.: Channel Press, 1958.

Block, Gertrude. *Legal Writing: Questions and Answers.* New York: William S. Hein & Co., 2004.

Boorde, Andrew. *The Fyrst Boke of the Introduction of Knowledge, the Whych Dothe Teache a Man to Speake Parte of All Maner of Languages, and to Knowe the Vsage and Fashion of Al Maner of Countreys.* London, [1555?].

Boswell, James. *Boswell: The Ominous Years, 1774–1776.* Ed. Charles Ryskamp and Frederick A. Pottle. New York: McGraw-Hill, 1963.

————. *The Life of Samuel Johnson, LL.D.* Ed. G. B. Hill. Rev. L. F. Powell. 6 vols. Oxford: Clarendon Press, 1934–64.

Boyle, Charles, Earl of Orrery [i.e., Francis Atterbury]. *Dr. Bentley's Dissertations on the Epistles of Phalaris, and the Fables of Æsop, Examin'd.* London, 1699.

Briggs, L. B. R. "The Harvard Admission Examination in English." In *Harvard University: Twenty Years of School and College English*, pp. 17–32. Cambridge, Mass.: Harvard University Press, 1896.

Brightland, John. *Reasons for an English Education, by Teaching the Youth of Both Sexes the Arts of Grammar, Rhetoric, Poetry, and Logic, in Their Own Mother-Tongue.* London, 1711.

The British Letter-Writer; or, Letter-Writer's Complete Instructor: Containing a Course of Letters on the Most Useful, Important, Instructive, and Entertaining Subjects, . . . the Whole Calculated to Enable the Reader to Write Letters on Every Occasion of Life, Without Any Further Instructions: To Which Is Added, a Plain and Easy English Grammar, and Instructions for Addressing Persons of All Ranks Either in Writing or Discourse. London, [1765?].

Bruce, Lenny. *The Essential Lenny Bruce.* Ed. John Cohen. New York: Ballantine Books, 1967.

Bunce, Oliver Bell. *Don't: A Manual of Mistakes & Improprieties More or Less Prevalent in Conduct & Speech.* London, 1884.

Burchfield, Robert. "Four-Letter Words and the *OED*." *TLS*, October 13, 1972, p. 1233.

————. "The Fowlers: Their Achievements in Lexicography and Grammar." In *Unlocking the English Language*, pp. 125–46. London: Faber and Faber, 1989.

————. "The *Oxford English Dictionary* and Its Historical Principles." In *Unlocking the English Language*, pp. 166–76. London: Faber and Faber, 1989.

————. "The Treatment of Controversial Vocabulary in the *Oxford English Dictionary*." In *Unlocking the English Language*, pp. 83–108. London: Faber and Faber, 1989.

————. "The Turn of the Screw: Ethnic Vocabulary and Dictionaries." In *Unlocking the English Language*, pp. 109–15. London: Faber and Faber, 1989.

Butterfield, Jeremy. *Damp Squid: The English Language Laid Bare.* Oxford: Oxford University Press, 2008.

Bynack, V. P. "Noah Webster's Linguistic Thought and the Idea of an American National Culture." *Journal of the History of Ideas* 45, no. 1 (January–March 1984): 99–114.

Campbell, George. *The Philosophy of Rhetoric*. 2 vols. London, 1776.

Campbell, Thomas. *Dr. Campbell's Diary of a Visit to England in 1775*. Ed. James L. Clifford. New York: Macmillan, 1947.

Carlin, George. *Class Clown*. New York: Little David, 1972.

Carlin, John. "Yo, Homeys! English Has Got a Fat New Flava, Nome Same? John Carlin in Washington Tries His Hand at Ebonics, the Newly Recognised 'Language' of American Blacks." *Independent*, January 12, 1997, p. 14.

Carroll, Joe. "To Is or Not to Is, That Be the Question." *Irish Times*, January 4, 1997, p. 11.

Caxton, William. *Here Fynyssheth the Boke of Eneydos, Compyled by Vyrgyle, Which Hathe Be Translated oute of Latyne in to Frenshe, and oute of Frenshe Reduced in to Englysshe by Me Wyll[ia]m Caxton, the Xxij. Daye of Iuyn. The Yere of Our Lorde. M.iiij.Clxxxx*. London, 1490.

Chaucer, Geoffrey. *The Riverside Chaucer*. Ed. Larry Dean Benson. 3rd ed. Boston: Houghton Mifflin, 1987.

Chesterfield, Philip Dormer Stanhope, 4th earl of. Review of Johnson's *Dictionary. The World, for the Year . . . by Adam Fitz-Adam*. 4 vols. London, 1753–57.

Chomsky, Noam. *Language and Problems of Knowledge—The Managua Lectures*. Cambridge, Mass.: MIT Press, 1988.

———. *Syntactic Structures*. The Hague: Mouton, 1957.

The Compleat Letter Writer; or, New and Polite English Secretary: Containing Letters on the Most Common Occasions in Life: Also, a Variety of More Elegant Letters for Examples, . . . to Which Is Prefix'd, Directions for Writing Letters, . . . Also, a Plain and Compendious Grammar of the English Tongue. 3rd ed. London, 1756.

Considine, John. *Dictionaries in Early Modern Europe: Lexicography and the Making of Heritage*. Cambridge: Cambridge University Press, 2008.

Cooke, Thomas. *The Universal Letter-Writer; or, New Art of Polite Correspondence*. London, [1770?].

Coulmas, Florian. *Writing Systems*. Cambridge: Cambridge University Press, 2003.

Crystal, David. "2B or Not 2B? Despite Doom-Laden Prophecies, Texting Has Not Been the Disaster for Language Many Feared." *Guardian*, July 5, 2008.

———. *The Fight for English: How the Language Pundits Ate, Shot, and Left*. Oxford: Oxford University Press, 2006.

————. *The Stories of English*. Woodstock, N.Y.: Overlook Press, 2004.

Curme, George O. "The Split Infinitive." *American Speech* 2, no. 8 (May 1927): 341–42.

Curzan, Anne. "The Compass of the Vocabulary." In *Lexicography and the "OED": Pioneers in the Untrodden Forest*, pp. 96–109. Ed. Lynda Mugglestone. Oxford: Oxford University Press, 2000.

DeBose, Charles E. "The Ebonics Phenomenon, Language Planning, and the Hegemony of Standard English." In *Talkin Black Talk: Language, Education, and Social Change*, pp. 30–42. Ed. H. Samy Alim and John Baugh. New York: Teachers College, Columbia University, 2007.

Defoe, Daniel. *The Complete English Tradesman, in Familiar Letters: Directing Him in All the Several Parts and Progressions of Trade*. London, 1726.

————. *Essays upon Several Projects; or, Effectual Ways for Advancing the Interest of the Nation*. London, 1702.

————. *The Life and Strange Surprizing Adventures of Robinson Crusoe, of York, Mariner*. Ed. J. Donald Crowley. Oxford: Oxford University Press, 1972.

Dempsey, David. "According to Evans." Review of Bergen and Cornelia Evans, *A Dictionary of Contemporary American Usage*. *New York Times*, September 5, 1957, p. BR18.

Dickens, Charles. *The Pickwick Papers*. Ed. James Kinsley. Oxford: Clarendon Press, 1986.

Dryden, John. *Astræa Redux: A Poem on the Happy Restoration & Return of His Sacred Majesty Charles the Second*. London, 1660.

————. *The Critical and Miscellaneous Prose Works of John Dryden, Now First Collected*. Ed. Edmond Malone. 4 vols. London, 1800.

————. *The Letters of John Dryden: With Letters Addressed to Him*. Ed. Charles E. Ward. Durham, N.C.: Duke University Press, 1942.

————. *The Satires of Decimus Junius Juvenalis Translated into English Verse by Mr. Dryden and Several Other Eminent Hands: Together with the Satires of Aulus Persius Flaccus, Made English by Mr. Dryden: With Explanatory Notes at the End of Each Satire: To Which Is Prefix'd a Discourse concerning the Original and Progress of Satire*. London, 1693.

————. *The State of Innocence and the Fall of Man: An Opera, Written in Heroique Verse and Dedicated to Her Royal Highness, the Dutchess*. London, 1677.

———. *Troilus and Cressida; or, Truth Found Too Late: A Tragedy, As It Is Acted at the Dukes Theatre: To Which Is Prefix'd, a Preface Containing the Grounds of Criticism in Tragedy.* London, 1679.

Dunford, Gary. "Boiling McMad: McDonald's Head Cheese Takes Merriam-Webster to McTask." *Toronto Sun*, November 13, 2003, p. 6.

Emblen, D. L. *Peter Mark Roget: The Word and the Man.* New York: Thomas Y. Crowell, 1970.

Evelyn, John. *The Diary of John Evelyn, Esq., F.R.S.* Ed. William Bray. 3 vols. London: Macmillan, 1906.

Fischer, Steven Roger. *A History of Language.* London: Reaktion Books, 1999.

———. *A History of Reading.* London: Reaktion Books, 2003.

———. *A History of Writing.* London: Reaktion Books, 2001.

Fletcher, Michael A. "Furor Erupts over Racial Epithet: Activists Seek to Drop or Redefine 'Nigger' in Merriam-Webster Dictionary." *Washington Post*, October 8, 1997, p. A16.

———. "Offensive Words May Get Less-Offending Definitions." *Washington Post*, March 13, 1998, p. A1.

Florio, John. *A Worlde of Wordes, or Most Copious, and Exact Dictionarie in Italian and English.* London, 1598.

Flynn, Seán. "Texting Damages Standards in English, Says Chief Examiner." *Irish Times*, April 25, 2007.

Follett, Wilson. "Grammar Is Obsolete." *Atlantic Monthly* 205, no. 2 (February 1960): 73–76.

———. *Modern American Usage: A Guide.* New York: Hill & Wang, 1966.

Follett, Wilson, and Erik Wensberg. *Modern American Usage: A Guide.* 1st rev. ed. New York: Hill & Wang, 1998.

Fowler, H. W. *A Dictionary of Modern English Usage.* Oxford: Clarendon Press, 1926.

Fowler, H. W., and F. G. Fowler. *The King's English.* Oxford: Clarendon Press, 1906.

Franklin, Benjamin. *Autobiography and Other Writings.* Ed. Ormond Seavey. Oxford: Oxford University Press, 1998.

———. "A Scheme for a New Alphabet and Reformed Mode of Spelling; With Remarks and Examples concerning the Same." In *Political, Miscellaneous, and Philosophical Pieces.* London, 1779.

Freeman, Jan. "When in Rome." *Boston Globe*, July 1, 2007, p. D2.

Friend, Joseph H. *The Development of American Lexicography, 1798–1864.* The Hague: Mouton, 1967.

Fussell, Paul. "Can Graham Greene Write English?" In *The Boy Scout Handbook and Other Observations*, pp. 95–100. New York: Oxford University Press, 1982.

———. *Wartime: Understanding and Behavior in the Second World War*. New York: Oxford University Press, 1989.

Gedoyn, Abbé. "A Dissertation upon What Was Called Urbanity or Politeness of the Romans." In *Select Discourses Read to the Academy of Belles Lettres and Inscriptions at Paris*, pp. 394–426. London, 1741.

Gledhill, Ruth. "*OED* Editors Never at a Loss for Words." *Times* (London), March 30, 1989.

Goldsmith, Oliver. *She Stoops to Conquer; or, The Mistakes of a Night: A Comedy*. London, 1773.

Gove, Philip B. "Lexicography and the Teacher of English." *College English* 25, no. 5 (February 1964): 344–52, 357.

———. "A Perspective on Usage." In *Language, Linguistics, and School Programs: Proceedings of the Spring Institutes, 1963, of the National Council of Teachers of English*, pp. 55–61. Champaign, Ill.: National Council of Teachers of English, 1963.

Grossman, Lev. "Cashing in on Cute Cats." *Time*, July 12, 2007.

H., R. [pseud.]. *New Atlantis: Begun by the Lord Verulam, Viscount St. Albans: And Continued by R.H. Esquire: Wherein Is Set Forth a Platform of Monarchical Government*. London, 1660.

Harris, George. *Observations upon the English Language: In a Letter to a Friend*. London, 1752.

Hart, John. *An Orthographie, Conteyning the Due Order and Reason, Howe to Write or Paint Thimage of Mannes Voice, Most Like to the Life or Nature: Composed by I. H. Chester Heralt*. London, 1569.

Hill, George Birkbeck, ed. *Johnsonian Miscellanies*. 2 vols. Oxford: Clarendon Press, 1897.

Hinckley, David. "Talk Radio Hooked on Ebonics Debate: Controversial Language Issue Proves to Be Anything but Black and White as Some Folks Let Their Bias Do the Talking." *New York Daily News*, January 7, 1997, p. 30.

Hirst, Christopher. "Why Not Sprinkle Organic Soil on Your Vegetables?" *Independent*, May 11, 2000.

Horace. *Horace's Art of Poetry Translated: Inscribed to the Right Honourable the Earl of Halifax*. Trans. William Popple. London, 1753.

———. *Q. Horatii Flacci Epistola ad Pisones, de Arte Poetica: The Art of Poetry: An Epistle to the Pisos*. Trans. George Colman. London, 1783.

Horne Tooke, John. Επεα Πτεροεντα; *or, The Diversions of Purley.* London, 1786.

Howard, Philip. "Dictionary Definition of 'Jew' Action Fails." *Times* (London), July 6, 1973, p. 1.

Hughes, Geoffrey. *A History of English Words.* Oxford: Blackwell, 2000.

———. *Swearing: A Social History of Foul Language, Oaths and Profanity in English.* Oxford: Blackwell, 1991.

Hume, David. *Essays, Moral and Political.* Edinburgh, 1741.

———. *Letters of Eminent Persons, Addressed to David Hume.* Ed. John Hill Burton. Edinburgh and London, 1849.

———. *The Philosophical Works of David Hume.* 4 vols. Edinburgh, 1826.

Humphrys, John. "I H8 Txt Msgs: How Texting Is Wrecking Our Language." *Daily Mail,* September 24, 2007.

Jefferson, Thomas. *Writings.* Ed. Merrill D. Peterson. New York: Library of America, 1984.

Johansson, Sverker. *Origins of Language: Constraints on Hypotheses.* Amsterdam and Philadelphia: John Benjamins, 2005.

Johnson, Samuel. *A Dictionary of the English Language.* 2 vols. London, 1755.

———. *The Letters of Samuel Johnson.* Ed. Bruce Redford. 5 vols. Princeton, N.J.: Princeton University Press, 1992–94.

———. *Lives of the Most Eminent English Poets; with Critical Observations on Their Works.* Ed. Roger Lonsdale. 4 vols. Oxford: Clarendon Press, 2006.

———. *London: A Poem, in Imitation of the Third Satire of Juvenal.* London, 1738.

———. *Samuel Johnson's Dictionary: Selections from the 1755 Work That Defined the English Language.* New York: Walker & Company, 2003.

Jones, Thomas. *History of New York during the Revolutionary War: And of the Leading Events in the Other Colonies at That Period.* Ed. Edward Floyd de Lancey. 2 vols. New York: New-York Historical Society, 1879.

Kennedy, Randall. *Nigger: The Strange Career of a Troublesome Word.* New York: Pantheon Books, 2002.

Kernan, Alvin B. *Printing Technology, Letters, & Samuel Johnson.* Princeton, N.J.: Princeton University Press, 1987.

Lakoff, Robin Tolmach. *The Language War.* Berkeley and Los Angeles: University of California Press, 2000.

Lambert, John. *Travels through Lower Canada.* London, 1810.

Lederer, Richard. *A Man of My Words: Reflections on the English Language*. New York: St. Martin's Press, 2003.

Levin, Bernard. "Pinched Buttock Stops Here." *Times* (London), August 29, 1991.

Lighter, Jonathan E. "Slang." In Algeo, *The Cambridge History of the English Language*, pp. 219–52.

Lily, William. *Institutio compendiaria totius grammaticae, quam et eruditissimus atq; idem illustrissimus Rex noster hoc nomine euulgari iussit, ut non alia quoque hæc una per totam Angliam pueris prælegeretur*. London, 1540.

Locke, John. *An Essay Concerning Human Understanding*. Ed. Peter H. Nidditch. Oxford: Clarendon Press, 1975.

Lowth, Robert. *A Short Introduction to English Grammar: With Critical Notes*. London, 1762.

Lynch, Jack. *Becoming Shakespeare: How a Provincial Playwright Became the World's Foremost Literary Icon*. New York: Walker & Company, 2007.

———. "Johnson's Encyclopedia." In *Anniversary Essays on Johnson's "Dictionary,"* pp. 129–46. Ed. Jack Lynch and Anne McDermott. Cambridge: Cambridge University Press, 2005.

Marjoribanks, Alexander. *Travels in New South Wales*. London, 1847.

Marryat, Frederick. *A Diary in America, with Remarks on Its Institutions*. 3 vols. London, 1839.

Matthews, Mitford M. *The Beginnings of American English: Essays and Comments*. Chicago: University of Chicago Press, 1931.

McMorris, Jenny. *The Warden of English: The Life of H. W. Fowler*. Oxford: Oxford University Press, 2001.

Mencken, H. L. *The American Language: An Inquiry into the Development of English in the United States*. 4th ed. 3 vols. New York: Alfred A. Knopf, 1936–48.

———. *A Carnival of Buncombe*. Ed. Malcolm Moos. Baltimore: Johns Hopkins University Press, 1956.

Merriam-Webster's Dictionary of English Usage. Springfield, Mass.: Merriam-Webster, 1994.

Micklethwait, David. *Noah Webster and the American Dictionary*. Jefferson, N.C.: McFarland, 2000.

Milroy, James, and Lesley Milroy. *Authority in Language: Investigating Standard English*. 3rd ed. London and New York: Routledge, 2000.

Mitchell, Richard. *The Leaning Tower of Babel and Other Affronts by the Underground Grammarian*. Boston: Little, Brown, 1984.

————. *Less than Words Can Say*. Boston: Little, Brown, 1979.

Monaghan, E. Jennifer. *A Common Heritage: Noah Webster's Blue-Back Speller*. Hamden, Conn.: Archon Books, 1983.

Montagu, Ashley. *The Anatomy of Swearing*. New York: Macmillan, 1967.

Moran, Terence P. "Public Doublespeak: On Expletives Deleted and Characterizations Omitted." *College English* 36, no. 6 (February 1975): 689–93.

Morgan, John S. *Noah Webster*. New York: Mason/Charter, 1975.

Morton, Herbert C. *The Story of Webster's Third: Philip Gove's Controversial Dictionary and Its Critics*. Cambridge: Cambridge University Press, 1994.

Mugglestone, Lynda. " 'An Historian Not a Critic': The Standard of Usage in the *OED*." In *Lexicography and the "OED": Pioneers in the Untrodden Forest*, pp. 189–206. Ed. Lynda Mugglestone. Oxford: Oxford University Press, 2000.

————. *Lost for Words: The Hidden History of the "Oxford English Dictionary."* New Haven, Conn.: Yale University Press, 2005.

————. " 'Pioneers in the Untrodden Forest': The *New* English Dictionary." In *Lexicography and the "OED": Pioneers in the Untrodden Forest*, pp. 1–21. Ed. Lynda Mugglestone. Oxford: Oxford University Press, 2000.

Mulcaster, Richard. *The First Part of the Elementarie Which Entreateth Chefelie of the Right Writing of Our English Tung, Set Furth by Richard Mulcaster*. London, 1582.

Murray, James A. H. *The Evolution of English Lexicography*. Oxford: Clarendon Press, 1900.

————. "Ninth Annual Address of the President to the Philological Society, Delivered at the Anniversary Meeting, Friday, 21st of May, 1880." *Transactions of the Philological Society* (1880–81): 117–74.

Murray, James A. H., et al., eds. *The Oxford English Dictionary*. 13 vols. Oxford: Oxford University Press, 1888–1928.

————. *The Oxford English Dictionary*. 2nd ed. 20 vols. Oxford: Oxford University Press, 1989.

Murray, K. M. Elisabeth. *Caught in the Web of Words: James A. H. Murray and the "Oxford English Dictionary."* New Haven, Conn.: Yale University Press, 1977.

Murray, Lindley. *English Grammar, Adapted to the Different Classes of Learners: With an Appendix, Containing Rules and Observations for Promoting Perspicuity in Speaking and Writing*. York, 1795.

Newman, Edwin. *A Civil Tongue*. Indianapolis, Ind.: Bobbs-Merrill, 1976.

———. *I Must Say: Edwin Newman on English, the News, and Other Matters*. New York: Warner Books, 1988.

———. *Strictly Speaking: Will America Be the Death of English?* Indianapolis, Ind.: Bobbs-Merrill, 1974.

Noble, Kenneth B. "Issue of Racism Erupts in Simpson Trial." *New York Times*, January 14, 1995, p. 7.

Novak, Maximilian E. *Daniel Defoe: Master of Fictions; His Life and Ideas*. Oxford: Oxford University Press, 2001.

Nunberg, Geoffrey. *Going Nucular: Language, Politics and Culture in Confrontational Times*. New York: PublicAffairs, 2004.

Oldmixon, John. *Reflections on Dr. Swift's Letter to the Earl of Oxford, about the English Tongue*. London, 1712.

Oxford Dictionary of National Biography: From the Earliest Times to the Year 2000. Ed. H. C. G. Matthew and Brian Howard Harrison. 61 vols. Oxford: Oxford University Press, 2004.

Partridge, Eric. *Usage and Abusage: A Guide to Good English*. New ed. London: Hamish Hamilton, 1957.

Payack, Paul J. J. *A Million Words and Counting: How Global English Is Rewriting the World*. New York: Citadel Press, 2008.

Phillips, Edward. *The New World of English Words; or, A General Dictionary*. London, 1658.

Pinker, Steven. "The Language Mavens." In *The Workings of Language: From Prescriptions to Perspectives*, pp. 3–14. Ed. Rebecca S. Wheeler. Westport, Conn.: Praeger, 2000.

Pinker, Steven, and Paul Bloom. "Natural Language and Natural Selection." *Behavioral and Brain Sciences* 13, no. 4 (1990): 707–84.

Piozzi, Hester Lynch. *British Synonymy; or, An Attempt at Regulating the Choice of Words in Familiar Conversation*. 2 vols. London, 1794.

Plutarch. *Plutarch's Lives: Translated from the Greek, by Several Hands*. 5 vols. London, 1703.

Pope, Alexander. *An Essay on Criticism*. 2nd ed. London, 1713 [i.e., 1712].

———. *The Iliad of Homer, Translated by Mr. Pope*. 6 vols. London, 1715–20.

Priestley, Joseph. *Experiments and Observations on Different Kinds of Air*. 2nd ed. 2 vols. London, 1776.

———. *Memoirs of the Rev. Dr. Joseph Priestley, to the Year 1795, Written by Himself: With a Continuation, to the Time of His Decease, by His Son, Joseph Priestley*. London, 1809.

———. *Miscellaneous Observations relating to Education: More Especially, as It Respects the Conduct of the Mind: To Which Is Added, an Essay on a Course of Liberal Education for a Civil and Active Life*. Bath, 1778.

———. *The Rudiments of English Grammar; Adapted to the Use of Schools: With Observations on Style*. London, 1761.

———. *The Rudiments of English Grammar; Adapted to the Use of Schools: With Notes and Observations, for the Use of Those Who Have Made Some Proficiency in the Language*. 2nd ed. London, 1768.

Read, Allen Walker. "American Projects for an Academy to Regulate Speech." *PMLA* 51, no. 4 (December 1936): 1141–79.

———. "The First Stage in the History of 'O.K.'" *American Speech* 38, no. 1 (February 1963): 5–27.

———. "The Folklore of 'O.K.'" *American Speech* 39, no. 1 (February 1964): 5–25.

———. "Later Stages in the History of 'O.K.'" *American Speech* 39, no. 2 (May 1964): 83–101.

———. "An Obscenity Symbol." *American Speech* 9 (December 1934): 264–78.

———. "The Second Stage in the History of 'O.K.'" *American Speech* 38, no. 2 (May 1963): 83–102.

Reed, Joseph W. "Noah Webster's Debt to Samuel Johnson." *American Speech* 37, no. 2 (May 1962): 95–105.

Rice, Wallace. "The Split Infinitive." *English Journal* 26, no. 3 (March 1937): 238–40.

Richardson, Charles. *Illustrations of English Philology*. London, 1815.

Richardson, Samuel. *Letters Written to and for Particular Friends, on the Most Important Occasions: Directing Not Only the Requisite Style and Forms to Be Observed in Writing Familiar Letters; but How to Think and Act Justly and Prudently, in the Common Concerns of Human Life*. London, 1741.

Right Spelling Very Much Improved: Teaching the Speediest and Surest Way to Write True English; by Rule and Not by Rote. London, 1704.

Robinson, T. *A Sermon against Prophane Cursing and Swearing: Being a Charitable Admonition to Her Majesty's Fleet*. London, 1710.

Roget, Peter Mark. *Thesaurus of English Words and Phrases, Classified and Arranged So as to Facilitate the Expression of Ideas and Assist in Literary Composition*. London, 1852.

The Sacco-Vanzetti Case: Transcript of the Record of the Trial of Nicola Sacco and Bartolomeo Vanzetti in the Courts of Massachusetts and Subsequent Proceedings, 1920–7. 5 vols. New York: H. Holt & Co., 1928.

Safire, William. "Balloon Goes Up on War Words." *New York Times,* February 3, 1991, p. 8.

———. "Growing Down Grows Up." *New York Times,* November 15, 1992, section 6, p. 12.

———. *Quoth the Maven.* New York: Random House, 1993.

———. *Take My Word for It: More on Language.* New York: Times Books, 1986.

———. "Words at War." *New York Times,* July 4, 1982, p. 6.

Sampson, George. *English for the English: A Chapter on National Education.* Cambridge: Cambridge University Press, 1925.

Scot, Patrick. *The Tillage of Light; or, A True Discouerie of the Philosophicall Elixir, Commonly Called the Philosophers Stone Seruing, to Enrich All True, Noble and Generous Spirits, as Will Aduenture Some Few Labors in the Tillage of Such a Light, as Is Worthy the Best Obseruance of the Most Wise.* London, 1623.

Scragg, D. G. *A History of English Spelling.* Manchester: Manchester University Press, 1974.

Senner, Wayne M., ed. *The Origins of Writing.* Lincoln: University of Nebraska Press, 1989.

Seymour, George. *The Instructive Letter-Writer, and Entertaining Companion.* London, 1763.

Shakespeare, William. *The Works of William Shakespeare.* Ed. Samuel Johnson. 8 vols. London, 1765.

Sharman, Julian. *A Cursory History of Swearing.* London, 1884.

Shaw, George Bernard. *George Bernard Shaw on Language.* Ed. Abraham Tauber. New York: Philosophical Library, 1965.

Sheffield, Emily. "Jackdaw." *Guardian,* June 18, 1996, p. 13.

Sheidlower, Jesse, ed. *The F-Word.* New York: Random House, 1995.

Sheridan, Thomas. *A Course of Lectures on Elocution: Together with Two Dissertations on Language; and Some Other Tracts Relative to Those Subjects.* London, 1762.

Shippey, Tom, with Martin Arnold. *Appropriating the Middle Ages: Scholarship, Politics, Fraud.* Cambridge: D. S. Brewer, 2001.

Shoemaker, Ervin C. *Noah Webster: Pioneer of Learning.* New York: Columbia University Press, 1936.

Simon, John. "The Corruption of English." In *The State of the Language.* Ed. Leonard Michaels and Christopher Ricks, pp. 35–42. Berkeley and Los Angeles: University of California Press, 1980.

————. *Paradigms Lost: Reflections on Literacy and Its Decline.* New York: C. N. Potter, 1980.

Skelton, John. *The Boke of Phyllyp Sparowe Compyled by Mayster Skelton Poete Laureate.* London, [1545?].

Sledd, James, and Wilma R. Ebbitt, ed. *Dictionaries and That Dictionary.* Chicago: Scott, Foresman, 1962.

Sparks, Jared, ed. *The Diplomatic Correspondence of the American Revolution.* 12 vols. Boston, 1829–30.

Spenser, Edmund. *The Shepheardes Calender.* London, 1579.

Spingarn, J. E., ed. *Critical Essays of the Seventeenth Century.* 3 vols. Oxford: Clarendon Press, 1908–9.

Sprat, Thomas. *The History of the Royal-Society of London for the Improving of Natural Knowledge.* London, 1667.

Stafford, Jean. "Plight of the American Language." *Saturday Review World,* December 4, 1973, pp. 14–18.

Stiles, Ezra. *The Literary Diary of Ezra Stiles, DD., LL.D.* Ed. Franklin Bowditch Dexter. 3 vols. New York: Scribner's, 1901.

Stockwell, Peter. *Sociolinguistics: A Resource Book for Students.* London and New York: Routledge, 2002.

Strunk, William Jr., and E. B. White. *The Elements of Style.* 3rd ed. New York: Macmillan, 1979.

Swift, Jonathan. *A Letter to a Young Gentleman, Lately Enter'd into Holy Orders.* London, 1721.

————. *A Proposal for Correcting, Improving and Ascertaining the English Tongue; in a Letter to the Most Honourable Robert Earl of Oxford and Mortimer, Lord High Treasurer of Great Britain.* 2nd ed. London, 1712.

————. *The Works of Jonathan Swift: Containing Additional Letters, Tracts, and Poems Not Hitherto Published; with Notes, and a Life of the Author.* Ed. Sir Walter Scott. 2nd ed. 19 vols. Edinburgh, 1824.

————. *The Works of the Rev. Dr. Jonathan Swift, Dean of St. Patrick's, Dublin: Arranged, Revised, and Corrected, with Notes.* Ed. Thomas Sheridan. 17 vols. London, 1784.

The Tatler; or, The Lucubrations of Isaac Bickerstaff Esq; Revised and Corrected by the Author, 5 vols. London, 1712.

Thomason, Sarah Grey, and Terence Kaufman. *Language Contact, Creolization, and Genetic Linguistics.* Berkeley and Los Angeles: University of California Press, 1988.

Trench, Richard Chenevix. *On Some Deficiencies in Our English Dictionaries: Being the Substance of Two Papers Read before the*

Philological Society, Nov. 5 and Nov. 19, 1857. 2nd ed. London, 1860.

Trollope, Frances Milton. *Domestic Manners of the Americans.* 4th ed. 2 vols. London, 1832.

Trusler, John. *The Difference, between Words, Esteemed Synonymous, in the English Language; and, the Proper Choice of Them Determined.* 2 vols. London, 1766.

Turnbull, George. *Observations upon Liberal Education, in All Its Branches.* London, 1742.

Valli, Clayton, and Ceil Lucas. *Linguistics of American Sign Language: An Introduction.* 3rd ed. Washington, D.C.: Clerc Books and Gallaudet University Press, 2000.

The Vulgarities of Speech Corrected: With Elegant Expressions for Provincial and Vulgar English, Scots, and Irish; for the Use of Those Who Are Unacquainted with Grammar. 2nd ed. London, 1829.

Wallace, James. *Every Man His Own Letter-Writer.* London, ca. 1782.

Waller, Edmund. *Poems, &c. Written upon Several Occasions, and to Several Persons.* London, 1686.

Walsh, William. *A Dialogue concerning Women: Being a Defence of the Sex: Written to Eugenia.* London, 1691.

Warfel, Harry R. *Noah Webster: Schoolmaster to America.* New York: Macmillan, 1936.

Warton, Joseph. *An Essay on the Writings and Genius of Pope.* 2 vols. London, 1756–82.

Webster, Noah. *An American Dictionary of the English Language: Intended to Exhibit, I. The Origin, Affinities and Primary Signification of English Words, as Far as They Have Been Ascertained; II. The Genuine Orthography and Pronunciation of Words, According to General Usage, or to Just Principles of Analogy; III. Accurate and Discriminating Definitions, with Numerous Authorities and Illustrations: To Which Are Prefixed, an Introductory Dissertation on the Origin, History and Connection of the Languages of Western Asia and Europe, and a Concise Grammar of the English Language.* New York, 1828.

———. *An American Selection of Lessons in Reading and Speaking. Calculated to Improve the Minds and Refine the Taste of Youth.* 3rd ed. Philadelphia, 1787.

———. *A Collection of Essays and Fugitiv Writings: On Moral, Historical, Political and Literary Subjects.* Boston, 1790.

———. *A Collection of Papers on Political, Literary, and Moral Subjects.* New York, 1843.

————. *A Compendious Dictionary of the English Language: In Which Five Thousand Words Are Added to the Number Found in the Best English Compends; the Orthography Is, in Some Instances, Corrected; the Pronunciation Marked by an Accent or Other Suitable Direction; and the Definitions of Many Words Amended and Improved*. Hartford and New Haven, 1806.

————. *Dissertations on the English Language: With Notes, Historical and Critical: To Which Is Added, by Way of Appendix, an Essay on a Reformed Mode of Spelling, with Dr. Franklin's Arguments on That Subject*. Boston, 1789.

————. *A Grammatical Institute, of the English Language: Comprising, an Easy, Concise, and Systematic Method of Education, Designed for the Use of English Schools in America: In Three Parts: Part I. Containing, a New and Accurate Standard of Pronunciation*. Hartford, 1783.

————. *A Letter to the Governors, Instructors and Trustees of the Universities, and Other Seminaries of Learning, in the United States, on the Errors of English Grammars*. New York, 1798.

————. *Letters of Noah Webster*. Ed. Harry R. Warfel. New York: Library Publishers, 1953.

————. *Noah Webster's American Spelling Book*. Intro. by Henry Steele Commager. New York: Columbia University Teachers College, 1958.

White, E. B. Introduction to William Strunk Jr. and E. B. White, *The Elements of Style*. 3rd ed. New York: Macmillan, 1979.

White, Richard Grant. *Every-Day English*. London, 1880.

————. *Words and Their Uses, Past and Present: A Study of the English Language*. New York, 1870.

————. *Words and Their Uses, Past and Present: A Study of the English Language*. 3rd ed. New York, 1880.

Whitefield, George. *The Heinous Sin of Profane Cursing and Swearing: A Sermon Preached at the Parish Church of St. Nicholas Cole-Abby*. London, 1738.

Williams, Evan. "Mob Rules in Amusing Mix." *Weekend Australian*, May 6, 2006, p. 22.

Williams, Robert, ed. *Ebonics: The True Language of Black Folks*. St. Louis, Mo.: Institute of Black Studies, 1975.

Willinsky, John. *Empire of Words: The Reign of the "OED."* Princeton: Princeton University Press, 1994.

Wilson, Thomas. *The Many Advantages of a Good Language to Any Nation: With an Examination of the Present State of Our Own:*

As Also, an Essay Towards Correcting Some Things That Are Wrong in It. London, 1724.

Wolman, David. *Righting the Mother Tongue: From Olde English to Email, the Tangled Story of English Spelling*. New York: Collins, 2008.

X, Malcolm. *The Autobiography of Malcolm X*. New York: Grove Press, 1965.

Index

A Note on the Author

JACK LYNCH is a professor of English at Rutgers University. He is the author of *Becoming Shakespeare* and the editor of *Samuel Johnson's Dictionary* and *Samuel Johnson's Insults*. He has also written journal articles and scholarly reviews addressing Johnson and the eighteenth century, and hosts a Web site devoted to these topics at http://andromeda.rutgers.edu/~jlynch/18th.